Benjamin Fiske Barrett

Heaven Revealed

Being a Popular Presentation of Swedenborg's Disclosures About Heaven

Benjamin Fiske Barrett

Heaven Revealed

Being a Popular Presentation of Swedenborg's Disclosures About Heaven

ISBN/EAN: 9783744692526

Printed in Europe, USA, Canada, Australia, Japan

Cover: Foto ©Thomas Meinert / pixelio.de

More available books at **www.hansebooks.com**

HEAVEN REVEALED.

BEING

*A POPULAR PRESENTATION OF SWEDEN-
BORG'S DISCLOSURES ABOUT HEAVEN,*

WITH THE

CONCURRENT TESTIMONY OF A FEW COMPE-
TENT AND RELIABLE WITNESSES.

BY

B. F. BARRETT,

AUTHOR OF "THE NEW VIEW OF HELL," "THE NEW DISPENSATION," "FOOT-
PRINTS OF THE NEW AGE," "THE QUESTION ANSWERED," ETC., ETC.

*"If the phenomena of the Spiritual World are real, in the nature of things they ought
to come into the sphere of Law."*—HENRY DRUMMOND.

PHILADELPHIA:

THE SWEDENBORG PUBLISHING ASSOCIATION,

GERMANTOWN, PA.

PREFACE.

IT is nearly fifty years since the author of the present work commenced a serious and thorough examination of the theological writings of Emanuel Swedenborg. He was told that this illustrious seer claimed to have enjoyed open intercourse with the denizens of the spiritual world for many years, and to have been divinely commissioned to write a detailed account of what he heard and saw in that world; and the treatise known as " Heaven and Hell " was placed in his hands for perusal. After reading a few pages, the book was laid aside, the present writer saying to himself: "All this *may* be true, or it may *not*. We have no means of knowing. There is no adequate test whereby the truth or falsity of such alleged disclosures can be determined. Why, then, should I waste time over such a book?"

It is easy for me, therefore, to pardon the incredulity of Christians touching this astounding claim of the great seer, and to excuse the prevailing reluctance to give any thought or attention to his alleged disclosures concerning the other world. For probably most of them think as I did, that we have no means of proving either the truth or falsity of such pretended revelations.

What is to be gained, therefore, by an examination of something which can neither be proved nor *dis*proved? Will it not be a waste of time?

But when, after thorough and careful study of Swedenborg's theological system, I found myself compelled by irresistible force of evidence to accept it for just what it claims to be—a divinely authorized revelation of new and heavenly truth—I was satisfied that he was a man ordained and sent of God, and that his disclosures concerning Heaven and Hell must also be true. Then turning my attention to his pneumatology, I very soon found that this, too, rests on a foundation not less solid and secure than his theology; and that its truth is susceptible of proof to an extent I had not suspected—susceptible of a verification, indeed, closely approximating the demonstrations of exact science.

The purpose of the present volume is, to lay before the reader some of the evidence which carried conviction to the writer's own mind, that what Swedenborg has revealed concerning the heaven of angels is no mere fancy sketch, but literally and unquestionably true. A number of reliable and independent witnesses have been summoned in the case,—such as Scripture, reason, analogy, human experience, the known laws of our mental and moral constitution, the hopes and perceptions of the wisest and best men, the revealed character of the Heavenly Father, and the

undeniably wholesome and benign tendency of the disclosures themselves.

Now, if we have the concurrent testimony of all these witnesses in support of the truth of Swedenborg's dis-closures, what is the verdict we might reasonably expect on the subject, from an intelligent and fair-minded jury? Had he performed miracles like those recorded in the New Testament, and had his miraculous power and deeds been ever so well authenticated, would this have been half as convincing to a rational and truth-seeking mind, as the agreeing testimony of the above named witnesses? Or would it have been half as well suited to the requirements of a reasoning and reflecting age?

Probably every Christian minister is plied with ques-tions now and then concerning the life beyond the grave, which he would be glad to answer, but feels his utter inability to do so; and most ministers would, no doubt, greatly rejoice to have a full and strictly accurate account of the spiritual world, its nature, inhabitants, phenomena and laws—an account as full and reliable as an honest and intelligent traveler who had spent twenty years or more in Japan, might be expected to give us of that country. They would doubtless find it an im-mense aid in their work of helping souls on the way to heaven.

And the author believes that every minister who reads this volume with close attention and without prejudice,

1 *

will be satisfied that such a report of the world beyond *has* actually been made. And he has himself derived so great satisfaction and spiritual help from the disclosures to which he here invites attention, and is so anxious that others should share what has been to him such a rich repast, that he feels like making personally a large discount from the price of the present volume, to every minister and theological student in our land, who will promise to read it with close attention and a sincere desire to know the truth.

On several of the subjects treated in these pages, the author is fully aware that most of the churches of to-day have outgrown and rejected the views that were entertained a hundred years ago; such, for example, as "Work in Heaven," "Sex and Marriage in Heaven," "Children in Heaven," "A Heaven for the non-Christian World," etc. And the fact that the views commonly held and taught on these subjects to-day, are in substantial agreement with those revealed through Swedenborg, should be taken as presumptive evidence that his disclosures on other subjects also are true.

And if a minister's ecclesiastical relations to-day, are in no wise affected by his open rejection of the old dogmas of the damnation of *some* infants and of *all* the Heathen, and of incessant oral prayer and psalm-singing in heaven, or by his acceptance of the new and more rational views on these subjects, there is no reason to believe that they would be seriously affected by his embracing and teaching the entire pneumatology of Swedenborg, so far, at least, as this can be shown to be in agreement with Scripture, reason, experience, and the known laws of the human soul.

But the strongest evidence of the truth of Swedenborg's revealings about Heaven, and that which, above all else, should commend them to the thoughtful and earnest inquirer, is their wholesome *practical* tendency— their unquestionably elevating and ‘benign influence upon the believer's life and character. The author hopes that the reader will not lose sight of this consideration, nor forget to give to it the weight which its importance demands: Remembering these divine words:

"For every tree is known by his own fruit. For of thorns men do not gather figs, nor of a bramble-bush gather they grapes."

And no more should we expect that wholesome and benign influences would be shed forth upon the believer's mind and heart, from false or fantastic teachings, from the speculations of a mere theorist, the hallucinations of a dreamer, or the oracular utterances of an innocent but self-deluded fanatic.

B. F. B.

GERMANTOWN, June 24, 1885.

CONTENTS.

HEAVEN REVEALED.

ABBREVIATIONS

OF THE WORKS OF SWEDENBORG QUOTED IN THE FOLLOWING
PAGES.

A. C.	stand for	Arcana Cœlestia.
H. H.	"	Heaven and Hell.
A. R.	"	Apocalypse Revealed.
A. E.	"	Apocalypse Explained.
D. P.	"	Divine Providence.
C. L.	"	Conjugial Love.
L. J.	"	Last Judgment.
Spl. D.	"	Spiritual Diary.
D. W.	"	Divine Wisdom.
Doc. L.	"	Doctrine of Life.
T. C. R.	"	True Christian Religion.
N. J. D.	"	Doctrine of the New Jerusalem.
D. L. W.	"	Divine Love and Wisdom.

xii

Heaven Revealed.

I.

SWEDENBORG THE CHOSEN INSTRUMENT.

MANY people nowadays know something of the claims of Emanuel Swedenborg, however deficient the great majority may still be in any correct knowledge of his teachings. It is generally known that he claimed, among other things, to have had his spiritual senses so opened as to enable him to see and converse with the denizens of the spiritual world as men see and converse with each other; and this continually for a period of nearly thirty years, embracing the ripest portion of his earthly life. He made no secret of this claim, extraordinary and startling as he knew it to be; but boldly announced it on every suitable occasion, and repeatedly in his published works. In the commencement of his treatise known as " Heaven and Hell," occurs the following explicit declaration :—

"The arcana revealed in the following pages are those concerning heaven, together with the life of man after death.. The man of the church at this day knows

2   13

scarcely anything about heaven or hell, nor yet about his own life after death, although these things are all treated of in the Word. Nay, many even among those who were born within the church deny these things, saying in their hearts, Who has ever come thence and told us? Lest, therefore, such a negative principle, which rules especially among those who possess much worldly wisdom, should also infect and corrupt the simple in heart and faith, it has been granted me to associate with angels and to converse with them as one man with another, and also to see the things which are in the heavens as well as those which are in the hells, and this for the space of thirteen years; so that I can now describe them from what I have myself seen and heard,—which I do, in the hope that ignorance may thus be enlightened and incredulity dissipated."

The same claim in substance is often repeated in his writings. And he tells us how this extraordinary privilege was granted him, or in what way this alleged open intercourse with the inhabitants of the other world was effected. It was through the providential opening of his spiritual senses. These senses, he says, belong alike to every human being. They are inherent in the very constitution of an immortal spirit—are included among its powers or capabilities, just as natural sight, hearing, feeling, etc., are included in the capabilities of our material organism. And although these senses (for a wise and beneficent purpose which he has repeatedly explained) are ordinarily closed during our life on earth, they nevertheless may be and repeatedly have been opened in men while living in the flesh. And when opened, the individual is for the time intromitted into the spiritual world, and enjoys a sensible perception of its people and objects.*

We know very well how this claim is commonly regarded by those who have never examined the seer's disclosures with sufficient thoroughness to enable them to form an intelligent opinion of his pneumatology. They look upon his alleged open intercourse with spirits, as not only improbable, unreasonable and unsusceptible of proof, but as evidencing a want of mental balance—as, indeed, a species of monomania. Many who do not believe him a willful impostor, and who are ready to admit (for popular opinion is beginning to lean this way) that he saw truth on many subjects quite in advance of his age, treat with contempt and derision his claim to open intercourse with angels and spirits ; as if such visions as he has recorded were to be reckoned among things highly improbable if not impossible, and the record itself to be accepted as evidence of mental derangement.

This is the attitude of nearly every one in reference to the great Swede's alleged intercourse with the denizens of the other world, before he has given much thought.to the subject, or has examined the evidence by which his claim is supported. It was substantially the writer's own attitude before he had made himself familiar with the general character of the seer's disclos-

---

* The Bible furnishes evidence of the existence of spiritual senses in man, and of their having been occasionally opened during his earthly sojourn. See 2 Kings vi. 15–18; and other texts cited in the chapter on "The Rationale of Spirit-seeing" in *Doctrines of the New Church* by the author, pp. 208–213.

ures, and had duly considered the facts and laws which underlie his pneumatology, and prove it not only credible but indisputably true.

But Swedenborg's claim to a special illumination and open vision (if allowed), we shall be told, stamps his disclosures with the character of a divinely authorized revelation. And not only do people nowadays find it hard to believe in any new revelation (multitudes are coming to disbelieve in *any* revelation, unless its truth can be *scientifically* demonstrated), but the claim itself seems to them ridiculous, and quite sufficient to discredit him who makes it; sufficient, indeed, to prove him a deluded fanatic or a wicked impostor. Nor are we surprised at this, seeing how many " false Christs and false prophets "—how many pretenders to a special divine commission—have from time to time appeared, and how many have been deceived by them. But people do not reason thus on other subjects. On the contrary, they admit that a *counterfeit* is conclusive evidence that there *is* such a thing as genuine coin.

It is quite true that Swedenborg's disclosures come to us professedly as a new and divinely authorized revelation; a revelation, however, not contrary nor supplementary to the Sacred Scripture, yet necessary to its complete fulfillment and to the better understanding and fuller efficacy of its teachings; a revelation meant and fitted for the spiritual edification of all who are longing for instruction on the sublimest themes, and are willing to receive it. But these disclosures, notwithstanding they come professedly as an authorized revelation, claim no authority and ask no consideration merely on that ground. They ask to be received solely upon the ground of their intrinsic reasonableness, or their clearly perceived agreement with the deepest intuitions of human reason and the verdict of the most enlightened understanding. They appeal to no miraculous evidence in attestation of their truth, but to evidence of a higher kind. Scripture, reason, analogy, observation, history, individual experience, well-authenticated facts, the principles of sound philosophy, the known laws of our mental and moral constitution, the wisdom and beneficence of God as revealed in his Word and works and in the wondrous ways of his Providence —these are the witnesses which are confidently appealed to. What if these should all unite in affirming the validity of this man's claim and the truth of his disclosures? Shall we reject or disregard the concurrent testimony of such witnesses?

Already there is a large and continually increasing class of minds—among them are persons by no means deficient in intellectual grasp, logical acumen or judicial candor—who, after years of careful examination of the disclosures in question, have been constrained to acknowledge their truth; and this, too, in spite of the influence of early education, preconceived opinions, popular prejudice, the sneers of the multitude, and the pity if not the frowns of near and valued friends: When all this is duly considered, we submit to the honest and independent seekers after truth, whether it does not entitle this new revelation to, at least, a candid examination. Certainly the acceptance of any revelation or theory by wise and good men, is not sufficient evidence of its truth; for wise and good men have sometimes embraced error,—yes, and clung to it with surprising tenacity. But the profound conviction of many such men, *is*, we think, a sufficient reason for giving their views a candid examination before pronouncing them erroneous. Our judgment is unintelligent, and therefore valueless, until we have carefully weighed the evidence which carried conviction to their minds. The Jews, when they crucified the Divine Saviour, knew not what they did. And Christians at the present day know as little what they do, when, without serious examination, or any weighing of the evidence, they reject and ridicule the disclosures made through the Swedish seer. May they not in this be imitating the example of the Jews more closely than they imagine?

But the very claim, we are told, which Swedenborg sets up—the claim to have enjoyed long and open intercourse with the spirits of deceased men, and to have been thereby enabled to reveal the arcana of the spiritual world, is of itself sufficient to stamp him as a deluded fanatic. It is assumed that such intercourse is impossible in the nature of things; and on the ground of this assumption, Christians proceed to justify themselves in their neglect to examine his disclosures. But if this *be* a sufficient justification, or if Swedenborg's claim alone be evidence of self-delusion, then what is to be said of Isaiah and Ezekiel and Paul and John and a host of ancient worthies? If the mere fact of his claiming open intercourse with spirits, is sufficient proof of mental aberration in his case, then why should not a similar claim be accepted as evidence of a similar mental condition in the case of all other seers? Or will it be said that what was once reckoned among the credentials of heaven-illumined prophets, is now to be regarded as evidence of mental hallucination?

II.

OBJECTIONS ANSWERED.

IT is quite common to hear urged against Swedenborg's claim, such objections as these: That, after the closing of the sacred canon, there was never to be any further revelation; that his disclosures concerning the other world, if true, would be a revelation of mysteries which no one has a right to pry into or know anything about; that it would be an unveiling of the "secret things" which belong to God, and are no concern of ours.

But what reason have we to believe that God has limited Himself to precisely that measure of revealed truth vouchsafed to the world many centuries ago? Where is it written that He will never make any further revelation concerning Himself, his kingdom, or the grand realities of the spiritual world? The Bible contains no such declaration—no warrant, indeed, for any such belief. What reason, then, for believing that the Heavenly Father has denied to Himself the delight of communicating, or to men the blessed privilege of receiving, more truth concerning that world beyond the tomb which is to be the final home of all his children?

What reason for the belief that everything was revealed centuries ago, which ever was or ever is to be revealed? And if it should please God to lift the veil, and make a disclosure of things *once secret*, is it presumptuous for mortals to look upon them? However unlawful it may be to *pry into* the mysteries of the spirit-world, it surely cannot· be wrong to receive with thankfulness such disclosures as Infinite Wisdom has been pleased to make. ·True, it is written that "secret things belong unto the Lord our God;" but it is immediately added: that "those things which are *revealed*, belong unto us and to our children forever." (Deut. xxix. 29.)

And if there *be* a spiritual world (and the Scriptures plainly teach that there is), is it not reasonable to believe that more will ultimately be known about it, than was communicated to Christians 1800 years ago? Have we not reason to expect that the time will come when the mysteries of that world will be unveiled and its sublime realities disclosed—at least to man's mental or moral vision? Christ told his immediate followers that He had many things to say unto them, which they were not able to bear (John xvi. 12); but He never intimated that the same inability would belong to his disciples throughout the coming ages. On the contrary, He more than hinted, and on more than one occasion, that more truth might some day be expected than it was expedient at that time to impart. He told them that the time was coming when He would no longer speak in parables, but would show them plainly of the Father. He told them of a Comforter which He would send unto them, " even the *spirit* of truth ; " and this Comforter, He said, when He came, would teach them all things, would show them things to come, would guide them into all truth. (John xvi. 7–13.)

He spoke also of another coming of Himself, more searching, more glorious, more powerful in its operation upon the minds and hearts of men than his first appearing—a coming which He said would be "with power and great glory."

Now, who can say, *in limine*, that, in these prophetic intimations, no reference was had to that grand system of religious truth which was unfolded, or came professedly as a new revelation, more than a century ago? Who can say that the increasing light upon all subjects which has been flooding the world for the last hundred years, is not a veritable fulfillment of these prophecies, and in the sense intended? Who knows but the many interesting disclosures made through Swedenborg concerning the spiritual world, may be among the things which the Saviour had to announce, but which the men of 1850 years ago were "not able to bear"? Christ declared Himself to be "the Way," "the Truth," "the Life," "the Light of the world," "the Light which enlighteneth every man." And the apostle John says: "God is light, and in Him is no darkness at all." May not the predicted second coming of Christ, then, be the coming to human minds of more abundant light from Him who is declared to be "the true Light"?—of light more interior, searching and glorious than has hitherto dawned on our world?—the light of the spiritual sense of the Word breaking forth through the cloud of the letter,—coupled also with the coming to human hearts of a sweeter and more Christ-like spirit? And may not this light reveal, among other things, the nature, laws and phenomena of that world which is to be our eternal dwelling-place? Who knows, we say, but spiritual light —the light of the New Jerusalem which is beginning even now to gild and gladden with its splendors the world's moral horizon—light manifesting itself amid clouds of still existing error, the mists of ignorance, superstition and prejudice, the smoke of demoniacal passions and enmities—may be precisely what the Saviour referred to when He spoke of a second coming of the Son of Man "in the clouds of heaven, with power and great glory"? Who knows? And the way to acquire such knowledge is not, we submit, to treat with indifference or neglect everything that claims to be a new revelation, but to "watch"—not with the eyes of the body, but with the eyes of the mind, that is, with our intellectual and reasoning faculties.

We shall find, on careful reading and a thoughtful consideration of the whole subject, that the language of the New Testament clearly requires, for its complete fulfillment, *some* such revelation as that claimed to have been made through the seer of Stockholm. The past history and present state of the Christian church also, and the acknowledged ignorance of teachers of the Christian religion concerning the spiritual world, justify the same expectation.

The Bible, it is generally conceded, teaches the immortality of the soul—the immortality of *man.* The fair and logical conclusions from which are, that the soul, when the body dies, still continues to live in its own congenial realm which is spiritual, that is, homogeneous with itself; that this, therefore, necessitates the existence of a supersensuous or spiritual world vastly more populous than that in which we are now living,—a world into which tens of thousands of human beings are consciously introduced every hour; not a mere dream-land, or a region of unsubstantial shadows, but a *real* world inhabited by a countless host of rational and immortal spirits who were once invested with material bodies like our own. And this, too, is generally conceded.

But ask the ministers of Christ to-day—the ministers of that religion which is claimed to have brought "life and immortality to light"—about the spiritual world. Ask them in what condition we may expect to find ourselves when we shall have "shuffled off this mortal coil." Ask them if we shall still be in the human form, having eyes, ears, hands, feet, and other bodily organs; —if we shall retain the power of thinking, reasoning, remembering, loving, conversing and enjoying. Ask them if our departed friends still think of us and love us on "the shining shore;" if they are near us, interested in our welfare, and capable of exerting any influence upon us,—and if so, how, or according to what law. Ask whether, when we leave these mortal bodies, we shall join them in conscious visible association—be recognized and embraced by them, and recognize and embrace them in return. Ask whether the distinction of sex is preserved in the great Beyond, what kind of social life (if any) exists there, and what the law that governs in the association of spirits. Ask whether those who die in infancy and childhood retain forever their infantile form, or whether they grow to the full stature of men and women as in this world. Ask whether the righteous who die of old age, continue wrinkled, bowed and decrepid there as here, or whether they return to the bloom and vigor of their early manhood. Ask what is the nature of heaven and hell; what are the delights of good and what those of evil spirits (if the latter have any); what constitutes the happiness of the former, and what the misery of the latter. Ask if there be any industries or occupations beyond the grave, and what their nature; and whether there exists any sort of connection (and if so, what?) between spirits in the other world and men in this world. Ask ministers of the Gospel these and a hundred other similar questions (and they are questions which the human heart instinctively asks,—nay, cannot help asking), and what will they answer? Perhaps they will give you their *opinions*—their *conjectures;* and these may sometimes be quite sensible. But generally you will receive, in answer to all such inquiries, a frank confession of entire ignorance. They will tell you that they do not pretend to know anything about such matters, as nothing has ever been revealed; and, therefore, they cannot undertake to teach with confidence anything concerning them.

And is it reasonable to suppose that this state of confessed ignorance about things of such absorbing interest to rational and immortal beings, will always continue? Can we believe that the ministers of Christ are *never* to have anything but crude conjecture wherewith to answer inquiries upon such lofty and momentous themes?

If there *be* a spiritual world, according to the universal belief of Christians, is it reasonable to conclude that its arcana will never be revealed ?   Does such conclusion agree with what we believe and know of the goodness and mercy of God, the wants of the human soul, or the progress of our race in knowledge upon all other subjects?   The human mind has, for the last hundred years, made prodigious advances in knowledge of the material world, and in the means of satisfying the wants and increasing the comforts of our physical life.   The secrets of universal nature have been steadily disclosing themselves, as men needed the knowledge thereof, and were prepared to use it wisely.   And new and useful discoveries still succeed each other almost with the rapidity of thought.   Nor can we fix any limit to this progress in knowledge of the material universe.   *There is no limit.*   To fix one, were to limit the Infinite Himself, or to deny the indefinite enlargement and receptivity of the human mind.

Now, seeing that God is perpetually disclosing the secrets of this natural world for the benefit of his rational creatures, and since the liveliest imagination can set no bounds to the increase of knowledge in this direction, is it reasonable to suppose that all knowledge of the spiritual world will be forever denied us ?   Will the Heavenly Father vouchsafe to his children an unimaginable amount of truth concerning this world of matter, and keep that sublimer world of spirit which is to be our eternal home, forever shrouded in darkness ?   Will He never reveal to us anything concerning the life

3

beyond the grave, save the simple fact of the soul's immortality?

Whether we consult reason or revelation, therefore, we are brought to the same conclusion. We find ample warrant for the belief that some such disclosures concerning the other world as are found in Swedenborg's pneumatology, are clearly in accordance with the ways and workings of Divine Providence, and therefore to be expected sooner or later. And how could such disclosures be made without the aid of a human instrument? How, but by the opening of the spiritual senses of some chosen and duly qualified servant of the Lord, and his consequent intromission into that world while still an inhabitant of this? How, in short, but in the precise manner alleged by the illustrious Swede?

But we are met with another objection—or rather excuse for giving no serious attention to Swedenborg's pneumatology—which is: That a revelation concerning the spiritual world, even if true, could serve no valuable purpose; that it is needless, and might be worse than useless; that it could only gratify a morbid curiosity or a love of the marvelous, which had better be denied than gratified.

Those who make this objection, or offer this excuse in justification of their indifference respecting the disclosures in question, do so, we think, without sufficient consideration. The same persons would hardly be willing to say, that the astronomer, the student of the higher mathematics, the inventor or builder of telescopes, any one devoted to the acquisition and impartation of knowledge respecting our solar system and the stellar universe, is engaged in a useless occupation. On the contrary, they would tell us that any pursuit which tends to enlarge our knowledge of the material cosmos, to make us better acquainted with the heavenly bodies and the laws that govern their movements, is a high and noble use, even though it add nothing to our immediate physical comfort. Useless, indeed, so far as relates to supplying our bodily wants, may be the business of those engaged in astronomical observations. But are they not ministering to some deeper wants of our nature —wants not less real and imperative than those of the body? Have not the labors of the astronomer helped to enlarge our knowledge of the universe, and thus contributed to the growth and expansion of the mind, and the consequent intellectual and moral progress of our race?

But the grandeur of the material universe as disclosed to us by modern science, is nothing in comparison with the grandeur of that other universe—the universe of mind. Planets and suns with all their beautiful laws and phenomena, and all their quiet, orderly, rhythmic movements, are indeed wonderful ; but the human soul with all its endowments—its amazing powers of thought and affection, its faculty of boundless growth in knowledge and virtue, its untold and inconceivable capabilities of bliss and of suffering—this is far more wonderful. · By the side of this, how feeble and almost insignificant the glory and grandeur of all material orbs! How much more is this like God himself, than planets or suns or aught else in the created universe! And shall we conclude that a knowledge of the universe of souls—of its facts, phenomena and laws—can be of no value? That this is knowledge not worth revealing, or not worth examining when revealed? Shall knowledge of the material universe be considered wholesome and useful—enlarging, enriching and exalting the human soul —and knowledge of the spiritual universe, so much higher and nobler, be pronounced worthless? Is it probable that the former of these knowledges can reveal to us more of God, can more exalt our conceptions of his wisdom and love, or tend to bring us nearer to his moral likeness, than the latter? Can the study of natural astronomy enlarge and ennoble the pursuer, and the learning of that higher kind of astronomy which embraces the relations, laws and phenomena of the spiritual spheres, be useless? Is this reasonable, or even probable?

Again: Let the reader imagine himself a young man, intending to emigrate to some foreign country in the course of a few years, and to reside there during the remainder of his life. Would he not naturally desire some information about that country, and about the character, conduct and condition of its people? Would he not wish to know something of their manners and customs, their language and laws, their dispositions and habits, their occupations and modes of life? And might not such knowledge be very useful by enabling him the better to prepare himself for the honorable discharge of his duties as a citizen of that country? And suppose the country to have been previously visited by some distinguished traveler who had published a full account of his travels, of the country itself and the people living there;

would the time employed in reading his book be considered unprofitably spent? Would anybody think, or would the young man himself think, that, in reading it, he was merely gratifying an idle curiosity?

Well, then, we ask if the desire for some information about that country whither we are all going—going, we know not how soon, and going to remain forever—be not equally natural, yes, and equally lawful? And can we conceive of no higher use for such information, than merely to gratify a morbid curiosity? Who knows but it may be turned to good account in enabling us to fit ourselves more thoroughly for the duties and enjoyments of our future home? Who knows but a graphic picture of both the upper and the nether realms in the spirit-land—of life in heaven and life in hell—may kindle in our hearts a deeper desire for the former and a more intense loathing of the latter? Who knows but it may quicken our diligence and nerve our energies toward the attainment of the one and the avoidance of the other? It has generally been believed by Christians that there exists some sort of connection between the present life and the life to come. And who dares say that the knowledge of *how* our life hereafter is related to our life here, can be of no practical importance?

A wise parent in the education of his children, usually has some reference to the part they are expected to act when they shall have come to years of maturity. And it will not be denied that his knowledge of their future duties as husbands, fathers, wives, mothers—as members of society and citizens of the state—enables him to direct their education more wisely and profitably

3*

than he otherwise could. Why, then, should not *we* be able to give a wiser direction to *our own* education in this the childhood of our being, by a knowledge of the world into which we are sure of being ushered in our more mature manhood?—a knowledge of the laws, duties, occupations and enjoyments of the spiritual realm?

No *need* of a revelation concerning the other world! Look at the state of the Christian church at the time Swedenborg lived and wrote. Infidelity had well-nigh palsied every limb, and a cheerless, heartless, withering materialism was pressing like an incubus upon her vitals. Questions had been asked about the future life, which the wisest of the clergy were unable to answer. Many had come to deny, and many more to doubt, even the soul's immortality. To arrest this tide of skepticism, there was needed just such a disclosure of the future life and of the grand realities of the spiritual world, as that made through Swedenborg; and one accompanied with precisely that internal and rational kind of evidence, too, which alone could satisfy the demands of a reasoning and reflecting age.

A revelation concerning the spiritual world not needed! *Useless*, say you, even if true! Go ask that mother as she bends over the body of her departed child, and presses upon its marble brow the last fond tribute of a mother's love:—Ask her if she could find no solace in the assured conviction that her little one is now in the tender embrace of loving angels—yes, and brighter, healthier, happier, too, and fuller of exuberant life and bounding joy than ever before. Or ask that widowed wife, whose streaming eyes and pallid cheek and languid frame bespeak an agony too deep for words:—Ask her, as she sees the coffin-lid close over the remains of him to whom her affections clung with all the devotion of woman's love, whether it would not lighten somewhat the burden of her grief, to know something definite about that realm which her departed husband entered but yesterday :—Ask if it would not comfort her aching heart to *know* that he is more alive than ever before, and thinks of and loves her still; that his spirit is very near and fondly brooding over her own ; —breathing into her soul in gentlest whispers the blessed influences of heaven (if his heart were set on heavenly things); watching over her tenderly, inspiring her with generous thoughts and noble endeavors, cheering and strengthening her in every good work, and ready, perchance, when her earthly sojourn is ended, to clasp her again in love's embrace : Or ask that youth or maiden who stands o'erwhelmed with anguish by the bedside of a dying father, mother, sister or brother, and feels as if the extinction of this mortal life were the end of human joys and hopes : Or ask that sad and thronging crowd who mourn the departure of those they love, and whose dark apparel is but a faint emblem of their darker sorrow, and the funereal gloom that shrouds to them the spirit-land,—ask them if a truthful revelation of the realities of that world to which their friends have so lately gone, would bring no comfort to their riven hearts.   Ask if they would find no solace in the unwavering conviction that their loved ones are still near and watching over them for good—inspiring holy thoughts

and sweet affections and good resolutions and high endeavor—fuller of life and joy and action than ever before. Or, ask the thousands who have felt and therefore
know the sustaining power of this new revelation in
times of sore bereavement;—thousands who once looked
on death with dread dismay, but now contemplate it
with a cheerful serenity, sometimes even with a holy
joy. Ask them, and they will tell you the use of this
revelation—speaking from their own experience of its
blessings. They will tell you that not the splendor of
empires, nor the wealth of kingdoms, nor the honor of
thrones, nor all the gold and glory of the world, can
compare in value with the truths they have learned
about the great Hereafter from the writings of the
Swedish seer.

And yet in all that we have here said, we have
scarcely hinted at what we conceive to be the great
practical value of these disclosures. We mean their direct influence upon the life of the receiver, here and
now; their direct and powerful tendency to repress the
evil and develop the good, and to mould the character
into a heavenly form.

Here, then, we close our argument against the objections and in support of the need and use of this new
revelation. Here we rest our plea for its thorough and
serious examination. The candid inquirer will find here
a pneumatology as rational as it is beautiful; as satisfying to the sternest demands of the head, as it is to the
intensest cravings of the heart. And those who have
studied it most and understand it best, would scarcely
be believed were they to tell half they know of its com-

forts and satisfactions, its great practical value in the formation of character. Suffice it to add, that the Heavenly Father who understands our human needs, and who knows how to give good and *only* good gifts to his children, has mercifully vouchsafed this revelation in answer to a deep and growing want, and as one powerful means of drawing his children spiritually nearer to Himself and the shining ones around his throne. Infinite Wisdom saw the need, else the revelation would not have been made. And the use which it has already performed, the darkness and doubts it has so effectually dissipated, the peace and satisfaction it has afforded, and the support and solace it has ministered to thousands in times of sore bereavement, prove that it is neither the creation of a poet's fancy, nor the offspring of a disordered brain. And if the revelation be true, then it must have come from God out of heaven; and its thankful and reverent reception must tend to lead the receiver up to Him from whom it came.

But *is* it true?—is the question. *Is* there really a spiritual world, inhabited by spirits who are not mere phantoms, but real, substantial, human beings, with spiritual bodies in human form? If so, where is it, and of what concern is it to us? Are *we* spirits clad in material vestments which death will shortly relieve us of? And shall we then consciously enter the spirit-world as living, conscious, intelligent men and women—spirits in human form? And has God, indeed, been pleased to reveal the sublime realities of that world? If so, what is the evidence which is expected to satisfy inquiring and rational minds?

The answer to these questions, and some of the evidence which we think ought to satisfy candid minds, will be given in the following chapters.

III.

THE ORIGIN OF ANGELS.

THE subject of angelology, including the origin as well as the nature of angels, is one upon which Christians of every denomination have written from time to time; and on few subjects has there been a more general agreement than on this. And as artists sometimes endeavor to heighten the effect of a beautiful picture by contrasting it with something hideous, so we may be excused for placing the Old and the New doctrine concerning the origin of angels side by side, trusting that the truth and beauty of the latter may thereby be rendered the more striking by the contrast. Such presentation, too, will show the *need* there was of the revelation made through Swedenborg.

All who profess the Christian religion, believe in the existence of angels. They believe them to be spiritual beings—the wise and happy denizens of heaven. They could not deny their existence without denying the explicit teaching of the Bible. But the general belief hitherto has been, that angels are created intelligences of different orders intermediate between God and man; that they were created angels in the beginning, and have therefore never known any other place of abode than the heaven in which they are now living.* It has also been generally believed by Christians that a portion of these innocent and happy beings, once rose in rebellion against the government of heaven, and sought to overthrow the Ruler of the universe, and obtain for themselves the supremacy. To this foul revolt they are thought to have been instigated by one more wicked and powerful, but once more wise and glorious, than the rest;—by one who,

> " ——————— in the happy realms of light,
> Clothed with transcendent brightness, didst outshine
> Myriads though bright;"

but who,

> " ——————— with ambitious aim
> Against the throne and monarchy of God,
> Raised impious war in heaven and battle proud,
> With vain attempt."

It has been further believed that the leader in that great rebellion, being defeated in his impious undertaking, was cast out of heaven with his rebellious crew, and became the Prince or chieftain of the bottomless pit—the

---

* As to the precise time of their creation, whether prior or posterior to, or simultaneously with, the creation of the material world, Christians have not been agreed. Nor has there been entire agreement as to their nature. The prevalent opinion, however, has been, that they are incorporeal— pure spirits destitute of any kind of body, yet capable of assuming a body at pleasure. Some have supposed that they have bodies of the purest kind of air or ether; and one of the Christian Fathers even went so far as to give *form* to their aerial bodies, declaring his belief that they are *spherical.*

Satan whereof the New Testament speaks. To quote
again from Milton, who reflects the religious beliefs of
his times:

> "———— Him the Almighty power
> Hurled headlong from the ethereal sky,
> With hideous ruin and combustion, down
> To bottomless perdition, there to dwell
> In adamantine chains and penal fire,
> Who durst defy the Omnipotent to arms."

And that prime instigator of the supposed rebellion in
heaven, along with those who enlisted under his banner,
are what Christians have generally understood to be
meant by "the Devil and his angels," also by "the
fallen angels." Nor is it in poetry alone that this doctrine respecting the angels, is to be met with. We find
the same set forth in sober prose by both Catholic and
Protestant writers. And we are not aware that any different doctrine on the subject, has ever gained currency
among any considerable class of Christians outside of
the small body known as the New Christian Church.
(*See the London Encyclopædia, Art. Angel.*)

Now, look at this whole story about the angels, which
has gained currency in the church and made a part of
Christian theology—look at it in the light of reason and
common sense. Does it not wear very much the appearance of ancient fable? Does it not look like the
offspring of heathen superstition? For see what it requires us to believe. First, that God created an order
(or several orders) of intelligent creatures—pure spirits
destitute of any form or body, though capable of assuming both *ad libitum*—and far superior to man in knowl-

edge and wisdom, constituting a class of beings intermediate between the Creator and the human race.* Second, that one of the wisest and most exalted of these beings, conceived the idea—an idea such as no one but the veriest dolt and monster were capable of conceiving —of wresting the government of heaven from the hand of Omnipotence, and actually waged war against the Almighty in the hope of gaining the supremacy; and that, failing in the attempt, he and his followers were cast down from heaven into the gulf of despair, where they still cherish their hostility towards the Ruler of the universe. Bear in mind, also, that this insurrection, war, and ejectment from heaven, are predicated of pure spirits—incorporeal beings—creatures utterly destitute of any kind of body or shape! We submit that such extravagances are the very height of folly and nonsense. One would think they had only to be looked at in a little rational light, to be instantly repudiated.

Let us now turn to the doctrine on this subject as revealed through Swedenborg. He claims to have enjoyed long and open intercourse with the spiritual world, and to have made a truthful revelation respecting both angels and devils—their origin as well as their character and condition. The following are some of the

---

* This was the general belief of the old heathen philosophers, as it is of the Mahometans at the present day. The ancient Greeks believed that the *demons* (which word was used by them in a good sense) were created such, and held a middle rank between the gods and men. Thus Plutarch says : "Those seem to me to have solved very many and great difficulties or doubts, who place the demons εν μεσω θεων και ανθροπων—*intermediate between gods and men.*,

4

things he tells us about the human soul and the origin of angels:

"The spirit of man, or the soul, is the interior man which lives after death, and is an organized substance [spiritual, not material], being adjoined to the body during man's abode in the world."—A. C. n. 1594.

"The soul which is said to live after death, is none other than the man himself who lives in the body ; that is, it is the interior man who acts in the world by means of the body, and enables the body to live. This man when freed from the body, is called a spirit, and appears altogether in the human form; yet he cannot be seen with the eyes of the body but with those of the spirit, before which he appears as a man in the world, having the senses of touch, smell, hearing and seeing much more acute than in the world . . . together with all the members and organs that man possesses."—Ibid. n. 6054.

"From all my experience which is now of many years, I can declare that the form of the angels is in every respect human ; that they have faces, eyes, ears, breasts, arms, hands and feet; that they see, hear and converse with each other; in a word, that they lack nothing which belongs to man, except the material body. I have seen them in a light which exceeds by many degrees the noon-day light of the world; and in that light I observed all parts of their faces more distinctly and clearly than ever I did the face of men on earth.

"I have often told the angels that men in the Christian world are in such blind ignorance concerning angels and spirits, as to believe them to be minds without form, and mere thoughts, concerning which they have no other idea than as of something ethereal in which there is somewhat vital. And because they thus ascribe to them nothing human except a thinking principle, they imagine that they cannot see, because they have no eyes; nor hear, because they have no ears; nor speak, because they have neither mouth nor tongue. The angels said in reply, that they knew such a belief exists with many in the world; and that it is the prevailing belief among the learned, and also to their astonishment among the clergy."—H. H. n. 74, '5.

" The like may be said concerning a man in whom the church is, as concerning an angel in whom heaven is, that he is a church in the least form, as an angel is a heaven in the least form; and further, that a man in whom the church is, equally with an angel, is a heaven; for man was created that he might come into heaven and become an angel. Wherefore, he who has good [or is in good] from the Lord, is a man-angel."—Ibid. 57.

" It is altogether unknown in the Christian world that heaven and hell are from the human race. For it is believed that angels were created from the beginning, and that this was the origin of heaven; and that the devil or satan was an angel of light; but because he became rebellious, was cast down with his crew; and that this was the origin of hell. The angels wonder very much that such a belief should prevail in the Christian world; and still more that nothing whatever is known about heaven, when yet it is a primary point of doctrine in the church. And because such ignorance prevails, they rejoiced in heart that it has pleased the Lord at this time to reveal to mankind many things concerning both heaven and hell; and thereby to dispel, as far as possible, the darkness which is every day increasing, because the church has come to its end. Therefore they desire me to declare positively from their mouths, that there is not a single angel in the whole heaven who was originally created such, nor any devil in hell who was created an angel of light and cast down; but that all, both in heaven and hell, are from the human race; in heaven, those who lived in the world in heavenly love and faith; in hell, those who lived in infernal love and faith; and that hell in the whole complex is what is called the devil and satan."—H. H. n. 311.

"That heaven is from the human race may be further evident from this, that angelic minds and human minds are similar. Both enjoy the faculty of understanding, perceiving and willing. Both are formed to receive heaven; for the human mind is capable of wisdom as well as the angelic mind; but it does not become so wise in the world, because it is in an earthly body, and in that the spiritual mind thinks naturally.

"From these observations it may be seen that the internal of man, which is called his spirit is, in its essence, an angel; and when released from the earthly body it is in the human form the same as an angel. But when the internal of man is not open above but only beneath, then after its release from the body it is still in the human form, but hideous and diabolical; for it cannot look upward to heaven, but only downward to hell."—Ibid. n. 314.

Such is Swedenborg's uniform teaching on this subject, reiterated many times in his writings. Throughout all his theological works, which occupied him nearly thirty years in writing, we find nothing at variance with this. Let us now examine his assertions in the light of reason and Scripture.

The sum of what is taught in the passages we have quoted, is: That man was created with the capacity of becoming an angel, and consequently of enjoying eternal happiness in heaven: That the soul or spirit which continues to live in the spiritual world after the body dies, is in the human form, and is the real man or woman: That all the angels who are also in this form, having a spiritual and substantial organism, are from the human race, and were once inhabitants of this or some other earth; and the same is true of the devils: Consequently no angel or devil was ever created such; but every individual in heaven and in hell, has once had his abode or commenced his existence in the natural realm. Angels, therefore, are more perfect or fully developed men; and men—good men—are angels in embryo. The spiritual or heavenly is evolved from the carnal or earthly man, by an orderly divine process known to Christian theology as regeneration.

Now, is there anything unreasonable in this, as we have seen there is in the old doctrine? Is there not, on the contrary, something in it which strikes us agreeably on its first announcement?—Something which avouches its alliance to the general tenor of all God's arrangements?—Something which tallies with that universal law under which the higher and more perfect are successively evolved from the lower and less perfect forms of being?

All Christians believe in the immortality of the soul; and the soul or spirit is the real man. They all believe that the soul does not die, but survives when its material vestment has crumbled to decay. And if man, after the death of the body, continues to live *as man*, endowed with human attributes—possessing human affections, dispositions, thoughts and feelings—then he must exist in the human form. For to suppose human char-

4*

acter and attributes to exist apart from the human form, were contrary to all reason and all analogy.

Christians also believe that the world which every *good* man enters after death, is a higher and more perfect world than the one in which we are now living. If this be so, then the good man should be a better man— should be in a higher state as to affection and thought —in the other world than he is or has been in this. He should be more perfectly human in disposition and character, more wise, kind and loving; therefore he should be more truly human in *form.* In short, he should be in all respects a more perfect man than he was while on earth. In other words, he should be an angel. Otherwise there would not be that perfect agreement between himself and the increased perfections of the other world, which might reasonably be expected.

The new doctrine that angels are from the human race, and that good men are embryo angels, has the undeniable testimony of reason and analogy in its support. For no law is more clearly revealed in the volume of nature, than that of progress from the imperfect and rudimental to the perfect and mature;—from the lower and simpler to the higher and more complex forms of being. Where among all the works of God, do we find any living thing created full-formed and perfect in the beginning? There is no such thing. Every creature that swims, walks or flies, and every tree and plant that springs from the bosom of the earth, commences its existence in a comparatively simple and imperfect form, and goes on increasing in complexity and perfection as it advances towards the end for which it was created.

It is known to science that all animals commence their existence from eggs which are quite uniform in their shape and structure. There is, therefore, a stage in man's existence, when, to human eyes, he does not differ essentially from the rudimental form of a fish, a frog, or a viper. But as life unfolds from this primary form, the animal undergoes various changes, gradually ascending from lower and simpler to higher and more complex forms, or passing from a less to a more perfect state. A familiar illustration of this universal law, is seen in the changes which insects undergo before reaching the perfected form of butterflies. First, the egg; then succeeds the larva or worm, which is a higher form of life than the egg; next, the caterpillar; then the pupa or chrysalis; lastly, the creature dies—on the outside, at least—and out of that dead covering springs a beautiful butterfly, the perfected form of this insect life. And similar is the case with every other form of life whether belonging to the animal or the vegetable kingdom. From a simple, rudimental and comparatively imperfect form, it goes on steadily unfolding, and gradually assuming one that is higher and more perfect, until it reaches the end of its creation.

And the case is similar with man regarded merely as an inhabitant of the natural world, and as standing at the head of the animal kingdom. Scientists tell us that, previous to birth, he undergoes a variety of changes, and at different stages in his development simulates the forms of various lower orders of animals. However this may be, we know that at the time of birth he is but feebly and imperfectly developed. In his rudimental or infantile form, some of the organs which belong to him in his mature state are wanting, and others are very imperfect or but partially formed. Yet his form in general is human. There is the rudimentary man. But as to the higher capacities of his nature—as to those intellectual and moral powers which give to him the supremacy over all other creatures, and are the essential human characteristics—they do not manifest themselves at all at birth. No living creature is more destitute of the properly human faculties, than a new-born babe. But as this rudimental form unfolds beneath the salutary influences of heaven and earth, the *man* gradually comes forth, and increases in wisdom and in stature.

This law, then—the law of progress from the lower to the higher; or from the less to the more perfect, in everything endowed with life, until it reaches the fulness and perfection of its being—stands revealed on every page of the volume of nature. Nor do we meet with a solitary exception to this law. The Divine creative energy obeys it everywhere. "The principle of progressive advance," says Prof. Bush, "from the imperfect to the finished, from the rude to the refined, from the infantile to the mature, from primordial elements to elaborate formations, from tender germs to ripened fruits, from initial workings to ultimate consummations, is everywhere apparent." Yet what a palpable contradiction of this great law, is the doctrine that angels were created such, full-formed and perfect in the beginning!

Reasoning analogically, therefore, we are brought to the conclusion that angels, like all other created beings, must have had their initial or rudimental state. Where and what was that state? Where and what was the rudimental or embryo angel? Can the Old Theology answer this question? And if this world is not our final home, if we were created to live forever in another and a higher realm, what shall we be in that higher realm?—provided that we here obey the laws of our higher life, and thus give to our spirits a right direction in this their rudimental state. Shall we not be more fully developed and more perfect men? Shall we not be in a higher state of love and wisdom—nearer the · moral likeness of the Creator? In a word, shall we not be angels?

Reason and analogy, then, are clearly in favor of Swedenborg's teaching respecting the origin of angels, and as clearly opposed to the commonly received doctrine. Let us now turn to the Scripture and see what is its testimony on the subject.

And we remark first, that the Bible nowhere speaks of the *creation* of angels. It tells (in the literal sense) of the creation of everything else, of the sun and moon, the earth and the seas, the vegetable and the animal kingdoms, and lastly of man the crowning work of the Creator's hands ; but never of angels. As to the creation of an order of beings intermediate between God and men, the Scripture says not a word.

In the next place, the Bible teaches that " God created man in his own image " (Gen. i. 27). How, then, is it possible that there could be an order of beings above man? A different order of beings must needs have a different form from the human ; and if so, they would not be in the image of God. Stretch your imagination to the utmost, and you cannot conceive of an order of beings superior to man, yet differing from him in outward form. For in so far as their form should differ from the human, they would not be in the image of their Creator ; and therefore they would be *inferior* to man, unless we admit that an order of beings created in the Divine likeness, may be inferior to another order created in the likeness of something else—an admission which would be most absurd. For God is the only perfect One. Among finite beings, therefore, those must be most exalted and perfect who most nearly resemble Him.

Is it said that a moral likeness to his Maker is what is referred to in Gen. i. 27 ? Be it so. But who needs to be told that, among created objects, the form is ever in correspondence with the essence ?—That this is a sovereign and universal law in creation? Even children know that the properly human characteristics cannot exist under the form of a fish or a crocodile—under any form, indeed, other than the human.

No. We can conceive of a race of wiser and better men than any now existing, but they will not be a different order of beings. They will be simply an improved variety of the same order, more truly human, more perfect men both in their internal character and their outward form. They will still be *men*, and all the more so for being truer likenesses of their Maker The text in Genesis, therefore, warrants the assertion that there is not and cannot be any such order of beings between God and man as Christians have supposed angels to be; for the human form is the perfection of all forms, and true human life, therefore, the perfection of all life; and a good man such as an angel is declared to be, is the perfection of created beings.

That this conclusion is legitimate, may be further argued from the fact that the Lord Jesus Christ in whom dwelt "all the fulness of the Godhead bodily," was in the form of a man, not only while He tabernacled in the flesh, but when He subsequently appeared in the spiritual realm to the opened eyes of his disciples. A fact which proves that the human form is capable of receiving the divine love and wisdom in all fulness. Hence it must be the perfection of all forms; and among created beings, therefore, there cannot be any higher order—any nearer to the Divine image and likeness—than man.

But we have further and more conclusive evidence from Scripture. For many instances of the appearance of angels to men in the flesh, are therein recorded; and in every such instance they appeared in the human form—*as men.* Not only so, but they are often *called* men by the inspired writers. Thus when the Lord appeared to Abraham in the plains of Mamre through the medium of angels, it is said: "And he lifted up his eyes and looked, and lo, three *men* stood by him" (Gen. xviii. 2). So of the two angels that appeared to Lot as he sat in the gate of Sodom. These are afterwards called *men.* The Sodomites inquiring after them, said: "Where are the *men* who came in to thee this night" (Gen. xix. 5)? And Lot said: "Unto these *men* do nothing" (v. 8. See also vs. 10, 12, 16). Again,

when the angel of the Lord appeared to the wife of
Manoah, it is said: "The woman came and told her
husband, saying: A *man* of God came unto me, and
his countenance was like the countenance of an angel
of God" (Judges xiii. 6. Also vs. 9, 10). So, too, the
angel Gabriel whom the prophet Daniel saw in vision,
is called "the *man* Gabriel" (Dan. ix. 21). And the
man whom the prophet Zechariah beheld in vision
"among the myrtle trees," is immediately after called
"the angel of the Lord" (Zech. i. 8, 11). Again, when
the women came early in the morning to the Lord's
sepulchre, and had entered into it, Luke says: "Behold
two *men* stood by them in shining garments" (xxiv. 4).
And John says that they saw "two *angels* in white, sitting, the one at the head and the other at the feet where
the body of Jesus had lain" (xx. 12)—proving conclusively the human form of angels and their generic identity with the human race. Again, when the seer of Patmos fell down to worship before the feet of an angel,
the angel said: "See thou do it not; for I am thy fellow servant, and of thy brethren the prophets, and of
them which keep the sayings of this book"—thus plainly affirming his human nature, and his consequent kin-
ship to our race. And that an angel is none other than
a thoroughly regenerate man—one who has attained to
the full stature of spiritual manhood and laid aside his
material body, is evident from his measure as given in
the Apocalypse. For the inspired apostle tells us, that,
having measured the wall of the Holy City when he
was in the spirit, he found it to be "the measure of a
man [meaning a true or regenerate man], that is, of the

angel" (Rev. xxi. 17). It is as true in morals as in physics that two objects which are equal to, or having the same measure as, a third, must be equal to each other. So if the measure of the celestial city be that of a man and likewise of the angel, then the moral dimensions of a true man must be the same as those of an angel, and the two must belong to one and the same order of created intelligences.

Then consider the myriads of angels whom John saw, and whose hymns of thanksgiving and praise he heard, when "in the spirit"; all of whom appear to have been in the human form. And not only so, but we are told that "a great multitude" of that angelic host, were "of all nations and kingdoms and people and tongues," and "stood before the Lamb, clothed with white robes, and palms in their hands." And when it was asked, "What are these who are arrayed in white robes, and whence came they?" the answer was, "These are they who came out of great tribulation, and have washed their robes and made them white in the blood of the Lamb" —showing that they all belonged to the human race, and had once constituted a portion of the tempted and struggling ones of this mundane sphere.

What need of further evidence on the subject, from either the volume of nature or revelation?

But some may ask, What then are we to do with those passages in the Bible which speak of "the angels which kept not their first estate," but "sinned," and were therefore "cast down to hell"? (Jude vi. 2. Peter ii. 4). If the inquirer regards the Epistles as equally inspired, and therefore of equal authority, with the Gospels, we would simply refer him, for an answer, to the criticisms of these passages by Prof. Moses Stuart, whose orthodoxy was never called in question, and whose learning and research were such as to place him in the very foremost rank of biblical scholars. In his work on the Apocalypse, Prof. Stuart, after a very careful and thorough examination of these passages, does not hesitate to pronounce them quotations (doubtless from memory) from the apocryphal book of Enoch, and therefore wholly destitute of divine authority (see *Stuart on the Apoc.*, vol. i., pp. 50–73). The conclusions reached by the learned Professor, may be summarily stated thus :

1st. That this apocryphal book of Enoch was generally known to the early Christian writers—*so* generally as to render it highly probable that all were familiar with its contents. 2d. That it was held by them in high esteem, some of them regarding it as canonical and of divine authority. 3d. That the contents of this book are of such a nature as to leave no reasonable ground for doubt that the statements in regard to the apostate angels made by Jude and Peter, were derived from this source; for this book makes frequent mention of them, of their being bound in chains, kept in darkness and in prison, reserved for judgment, and the like; each of which circumstances is mentioned by these apostles.

Such, then, is the acknowledged foundation on which this absurd and heathenish doctrine concerning the pre-existence, apostasy and punishment of the angels rests. From the apocryphal book of Enoch as its source, through the epistles of Jude and Peter as channels, the doctrine has flowed into the minds of Christians and been generally accepted for divinely revealed truth. And as this book of Enoch is now regarded by all Protestant Christendom as utterly destitute of divine authority, therefore it must be conceded that the passages in Peter and Jude's epistles, obviously taken from this book, furnish no support to the absurd doctrine they have been so often cited to prove.

And now apply to each of these doctrines—the Old and the New—that highest and surest test of truth, its obvious *practical* tendency. Which is most benign and wholesome in its influence on the believer's life and character? According to the Old view, the angels are not *men*, and never were. They are quite outside the pale of our common humanity, created another and different order of beings from ourselves. What matters it to us, then, how wise and good and glorious they may be? For with all our strivings after the heavenly life, with all our acts of self-denial and self-crucifixion, with all our patient and persevering endeavors to follow the Lord in the regeneration, we can never become angels. Our human nature renders it impossible. We are a different order of beings.

Nor does the Old doctrine respecting the nature and origin of devils address itself to human fears, any more than that respecting the nature and origin of angels addresses itself to human hopes. For it teaches that the devils, too, are a different order of beings from us—different in their original nature and constitution ; that they are fallen angels, and consequently were never men like ourselves. Of what concern, therefore, is it to us to know the character or manner of life of the devils, since we can never become one of them. We belong to a different genus. No man, therefore, however wicked and unrepentant, is to be regarded as a rudimental devil.

But the New doctrine teaches that both angels and devils are from the human race; that they are all partakers of our common humanity, and were once men like ourselves. It teaches that we were all created with the capacity of ultimately becoming angels, and that the laws of our higher or spiritual nature are the very laws of the angelic life. And not only so, but that we shall actually become either angels or devils, according as we freely obey or disobey these divinely revealed laws. It teaches that this present world is the seminary of both the upper and the nether realms; that men in the flesh are rudimental angels or rudimental devils.

Thus the New doctrine brings us into close and vital relationship with the angels of heaven. It affirms our near affinity—nay, our absolute identity—with them, as to our nature or spiritual constitution. It reveals them to us as sympathizing and loving brothers, possessing a common nature with ourselves, having once like us experienced the bondage of selfishness and sin, and through a course of varied discipline suited to each one's state—through disappointments and sorrows, through struggles and sore temptations, through faith and prayer and repentance and self-denial—have become cleansed of their natural defilements, and elevated to their present state of heavenly wisdom and serene peace. Thus the New doctrine appeals strongly to human hopes. It discloses the grand capabilities of our nature, opens up to our mental vision sublime and glorious possibilities, and prompts us, by the hope of one day becoming wise, and happy angels, to a resolute and persevering struggle against the evils that infest our bosoms.

And by teaching us that the devils, also, are from the human race and were once men like ourselves, the New doctrine appeals no less to human fears than to human hopes. It discloses to us those marred and distorted forms of humanity—the denizens of the nether realms, yet created with the capacity of becoming angels—and proclaims the solemn truth that we, too, may become, yes, *shall* become just such inverted images of the Divine, if we turn our backs upon the Lord and disregard the precepts of his holy Word. In the revealed character and condition of the devils, we see disclosed our own final destiny if we live in the indulgence of our natural inclinations, and do not deny self, take up our cross and follow the Lord. Thus the New doctrine constrains the believer, through fear of all that is loathsome in the character and mournful in the condition of devils, to shun the paths which they have trod, to curb the propensities which they indulged, to seek "the way, the truth, and the life" which they ignored and forsook.

Yes. Angels and devils once were men. And angels *or* devils we, too, shall become. So teaches the New doctrine. And it is for each individual to choose which it shall be. A question of deep solemnity and supreme moment! How carefully should it be weighed! How watchful should such consideration make us over our

5 *

hearts and lives—our dispositions, motives and cherished purposes!

Considered, therefore, as to its influence on the believer's life and character—viewed as to its obvious *practical* tendency—which of these doctrines appears most worthy of acceptation, the Old or the New?   Which has the signature of infinite Wisdom and Love most legibly impressed upon it?   Which appears most in harmony with the Divine character and attributes as revealed in nature and the written Word?   Which looks most like heaven-descended truth, and which most like the vain imaginings of men?   Which is calculated to exert the most salutary influence on the soul of the believer?   The reader needs not our answer to these questions.   He can answer them for himself.

IV.

THE ESSENTIAL NATURE OF HEAVEN.

FEW terms are of more frequent occurrence in the Gospels, than *heaven* and *the kingdom of heaven.* And precisely what they mean, would seem, therefore, to be a matter of some practical importance to every believer of the Gospels.   What *is* heaven, viewed as to its essential nature?   Dr. E. H. Sears asks this question near the commencement of his *Foregleams of Immortality;* and immediately adds:

"We know of no subject so practical as this.   The whole business of the present life, with all its discipline of labor, sorrow and joy, is to prepare and ripen us for heaven ; and if it shall not do this, life will be a miserable failure. But how shall we prepare for it, unless we know what we are to prepare for ? How can we travel, unless we know the point of the compass towards which we are steering ? "

The Christian Scriptures are commonly regarded as a revelation from God. They are called, and are believed to be, the Word of God. And for what end was this revelation given ? Was it not, primarily, that men might be conducted to heaven ?—might become happy denizens of the kingdom of heaven, and thus realize the end for which they were created ? If this be so,—if the attainment of heaven be a matter of supreme moment, the very end for which the Lord created us, and would therefore have us strive for unceasingly ;—the end for which He came into the world, taught, suffered, died, rose from the sepulchre, and ascended to the Father ;— the end for which the church, the ministry, the institutions and ordinances of the Gospel were established ;— the end for which Christians erect houses of worship, and assemble there to hear preaching, unite in prayer and in songs of thanksgiving and praise ;—if heaven, we say, be the great end of all this stupendous machinery and these sublime events, then a clear understanding and a well-grounded belief of what heaven is and where it is, would seem to be matters of supreme importance.

Christians have hitherto believed and taught that heaven is a *place* into which a person may be admitted by an act of immediate Divine mercy. *Going to heaven,* therefore (if this old and once popular view be accepted) would mean simply to enter the *place* called heaven, as a man might go to a foreign country, or walk into a cathedral or a king's palace. And if entrance into heaven be from immediate mercy, and those who enter are admitted to its blissful enjoyments, why are not *all* admitted, whatever be their character? For God must desire the happiness of all, since He is a Being of infinite love. If, therefore, *going to heaven* means simply going to a *place* called heaven, and if people are admitted by an act of immediate mercy, then it is difficult to understand why everybody should not go there,—unless one accepts the old Calvinistic dogma of unconditional election, and believes that it is God's eternal purpose and desire that some of his intelligent creatures should be forever excluded from the abodes of bliss.

Now, contrary to the old and commonly received doctrine, Swedenborg teaches that heaven is not a place, but a certain state of the soul—a state of love to the Lord and the neighbor, which is one of spiritual likeness to our Maker. It cannot therefore be located in any region of space. Being purely spiritual and *within* men, it exists wherever human spirits exist that are in a heavenly state—and nowhere else. To cite the seer's own words :

" It is to be observed that heaven is not in any certain or determinate place, thus not on high according to the vulgar opinion, but it is where the Divine is; that is, with every one and in every one who is in charity and faith, for charity and faith are heaven because they are from the Divine."—A. C. n. 8931.

And speaking of discoursing with the angels on one occasion "when the interior heaven was opened to him," or in other words, when he was brought into a state similar to that of the angels by the opening of the interiors of his own soul, he says:

"Let it be remarked that, although I was in heaven, still I was not out of myself but in the body, for heaven is in man in whatever place; and so, whenever it pleases the Lord, a man may be in heaven and yet not be withdrawn from the body."—A. C. n. 3884.

"The love and wisdom in which the angels are and which constitute heaven, are not theirs but from the Lord, and are indeed the Lord in them. . . . The angels themselves confess that they live from the Lord; and from this it is evident that heaven is conjunction with the Lord."—D. C. n. 28.

"It can in no case be said that heaven is without one, but that it is within him; for every angel receives the heaven which is without him according to the heaven that is within him. This plainly shows how much he is deceived, who believes that to go to heaven is merely to be elevated among the angels, without regard to the quality of one's interior life; thus that heaven may be given to every one from immediate mercy; when yet, unless heaven is within a person, nothing of the heaven without him flows-in or is received."—H. H. n. 54; also 400, 518, 525.

And throughout his voluminous works the same doctrine is everywhere taught: Which is, that heaven is within men, and is to be thought of as a certain quality of life or condition of the soul—as an internal *state*, and not as an external *place*. It is a state of spiritual nearness to, or conjunction with, the Lord; and "conjunction with the Lord," we are repeatedly told, "is effected by means of the truths of the Word, and a life according to them." (A. R. n. 883.)

Every individual has some ruling love—a love that continually acts as an impelling force within him, even without his being conscious of its presence. This love is his life. It shapes his thoughts and words, and directs all his activities. The quality of his life, therefore, is that of his ruling love. Oftentimes this love lies deeply concealed, and does not reveal itself to others here on earth. But in the Hereafter all disguises are thrown off, and the interiors are laid open; and whatever had been assumed for the sake of appearance or credit among men, is rejected, and the ruling love is made manifest by being *acted out*. The individual then becomes the very image of his love—goes where his love leads him, does what his love prompts, seeks what his love craves, and *is* just what his love is, good or bad, according to its quality. If heaven, therefore, be a certain quality of life, then as surely as a man preserves his identity in the Hereafter, or carries his own life (and nothing else) with him into the other world, so surely must he carry his heaven with him if he hopes for an abode among the blessed.

But Swedenborg not only teaches that heaven is a state, but he has clearly revealed the nature of that state, or the kind of life that constitutes heaven. He tells us that love of the Lord and the neighbor is the ruling love of all the angels, and that this love flows into their hearts from the Lord, and is similar, therefore, to the love that He feels and exercises toward all his creatures. It is the Lord's own influent life operating within them, and leading them to love what He loves, and to delight in doing what He loves to have them do. It is the Divine Love received by the angels so as to become in them love of the Lord and of each other. Hence all in heaven are said to dwell in the Lord and the Lord in them; for they all abide in his love, and his love abides in them. Thus they are images and likenesses of the Lord, being conjoined to Him by love. And we may see from this why heaven is said to be a state of conjunction with the Lord; and what is meant by the Lord's own words to his disciples: "Abide in me and I in you." "He that abideth in me and I in him, the same bringeth forth much fruit." "If ye keep my commandments, ye shall abide in my love." (John xv. 4, 5, 10.) And the beloved apostle says: "God is love; and he that dwelleth in love, dwelleth in God and God in him." (1 John iv. 16.)

Love of the Lord, then, is the supreme love of all in heaven. But to love the Lord supremely, is not to love Him as a person, but it is to love the divine things which proceed from Him—innocence, justice, sincerity, charity—all the Christian graces; and these are really loved only by those who practise them as religious duties. Accordingly, Swedenborg says:

"To love the Lord is not to love his person, but to love those things that proceed from Him, for these are the Lord with man. Thus it is to love what is itself sincere, what is itself right, what is itself just; and since these things are the Lord, therefore in proportion as a man loves them and acts from them, he loves and acts from the Lord; and the Lord removes from him things insincere and unjust, even as to the very intentions and will."—A. E. n. 973.

Again:

"By loving the Lord is not meant to love Him as a person ; for by this love alone man is not conjoined with heaven, but by a love of the divine good and truth which are the Lord in heaven ; and these two are not loved by knowing, thinking, understanding, and speaking them, but by willing and doing them because they are commanded by the Lord, and therefore are of use.   Nothing is full until it is *done*, and what is done is the end for the sake of which the love is cherished."—Ibid. n. 1099.

We thus see what is meant by loving the Lord supremely, and how entirely this teaching, which is so often repeated by Swedenborg, agrees with the Lord's own. For He says : " He that hath my commandments and keepeth them, he it is that loveth me."   (John xiv. 21.) " Ye are my friends if ye *do* whatsoever I command you." (Ibid. xv. 14.)   " This is my commandment, that ye love one another as I have loved you " (v. 12).   And to love others as the Lord loves us, is not merely to refrain from doing them evil, but to intend and do them good, and seek to promote their highest welfare.

Such is the nature of the love that dwells in the bosom of the angels.   The Lord's own love constitutes their breath of life.   In the. atmosphere of this love, which seeketh not its own but always the good of others, they live and move and have their being.   From it they think and speak, and by it all their actions are prompted and controlled.   It is the very essence and life of heaven.

But truth of corresponding purity and elevation is conjoined with this love in angelic minds, as the sun's light is conjoined with heat, or as the lungs are conjoined with the heart in our bodies. Therefore the angels are as wise as they are good. They act from love, and according to truth which is the everlasting law of love. They obey the divine laws of charity because they *love* to obey them—because it is their supreme delight to do the will of the Lord.

And the unspeakable bliss of heaven all flows from the love which the angels receive and exercise. And as we can form but a faint conception of the purity and intensity of their love, therefore we can have but a faint conception of their exalted happiness. Swedenborg says the delights and blessedness which they enjoy are beyond the power of language to describe, and such as the natural man cannot conceive of.

" Heaven," he says, " is so full of delights, that, viewed in itself, it is nothing but delight and blessedness. . . The delights are ineffable and likewise innumerable ; yet not one can be known or believed by him who is in the mere delight of the body or flesh."—H. H. n. 397, '8.

" Heavenly joy, such as it is in its essence, cannot be described, because it is in the inmosts of the life of the angels. . . It is as if their interiors were wide open and free to receive delight and blessedness which is distributed to every single fibre, and so throughout the whole frame."—Ibid. n. 409.

" How great the delight of heaven is, may appear from this single circumstance, that it is delightful to all there to communicate their delights and blessings to each other. And because all in heaven are of this character,

6

it is obvious how immense is the delight of heaven; for there is in heaven a communication of all with each and of each with all. Such communication flows from the two loves of heaven, which are love to the Lord and love toward the neighbor; and it is the nature of these loves to communicate their delights. Love to the Lord is of this nature, because the Lord's love is the love of communicating all that He has to all his creatures, for He wills the happiness of all; and a similar love is in each of those who love Him, because the Lord is in them."—H. H. n. 399.

Now compare the Old with this New doctrine concerning heaven, and note the contrast. The former teaches that heaven is a *place*, into which people may be admitted arbitrarily—suddenly—by an act of immediate Divine mercy; the latter says it is *a state of life* into which people come gradually, and only through voluntary obedience to the laws of that life revealed in the Divine Word. The one teaches that admission into it is granted as a *reward* for certain acts done or refrained from here on earth; the other, that entrance is effected through the normal opening of the interiors by *religious obedience to the God-given laws of the soul.* The one presents it as a desirable locality to which the souls of the pious will be transferred when they leave the body; the other, as a certain kind of life that each one must carry with him—obscured though it be, and but partially developed here below. In the light of the Old doctrine, therefore, heaven seems to be an arbitrary gift of God, conditioned, it is true, on the receiver's faith and repentance; while the New doctrine reveals an organic and necessary connection between heaven and earth—between the angel and the man—between the life hereafter and the life here.

Therefore, according to the New doctrine, *going to heaven* is no obscure or mystical phrase, but one perfectly intelligible to the most ordinary understanding. For if heaven is not a place but a state, it is obvious that entrance into it can be had only by such as enter into the heavenly state. To long and labor and strive for heaven, therefore, is to long and labor and strive for that state of life which is heaven. And that state is one of love to the Lord and the neighbor—the very opposite of man's natural or hereditary state, which is one of supreme self-love. To seek heaven, therefore, is to seek the complete subjugation of our natural love of self and the world, and the exaltation or establishment of the Lord's own love and life in place of it. And this is to lose the old hereditary life, and to find a new life that is far higher and better. "He that loseth his life for my sake, shall find it," saith the Lord.

And now compare the two doctrines—the Old and the New. Which is most rational and which most Scriptural? If this seems doubtful to any mind, we hope in subsequent chapters to remove such doubt. Then look at the two as to their practical tendency—their obvious influence upon life and character. Which is most wholesome, most stimulating, most benign and potent in its operation upon the receiver's mind and heart?

V.

CHARACTER OF THE ANGELS.

FROM what has been said of the essential nature of heaven, it is plain to be seen what ought to be the general and particular character of the angels—what their prevailing dispositions and motives, and how they ought uniformly to feel and act. But Swedenborg has himself sketched their character in many parts of his writings. Let us see, then, whether his sketch be such as ought to follow by logical sequence from the alleged ruling loves of all in heaven; and whether their character as portrayed by him, be in agreement with the laws of love as revealed in Holy Scripture.

According to his disclosures, no one in heaven desires any good merely for himself; but it is the delight of every one there "to do good and communicate," hoping for nothing in return. Their highest happiness consists in freely imparting their joys to others. He says:

"Mutual love which reigns in heaven, consists in this: that each loves his neighbor more than himself. Hence the whole heaven constitutes, as it were, a single man, all being thus consociated by mutual love from the Lord. Hence it is, too, that the felicities of all are communicated to each individual, and those of each individual to all: and hence the heavenly form is such, that every one is, as it were, a kind of centre, whence he is a centre of the communications, consequently of the felicities, proceeding from all; which take place according to all the differences of that love, which are innumerable. And as they who are principled in that love perceive the highest happiness in this circumstance, that they are capable of communicating to others what they receive by influx themselves, which they do from the heart, the communication is thus rendered perpetual and eternal; in consequence of which the happiness of each increases in proportion to the increase of the Lord's kingdom."—A. C. 2057.

" When an angel does good to any one, he also communicates to him his own good, satisfaction and blessedness, so that he is willing to give everything to the other, and to retain nothing. When he is in such communication, good flows-in with satisfaction and blessedness to him in a much greater degree than he gives, and this continually with increase. But as soon as the thought occurs, that he wills to communicate what he has, to the intent that he may obtain that influx of satisfaction and blessedness in himself, the influx is dissipated; and still more so, if anything presents itself of thought concerning recompense from him to whom he communicates his good. This it has been given me to know from much experience. Hence also it may be manifest that the Lord is in singulars, for He is such that He wills to give Himself to all; hence satisfaction and blessedness are increased with those who become images and likenesses of Him."—Ibid. n. 6478.

Observe it is here said that "good flows-in with satisfaction and blessedness to him [who wills to give everything to others], in a far greater degree than he gives; and this with continual increase." Which agrees perfectly with these words of the Lord—spiritually interpreted: " Give, and it shall be given unto you; good measure, pressed down, shaken together and running over, shall men give into your bosom. For with the same measure that ye mete withal, it shall be measured to you again." (Luke vi. 38.) But if an angel "wills to communicate what he has, to the intent that he may obtain that influx of satisfaction and blessedness in himself, the influx is dissipated." And so, in respect to the purely disinterestedness of their love, and their desire to have others share their blessedness, the angels resemble the Lord Himself, whose delight it is to impart of his own life and blessedness to his creatures.

No one in heaven aspires to be great above others. No one desires to have others honor or serve him personally. All are more desirous of serving than of being served. "In heaven he is the greatest of all, who is the least of all," says Swedenborg; "for whosoever wills to be least, has the greatest happiness, and consequently is the greatest." Yet "heaven does not consist in desiring to be least with a view to being the greatest, for in such desire there lurks the lust of preeminence; but it consists in this, that every one should from the heart wish better to others than to himself, and should serve others with a view to their happiness, that is, from a principle of love that has no regard to selfish ends." (A. C. n. 452.) And the Lord says: "Whosoever will be great among you, let him be your minister; and whosoever will be chief among you, let him be your servant; even as the Son of Man came not to be ministered unto, but to minister, and to give his life a ransom for many." (Matt. xx. 26, '7, '8.)

Here, again, we trace the resemblance of the angels to the Lord—precisely as it should be, if they are filled and animated by his Spirit.

Then their humility, according to Swedenborg, is no less remarkable than their unselfish love. Notwithstanding their exalted wisdom, transcending by many degrees that of the wisest men on earth, they are not puffed up on account of it. They have no pride of intellect, no self-derived intelligence, no self-righteousness. They regard none of the goods or truths they possess as their own; but perceive and acknowledge and love to acknowledge that they are all the Lord's, and are his free and perpetual gift to them.

"Because the angels believe this, therefore they refuse all thanks on account of the good they do, and are displeased and recede if any one attributes good to them. They wonder that any one should believe that he is wise and does good from himself. Good done for the sake of one's self, they do not call good; because it is done from self; but good done for the sake of good, this they call good from the Divine; and this good, they say, is what makes heaven, because it is the Lord [for He is within it as its inmost principle. A. C. 1802, 3951, 8480]."—H. H. n. 9.

Again:

"He lives most, that is, most wisely and intelligently, most blessedly and happily, who is most confirmed in the belief that he does not live of himself; and this is the life of the angels, especially of the celestial who are the inmost or nearest to the Lord. . . . In heaven they are the greatest who are the least, and they are the wisest who perceive and think themselves the least wise; and they are the happiest who desire others to be most happy, but themselves least so. Heaven consists in desiring to be below all, but hell in desiring to be above all; therefore in the glory of heaven there is nothing at all of the glory of this world."—A. C. n. 2654.

This reveals the profound and beautiful humility of the angels; and in this consists their real exaltation. And there can be no spiritual exaltation of a finite being, without similar humility. As it is written: "For whosoever exalteth himself, shall be abased; and he that humbleth himself, shall be exalted." (Luke xiv. 11.)

The angels are further described by Swedenborg as abounding in charity or neighborly love. Under the influence of this principle, they seek perpetually to excite what is good and true in the minds of men and of each other; and they are ever ready to overlook, or put the best possible construction on, whatever they perceive as evil and false. They have no inclination to spy out others' faults, or to condemn any one on account of them, but rather to find what is good and true in every one.

"They who are in charity, scarcely see another's evils, but observe all that is good and true in him, and put a favorable interpretation upon what is evil and false. Such are all the angels; and they have this disposition from the Lord who turns all evil into good."—A. C. n. 1079.

"They who are not in charity, think only evil of their neighbor, and speak nothing but evil of him; or if they say what is good, they do it on their own account, or with a view to insinuate themselves into the favor of him whom they flatter with commendation. Those, however, who are in charity, think and speak nothing but what is good of their neighbor; and this not for their own sake, or to gain the favor of others, but from the Lord operating in charity. The former resemble the evil spirits, and the latter the angels who are attendant on man; for evil spirits always excite man's evils and falsities, and condemn him; whereas angels excite nothing but goods and truths, excusing what is evil and false. · Hence it is evident, that such as are not in charity are under the dominion of evil spirits, by whom man has communication with hell; and that such as are in charity are governed by angels, by whom he has communication with heaven."—A. C. n. 1088.

Such is the charity in which, we are told, the angels are. And is it not the very spirit of the Lord's own Gospel? Is it not in agreement with the spirit of the texts which counsel us not to judge, nor condemn, nor think evil of others; and not to be on the watch for a mote in a brother's eye, without thinking of the beam which needs first to be cast out of our own eye?

Look also at the *innocence* of the angels as portrayed by Swedenborg. And this word as employed by him, has a vastly deeper and more comprehensive meaning than is commonly given to it. It means not mere sinlessness, or freedom from wrong in thought or deed; but a state of the highest wisdom, such as only those are in who have been brought to see that their natural proprium is altogether evil, and that whatever good they have is not their own but the Lord's; and whose deep desire and purpose it is to be led of the Lord in all things, and who have no desire to lead themselves. It is, in short, the very *esse* of all goodness, for it is the Lord's own life in the soul. ·

"It is said in heaven that innocence dwells in wisdom, and that an angel has as much of wisdom as he has of innocence. That such is the case, they confirm by this, that those who are in a state of innocence attribute nothing of good to themselves, but regard all their

goods as gifts received, and ascribe them to the Lord;
that they wish to be led by Him, and not by themselves; that they love everything which is good, and
are delighted with everything which is true, because
they know and perceive that to love what is good, thus
to will and to do it, is to love the Lord; and to love
what is true, is to love their neighbor; that they live
contented with their own, whether it be little or much,
because they know that they receive as much as is profitable for them; little, if little be profitable, and much,
if much be profitable; and that they do not themselves
know what is best for them, this being known only to
the Lord, whose providence in all things contemplates
eternal ends. Hence they are not anxious about the
future. They call solicitude about the future, care for
the morrow, which they say is grief for the loss or non-
reception of things which are not necessary for the uses
of life. In their intercourse with others they never act
from an evil end, but from what is good, just and sincere. To act from an evil end, they call cunning, which
they shun as the poison of a serpent, since it is altogether contrary to innocence. Because they love nothing more than to be led of the Lord, and acknowledge
their indebtedness to Him for everything they receive,
therefore they are removed from their proprium; and
in the degree that they are removed from their proprium, in the same degree the Lord flows-in. . . . Such
is the innocence which is called the innocence of wisdom."—H. H. n. 278.

We further learn from this new revelation, that the
angels love even the worst of men, and constantly endeavor to do them all the good they can. They feel
only tenderest love and compassion for us, even in our
states of deepest guilt and sin. However we may resist their hallowing influences, and close our hearts

against the precious things they long to communicate, they never leave us, nor relax their efforts to do us good. They continually endeavor to withdraw and withhold us from evil—to rescue our souls from the dominion of infernal spirits. They do this, because the Lord's own love is in them and in active operation; and it is the nature of this love to do good to all, and to seek the salvation and happiness of all. The angels are, therefore, in the same ends as the Lord Himself, and desire the very things that He desires. Hence they are called his ministers or "ministering spirits." (Heb. i. 14. See also Ps. ciii. 21 : civ. 4.) They are images and likenesses of Himself. In them is fulfilled the great law of love delivered in these divine words: " Love your enemies; bless them that curse you; do good to them that hate you; and pray for them that despitefully use you and persecute you; that ye may be the children of your Father which is in heaven; for He maketh his sun to rise on the evil and on the good, and sendeth rain on the just and on the unjust.—Be ye, therefore, perfect, even as your Father which is in heaven is perfect." (Matt. v. 44–48.)

Such is a brief sketch of the character of the heavenly inhabitants, as portrayed by Swedenborg. And is it not precisely such as might be expected, if heaven in its essential nature be what he says it is? Is not every trait as here delineated, such as might be inferred from the alleged ruling loves of heaven?—such as follows by strict logical sequence from love to the Lord and love to the neighbor, when these loves rule supreme in the soul?

VI.

VERDICT OF REASON AND EXPERIENCE.

NOW is this doctrine respecting heaven, as thus far opened, true?   Let us see,—and we will first examine it in the light of reason, common observation and human experience.

However people's ideas of heaven may differ in other respects, they all agree in this: that whoever goes there, will find great and enduring happiness.   The Bible clearly warrants this belief.   But in what does human happiness consist?   What do reason, observation and experience teach on this point?   Certainly that it does not consist in any outward appliances of which time and space are predicable.   It is not those who are most comfortably lodged and luxuriously fed and royally apparelled, who are the happiest.   By no means.   True and enduring happiness is something which the wealth of the Indies cannot purchase.   For it does not depend on the character or condition of things without, but on the character and condition of the world within us—on the state of the soul.   *Locate* people as you may, place them in the midst of the loveliest surroundings, supply them with all the elegances, comforts and luxuries that wealth can furnish—houses, furniture, equipage, books, friends, companions, all that the natural man craves— and you will not thereby make them happy.   They may appear and even esteem themselves happy for a time; but it is only an external delight, a merely natural gratification which they experience, and which from its very nature must soon pass away. Every person of much reflection or self-intuition, knows that

> " The mind is its own place, and in itself
> Can make a heaven of hell, a hell of heaven."

The soul very soon stamps its own complexion on a man's entire surroundings. The outer soon acquires the color and the key of our inner world; becomes beautiful and harmonious if there be beauty and harmony within, but ugly and discordant if deformity and discord are in the soul. As one of our own poets sings:

> " It is the soul's prerogative, its fate
> To shape the outward to its own estate;
> If right itself, then all around is well;
> If wrong, it makes of all without a hell."

No. It is in vain that men seek, with any hope of finding, true happiness from without—from any new political, social, economic or industrial arrangements. We do not mean to say that some external arrangements may not be more useful than others in promoting internal and spiritual culture. But real happiness can never come from without, but only from within—from a regenerate and well-ordered state of the soul, yea, from the Lord's own presence therein. It is the normal result of obedience to the laws of our spiritual life. Let these laws be faithfully obeyed, and the soul is thereby opened to an influx of the Divine life, and the man is happy under almost any circumstances. But let them be violated, and no amount of purple and fine linen and sumptuous fare can ward off the evil consequences of such violation. The truly good man, however bereft of comforts and luxuries, is never really miserable; nor is the bad man, though crowned with abundant earthly treasures, ever truly happy. For true happiness never comes from without, but depends wholly on the condition of the soul. How clearly did Milton see this, when he sang in strains no less true than beautiful:

> " He that hath light within his own clear breast,
> May sit in the centre and enjoy bright day;
> But he that hides a dark soul and foul thoughts,
> Benighted walks under the mid-day sun,
> Himself is his own dungeon."

And another of England's poets says:

> " Know then this truth (enough for man to know),
> Virtue alone is happiness below.
> Condition, circumstance, is not the thing,—
> Bliss is the same in subject and in king."

And the same thing has been seen, if not sung, by every one who has received from the Creator a single spark of poetic inspiration.

If, then, all who go to heaven are to be happy there, and if true happiness on earth comes only from a regenerate and well-ordered state of the soul, the conclusion is forced upon us that heaven is not a *place* into which people may be admitted from immediate mercy, but a certain state of life. And it may be further inferred that it is a similar state (it may be far more exalted and perfect) to that which is known to be attended with the highest happiness on earth. And what is that state? Let reason, observation and experience testify.

Consider that God is Law and Order itself. He governs the material universe by fixed and determinate laws.

In every form and condition of matter, laws pervade and preside over it. We call them laws of matter, but they are really the Lawgiver's own vital presence in matter, —laws to which He continually subjects matter. And every infraction of these laws, we know, is attended with more or less suffering. Our corporeal frame has its laws —beneficent and God-ordained; and bodily health and comfort can be enjoyed only on condition of the strict observance of these laws. They cannot be transgressed with impunity. If we overwork our bodies or our brains, if we indulge our appetites to excess, if we take poison (be it food or drink) into the system, if we breathe a vitiated atmosphere or neglect all bodily exercise for a considerable time, we must suffer the penalty of every such infraction of the body's laws,—a penalty always proportioned to the extent of the violation.

Now, mind has its laws as well as matter. There are laws of the soul as well as of the body. And it is just as essential to the health of the soul—as essential, there-fore, to human happiness—that these spiritual laws be obeyed, as it is to the body's health and comfort that we obey the laws of our physical being. All these laws are divine—are God's laws; and none of them can be transgressed with impunity. If the soul's laws, there-fore, be violated, the soul will be sick and suffer, and un-happiness will ensue; as certainly as bodily sickness and suffering follow the transgression of the body's laws.

But where and what are the laws of the soul, on the observance of which human happiness is conditioned? They are all contained in the Word of the Lord. The Word is, indeed, *the Book of Life*, for herein are recorded all the laws of our spiritual life.   Yet some of these laws may be rationally inferred.   They may be learned from experience and observation.   Since they are God's laws, they must all be laws of love, and therefore good ; and if carefully obeyed, they must produce the greatest possible amount of happiness.   Obedience to divine laws can never be attended with unhappiness.   This is ever the result of disobedience.

Now every one knows that people are not happy who are governed by an inordinate self-love, and who seek their own good exclusively, regardless of the good of their neighbor.   Every one who has not wholly quenched the Divine Spirit within him, feels that, in obeying at all times the promptings of self-interest—living and acting with a supreme and exclusive regard to himself—he is not obeying the will of God, nor that law of life which God has ordained.   He is inwardly conscious of living and acting otherwise than the Heavenly Father would have him.   Nor is he happy—far from it—in the perpetual indulgence of his love of self.   He is restless and sour and hard and morose.   And not only does this love make the soul of its possessor unhappy, but its indulgence is attended with unhappiness to others.   Its tendency is altogether evil.   Let all men act in obedience to its promptings, and universal hatred, anarchy, war and wretchedness would be the inevitable consequence.

Nor are those persons happy who are in the lust of dominion—who seek to exalt themselves above others and to rule over others ; nor those who pride themselves on their attainments, and desire to be esteemed and honored above others on account of them ; nor those who cherish hatred and revenge, who indulge in bitter and vindictive feelings toward enemies. All such dispositions and feelings are the legitimate offspring of self love, and utterly opposed to the laws of life which God has revealed for the government of human spirits. And from the bosoms in which they dwell, they drive away all genuine peace, and induce a restless fever-heat which burns and burns to the core of life—a tormenting fire of hell.

Very different is the case with those who obey the laws of neighborly love; whose supreme desire is to render themselves useful—to do all the good they can in the world; who love, and seek to do good to, even their enemies ; who have no desire to rule over but only to serve others ; who care little for mere earthly rewards —the honors or praises of men ; who claim no merit on account of what they know or do, but in their hearts acknowledge their utter dependence on the Lord, and ascribe all the honor and glory to Him. These are the truly great, wise and noble ones of earth, however obscure their names or humble their abode. Viewed in the light of that truth by which all souls are to be finally judged, they shine like stars even in this world. They are the golden links in God's great chain of love, connecting men on earth with the angels in heaven. Men call them angels—for some perception of the quality of angelic life is vouchsafed to many here on earth.

And such persons, too, are the only ones who know what true and substantial happiness is. They are happy because they obey the highest laws—laws divinely ordained and revealed for the government of human be-

7 *

ings. And the nearer men approach to this state, or to the quality of angelic life as disclosed by Swedenborg—the more faithfully they obey all the revealed laws of the higher or regenerate life—the more pure, serene and exalted is their happiness. This has been the universal experience of mankind in all ages.

But Swedenborg does not teach that the happiness of heaven in all its fullness, can ever be enjoyed on earth. We must lay aside the material body before we can arrive at the perfection of that state denoted by the term *heaven.* The blessedness experienced here on earth resulting from strict conformity to the highest laws, or from the highest spiritual state to which we are capable of attaining here, is obscure and meagre when compared with that which regenerate souls will enjoy in the world beyond. Accordingly Swedenborg says:

"The man who is in the loves of self and the world, so long as he lives in the body feels delight from these loves, and also in each of the pleasures to which they give birth. But the man who is in love to God and the neighbor, does not, so long as he lives in the body, feel a manifest delight from these loves and from the good affections thence derived, but only a blessedness almost imperceptible, because it is stored up in his interiors, and veiled by the exteriors which are of the body, and blunted by worldly cares.

"But the states are entirely changed after death. The delights of the love of self and the world are then turned into painful and horrible sensations, which are called hell-fire, and occasionally into things defiled and filthy corresponding to their unclean pleasures which—strange to say—are then delightful to them. But the obscure delight and almost imperceptible blessedness which had been enjoyed by those in the world who were in love to God and in love toward the neighbor, are then turned into the delight of heaven, which becomes perceptible and sensible in all manner of ways; for that blessedness which lay stored up and hidden in their interiors when they lived in the world, is then revealed and brought forth into manifest sensation, because they are then in the spirit, and that was the delight of their spirit."—H. H. n. 401.

"All goods increase immensely in the other life. But man's life while in the body is such that he cannot go beyond loving his neighbor as himself, because he is in corporeal principles; but when these are removed the love becomes more pure, and at length angelic, which is to love the neighbor more than one's self. For in heaven it is delightful to do good to another, and not delightful to do good to themselves unless in order that the good may become another's, thus for the sake of another; and this is to love the neighbor more than themselves."—Ibid. n. 406.

Heaven, then, according to the New Christianity, is essentially a state of life. And if happiness must enter into our idea of it, as an essential element, then it can be no other than the very state that Swedenborg says it is ; and the angels, if human and subject to the laws ordained for the government of human beings, must be of precisely the character that he has so often and so vividly portrayed. The nature of the heavenly life can be none other than that he describes. This is the clear and undeniable testimony of enlightened reason, common observation, and all human experience. To suppose the character of the angels to be at all different from that revealed through him—to suppose them pos-

sessed of different dispositions and feelings, to be actuated by different motives, to desire and seek different
ends, would be to suppose them not thoroughly imbued
with the spirit of the Gospel, not subject to the laws of
the higher life as revealed in the Divine Word, not images and likenesses of the Lord, not children of the
Heavenly Father, and therefore *not* his "ministering
spirits sent forth to minister for them who shall be heirs
of salvation."

But what is the testimony of Holy Scripture on the
subject? We have incidentally introduced some of it
already ; but we will consider this question more in de-
tail, and answer it more fully, in the next chapter.

VII.

TESTIMONY OF SCRIPTURE.

THE next question to be considered is : Does this
doctrine concerning the essential nature of heaven
and the character of the angels as delineated by Swedenborg, agree with the teachings of the Bible ? If not,
devout and reverent souls will be slow, as they ought,
about accepting it. But right here, is the place to say,
that human rationality is as truly the gift of God as the
Sacred Scripture. And before accepting such an interpretation of Scripture as would make the Bible contradict the clear intuitions of reason and all human experience, we ought carefully to consider whether it does not

admit of some other interpretation more accordant with the testimony of these two witnesses. All who desire that the credit and authority of the Bible be maintained, must desire to see its language interpreted in such a manner (if this can be fairly done) as to make its teachings tally with the intuitions of our highest reason. Those who give to Scripture such an interpretation as requires (for its acceptance) the annihilation of reason or the repudiation of the lessons of experience, know not what they do. For in this way they are weakening the faith of thoughtful people in the divinity of the Scriptures, and engendering a skepticism none the less real and obstinate for being carefully concealed.

It is not the least among the merits of the New Christian Dispensation, that, while firmly based upon the inspired Word, it is yet a dispensation of rational religious truth. It holds that the Bible rightly interpreted, will ever be found in complete accord with the teachings of enlightened reason, true science, sound philosophy, human experience and the well-ascertained laws of our mental and moral constitution. If this claim be well-founded, we ought to be able to show that the new doctrine announced by Swedenborg and affirmed by reason and experience, concerning the essential nature of heaven, is fully sustained by the teachings of Scripture. See, then, if this be not actually the case. " To the Law and to the Testimony." If Swedenborg "speak not according to this Word, it is because there is no light in him." (Isa. viii. 20.)

First, it is not to be denied that the Bible, interpreted in its lowest or strictly literal sense, often speaks of heaven as if it were located in some region of *space*. The sacred penmen, when treating of it, make use of such terms as are uniformly employed in speaking of *places*. Thus they speak of *going to* heaven, of *looking towards* heaven, of *ascending up* into heaven, of *looking down* and *coming down* from heaven, etc.—language which, understood in its strictly literal sense, certainly favors the old idea of heaven as a place. Besides, it is sometimes *called* a place ; as where our Lord, speaking of the " Father's house " (by which Christians generally understand that heaven is meant), says : " I go to prepare a *place* for you. And if I go and prepare a *place* for you, I will come again and receive you unto myself; that *where* I am, *there* ye may be also." (John xiv. 2, 3.) This is one of the strongest passages cited to prove that heaven is a *place*. " The Bible calls it a *place*, and does not the Bible mean what it says ? "—is the usual form of the argument resorted to by the old theologians.

But the Bible, as we believe and as Swedenborg everywhere teaches, has both a natural and a spiritual sense related like body and soul. The spiritual is the true and *real* sense, as the soul is the true and *real* man; for the Bible was given to instruct mankind about spiritual and not about natural things. Accordingly all *places* mentioned in Scripture, signify, in their true spiritual sense, certain states of life—for place corresponds to state. And all words which, in their natural sense, refer to places and changes of place, in their spiritual sense refer to mental states and changes of state. Thus the Bible speaks of certain persons being *far from* the Lord, and of others as being *near* Him. It also invites us to *look* to Him, to *draw nigh* to Him, *follow after* Him, *come unto* Him, etc. And is it to be understood from this, as really teaching that some people are nearer to God than others *as to space*, or according to the natural idea? Or that, to *look unto* Him we must turn our natural faces to some particular point of the compass? —or to *follow* Him or *come unto* Him, our bodies must pass through a portion of space? This is what it *appears* to teach—what it actually *does* teach if its words must be interpreted in their merely natural sense.

But every one sees that such a literal interpretation would be most absurd. Every one knows that, to be *far from* the Lord, is to be far from Him spiritually— distance from Him being difference in state, remoteness from that state of pure and unselfish love in which He is, and which is Himself. And to *look unto* Him, is to look with the understanding, or the mind's eye, to those divine-human qualities revealed in the person of Jesus Christ. To *follow* Him, or *draw nigh unto* Him, is not to pass through any natural space, but to pass from a low, carnal, selfish state, to one more internal, pure and unselfish—more like that of the Lord Himself. We *follow* Him when we obey his precepts—deny self—engage in spiritual conflict with the hells within us, as He did while glorifying the assumed human. And we thus approach nearer to Him by becoming spiritually more like Him—receiving more of his own divine-human life into our hearts. So, too, when the angels are said to *descend* from heaven to men, we are not to understand that they come down through *space*, but that they descend to men's states with heavenly gifts suited to their wants and their capacity to receive; comparatively as a wise teacher *comes down* to the states of little children with instruction adapted to their feeble capacity. And when the Lord says, " I *came forth* from the Father, and am *come* into the world; again I leave the world and *go to* the Father," no one understands Him as meaning that He came from or passed through any particular region of *space.* He *came* by assuming a material body, whereby He was enabled to descend to the very ultimates of humanity with regenerating and saving power. And from this lowest state He (as to his assumed human) passed, by a process of glorification of which our regeneration is an image, through all superior states, even to a full and perfect union with the Divine. This is the way in which He again left the world, as He says, and *went to* the Father. And in this way, too, He prepared a *place* in the Father's house for all his faithful followers; that is, He made possible, henceforward, the salvation and happiness of all who should, by his divine aid, be brought into states of genuine good and truth however humble.

But the Scripture furnishes testimony on this subject still more explicit and conclusive. We read that the Pharisees, on one occasion, asked our Lord ".when the kingdom of God should come." And this was his answer: " The kingdom of God cometh not with observation: Neither shall they say, Lo, here! or lo, there! For behold the kingdom of God is within you." (Luke xvii. 20, 21.) Now the kingdom of God and the kingdom of heaven mean one and the same thing; for heaven is his kingdom. (Compare Matt. v. 3 with Luke vi. 20: also Matt. iv. 17 with Mark i. 15; and Matt. xix. 14 with

Mark x. 14.) We have, then, the plain testimony of Scripture, that heaven or the kingdom of heaven is not without but within the soul. It cannot, therefore, be located. It cannot be said to be in any particular *place*, for it is in all heavenly-minded people wherever they may be. Therefore it must be a state of life. But does the Scripture tell us what is the nature of that state? And if so, how does its teaching tally with Swedenborg's?

And here the primitive meaning of the original Greek and Hebrew word for heaven, should first receive attention. The Hebrew word for it is *shâma-yim*, which means the *firmament*, or *the region of space above the earth.* It comes from an obsolete root *shâmâ*, the meaning of which in the cognate Arabic language is, *to be high* or *lifted up.* And to this Arabic radical lexicographers refer the Hebrew term as denoting a *high locality.* The Greek *ouranos* which answers to the Hebrew *shâma-yim*, and is also translated by our English *heaven*, means the same as the Hebrew—the region above or the vast concave surrounding the earth. (*See Schleüsner's Greek and Latin Lexicon.*) And most philologists derive it from the Greek *orao, to see*—as referring to the space above or around the earth, that is pervaded by the light of the sun.

Heaven, then, according to the *literal* meaning of the term in both the Hebrew and Greek, denotes an *elevated place.* And in the Bible it is said to be *high*, and to be located *on high.* Accordingly, it is common for little children to think and speak of heaven as a place up in the sky; for it is not to be expected that they should think otherwise than according to the sense of the let-

8

ter. And many adults have not advanced beyond this natural childish thought. Now why is it that a state of angelic love and bliss, should be designated in Holy Scripture by a word which, in its strictly literal sense, means a *high place?* Swedenborg furnishes a satisfactory answer to this question in his doctrine concerning the Scripture, teaching us that it contains both a natural and spiritual sense which correspond like body and soul. Accordingly there is natural height and spiritual height; or elevation in space, and elevation of state. Whenever a high *place*, therefore, is mentioned in the Word, a high mental or spiritual *state* is what is denoted in the spiritual and true sense.

But what is a high spiritual state? Is it any other than a state of elevated thought, affection and purpose? —a state of pure and unselfish love?—a state in which we think of and seek after, not merely our own good, but the highest good of our neighbor also, in the largest as well as the smallest form. Persons of this character are spiritually near the Lord, and may well be said to dwell *on high*. They are spiritually on high, for they live above the world while in it. Hence it is often said of such, whose lives are devoted to lofty and beneficent ends, that they are *superior* persons—persons of *elevated* desires, *exalted* views, *lofty* aims, etc. And the Scripture saith, " He that humbleth himself, shall be *exalted.*" Every one perceives that spiritual exaltation is what is here meant, or that elevation of state which comes from subduing our selfish and infernal propensities—from humbling self, and permitting the Lord alone to be exalted to the supreme place in the soul.

The state of life, therefore, in which Swedenborg tells us the angels are, is clearly a *high* state. Hence we may understand why heaven is said to be *on high*, and why the word itself in both the Greek and Hebrew, according to its primitive literal import, means a locality that is high. And we may see, too, why man is said to have been made "a little *lower* than the angels." In his fallen or unregenerate state, he is a great deal lower.

Because the word *high* when used in Scripture has such spiritual signification, denoting elevation of state, or purity of love and exaltation of wisdom, therefore the Lord is called the *Most High*, and is said to dwell *on high*, *above* the earth and *above* the heavens. Certainly natural or spatial elevation is not to be thought of, when such things are predicated of the omnipresent Jehovah. No. It is because He is the highest as to state or quality of life—infinitely exalted above men and angels as to the quality and degree of his love and wisdom, that He is said to be the Highest, above the earth and the heavens. And what is it that really exalts men, or makes them spiritually high, but such a reception of the Lord's love and wisdom as recreates them in his own image and likeness? This lifts. their souls on high. We know it is not uncommon for Christians, when in a cold, external, or very low state of mind, to pray that the Lord would *lift them up* out of that state. And the Psalmist speaks of God's setting certain ones "*on high*," and of others being "brought *low*"—where it is plain that these terms have no reference whatever to space, but to mental state.

But the Bible furnishes still more positive evidence

concerning the essential nature of heaven. It contains, as Christians generally believe, all the laws of our spiritual life. And these laws must be in their nature eternal as the soul itself, for they are laws of the soul. They are spiritual laws, and must therefore exist and operate wherever human spirits exist—in the Hereafter as well as here. Whatever laws, therefore, the Bible contains for the government of human beings here on earth, are the very laws to which the angelic hosts are subject. "Forever, O Jehovah, thy Word is established in heaven," says the inspired Psalmist: Which clearly authorizes the conclusion that the truth of God's Word is the law of life for the angels in heaven. And the Lord Himself, when speaking as the Word incarnate, says: "I am the living bread which came down from heaven." The living·bread from heaven can be none other than the Lord's own love and wisdom, the goods and truths of his Word; and these are Himself. These are what feed and nourish the angels, and coming down from heaven (that is, being properly clothed, and accommodated to our low human condition) give life—spiritual and eternal life—to the world. To receive the goods and truths of the Word in such a manner as to make them of our life, to have our souls filled and vitalized by them, is to receive the Lord Himself. It is to eat his flesh and drink his blood. This is "the bread of life"—"the true bread from heaven." "If any man eat of this bread, he shall live forever." And there can be no true spiritual life without it. "Except ye eat the flesh of the Son of Man and drink his blood, ye have no life in you," saith the Lord. That no material flesh or blood is here meant, but the good of the Lord's own love and the truths of wisdom with which his Word is all aglow, is plain enough; for, as if to place the meaning beyond all doubt, this is immediately added: "It is the spirit that quickeneth; the flesh profiteth nothing: the words that I speak unto you, they are spirit and they are life." (John vi. 51–63.) And so we have Divine authority for affirming that the Lord's words are the living bread of heaven—the food on which the angels live.

Furthermore, we are taught to pray that the Lord's will may be done on earth as it is done in heaven. What can this mean but that men on earth should desire and seek after the life of heaven?—Should cherish such loves as the angels cherish, act from such motives as the angels act from, aim at such ends as the angels aim at, and in all things endeavor to conform their lives to the revealed laws or will of the Lord as the angels do.

Now if we can learn from the written Word what is the essential nature of the life which men on earth are capable of receiving, and which God desires they should receive, we may then know what kind of life the angels receive, or what is the essential nature of heaven. In other words, we may learn how the angels live, by seeing how the Lord requires those to live whom He desires and is endeavoring to make angels.

We read in the prophecy by Micah: "He hath showed thee, O man, what is good; and what doth Jehovah require of thee, but to do justly, and to love mercy, and to walk humbly with thy God?" (vi. 8.)

8*

And in the gospel by Matthew: "Thou shalt love the Lord thy God with all thy heart, and with all thy soul, and with all thy mind. This is the first and great commandment. And the second is like unto it, Thou shalt love thy neighbor as thyself. On these two commandments hang all the law and the prophets." (xxii. 37–40.) The meaning of which is, that the sum and substance of all that the law and the prophets teach, is comprehended in these two commandments. In other words, that these are the comprehensive principles or leading ideas which the Scripture everywhere inculcates. And if these ought to be men's governing principles or ruling loves, then they must be the ruling loves of people in heaven. Again we read "God is love; and he that dwelleth in love, dwelleth in God and God in him. . . . And this commandment have we from Him, That he who loveth God, love his brother also." (1 John iv. 16, 21.) And again: "All things whatsoever ye would that men should do to you, do ye even so to them; for this is the law and the prophets:" Again teaching us that love is the vital and pervading principle of the whole of the inspired Word. And if such be the revealed law of life for men on earth, must it not also be the law of life for those in heaven?

We thus see that the Bible affords abundant confirmation of the truth of what Swedenborg has told us in regard to the essential nature of heaven, or the kind of life that prevails there. And when love of the Lord and the neighbor is the ruling love in any mind, it is clear that all subordinate loves thence proceeding must needs be good. Those in whom this love bears rule, can have no narrow or selfish aims. Their supreme desire and purpose will be, to serve others by performing the highest use they are made capable of performing. They will not forget "to do good and communicate," knowing that, "with such sacrifices God is well pleased." They will intend nothing and do nothing but what will contribute to the welfare and happiness of their neighbor. In short, they will study to know, and in all things seek to do, the will of their heavenly Father. And this, according to Swedenborg, is precisely what the angels intend, seek, love and do.

Thus far in our inquiry, we have found the truth of Swedenborg's disclosures to be amply sustained by reason and Scripture and the known laws of the human soul. We have seen that angels were not created such, but were all once inhabitants of the natural world; that they are all human—men advanced to a higher and more perfect state. This view presents the angelic host, not at an immeasurable distance from, but in a near and brotherly relation to, people here on earth; while at the same time it reveals the possibility, and can hardly fail (one would think) to kindle in the hearts of believers the desire of some day becoming angels themselves.

It has been further shown that every man takes his own life with him into the other world, and that his life is his ruling love. This is the soul's real life. And such as is the nature or quality of this love at the time of death, such it remains. And since heaven is essentially a state of life, therefore all who go to heaven must carry their heaven with them; at least they must carry its germ, its essence, something of that unselfish love which, in its full and final expansion, makes heaven and its delights. We can carry with us into the other world no other life, and can *have* no other there, than that which we have sought and in some degree formed for ourselves while in the flesh. Therefore none can enter heaven, save those who have learned to love and live the life of heaven—have learned to think and feel and will and act to some extent like the angels.

Look, now, at this teaching in a practical point of view. What is its manifest and legitimate tendency? Can we conceive of anything calculated to exert a more benign influence on the hearts and lives of those who receive it?—anything better fitted to lift men above a mean selfishness and sordid avarice, to enlarge their hearts, purify their motives and exalt their aims?—any instruction more healthy and stimulating, or better calculated to make the receiver honest and unselfish, kind and forgiving, just and generous, meek and pure and lowly in heart?—any that offers a stronger inducement to deny self, take up the cross, and follow the Lord in the regeneration?

In the light of this new doctrine it is clear that if we ever go to heaven we must begin on earth to form a heavenly character. We see the weight of an endless eternity pressing upon each day and hour of our existence here below; and seeing this, we shall see and feel the need of continual repentance, earnest prayer, daily watchfulness and ceaseless effort to subdue within us (with Divine assistance) whatever is contrary to the life of heaven;—the need of continual striving to think, will and act under the influence of the Lord's own love, and according to the revealed laws of angelic life. Is it good and useful to mingle in the society, read the biographies and contemplate the character of true and righteous men? Does it quicken our aspirations, exalt our aims and incite us to higher and nobler endeavor? How much more quickening and exalting in its tendency, then, must be that pure and lofty standard of humanity as revealed through Swedenborg in the character of the angels! Its tendency is to raise us to the stature of spiritual manhood; for it discloses the sublime capabilities of the human soul—reveals the true " measure of a man, that is, of the angel." (Rev. xxi. 17.)

Let the hearts and lives of all men be formed after this heavenly pattern, and what a different world would this of ours be! The wilderness would indeed be changed to Eden, the desert to the garden of the Lord. People of different ranks and professions, of various climes and colors, would then form a shining band of brothers, bound each to each by the golden links of love. No hate, no scorn, no pride, no avarice, no self-seeking, no injustice, no tyranny, no violation of any of the divine laws of brotherhood, but mutual love and mutual help, united with deep humility and confiding trust, would be here. The Father's will would be done on earth as it is done in heaven. Men would be, as the angels are, God's ministering servants, striving mutually to aid and bless each other. A great family of loving, joyous, happy, obedient children, all looking up with filial love and reverence to their heavenly Father, and suffering themselves evermore to be led by his unerring hand.

Such would this world be if the life in heaven as disclosed to us by Swedenborg, were brought down to earth. And the whole object of this New Revelation is to prepare suitable recipient vessels, and thus aid in bringing it down. And what would this be, but a practical exemplification of the true Christian Religion?—the grand predicted triumph of the gospel of peace and love?—the promised second coming of the Lord, "with power and great glory"?—the blissful period of the church foreshadowed in the Revelation under the figure of "the Holy Jerusalem descending out of heaven from God, having the glory of God:" when "the tabernacle of God shall be with men, and He will dwell with them, and they shall be his people, and God Himself shall be with them, their God." (xxi. 3.)

But the ruling loves of the angels are not the loves of any of us in our natural or unregenerate state. They are not such loves as we receive hereditarily, but loves that are born of God. Before we can become angels, therefore, a radical change must take place within us. What is the nature of this change, and how is it to be wrought? In other words, how is the heavenly state to be attained? What is the sure pathway to the abodes of bliss? We will answer this question in the next chapter.

VIII.

THE SURE WAY TO HEAVEN.

A SUBJECT of transcendent interest and importance,—and this seems as suitable a place as any for its treatment. It is none other, indeed, than an inquiry as to the sure way of attaining the end for which we were created—a state of internal and spiritual conjunction with the Lord; which is the highest and most perfect state that a human being is capable of attaining—a state of unutterable bliss.

We have already shown—we trust with sufficient clearness—that heaven is not a place, but a state of life. And the nature of that state has also been made sufficiently plain. But we are none of us naturally or by inheritance in the state denoted by heaven, but in one quite the opposite; for we are naturally dominated by a supreme love of self, which is the ruling love of those in hell. If we ever reach the kingdom of heaven, therefore, our hereditary state must be wholly changed, and a new state be formed, by a process which the Bible calls regeneration, or a *new creation.* Thus the old hereditary life of self-love and the love of the world must be cast aside or die, and a new and higher life be received from the Divine Humanity—the life of love to the Lord and the neighbor.

It needs no argument to prove that the state of the natural man is the very opposite to that of heaven. This is well known to all. Look at the character and conduct of men who follow their natural bent, who never think of practising self-denial, but always yield to the promptings of their hereditary inclinations. Do such men live and act like the angels? Do they seek *first* —that is, as the thing of supreme moment—the kingdom of God and his righteousness? Do they regard their neighbor's good—the good of the .community, the state, the church, the Lord's kingdom—as paramount to their own, or as a matter of even equal concern? Do they not, on the contrary, act with sole reference to their own private interests, regardless of the welfare or the rights of their neighbor? Do not the past history and present condition of mankind prove that an absorbing and predominant selfishness is the withering curse of our race? Has it not eaten like a canker into the souls of men, and left its sad and sickening blight on every feature of human society?

And if we look into our own hearts, do we not there learn the same melancholy fact? Do we not find that self-love is naturally our ruling love? Is it not a difficult task—one that requires us to struggle against our natural inclination—to do always the thing which we know to be right in the sight of God?—to obey the revealed laws of neighborly love?—to do to others as we would have them do to us?—to return good for evil, blessing for cursing?—to love, bless, do good to and pray for our enemies? Every one knows that, to do this, often requires much self-denial and self-compulsion, and sometimes a pretty severe internal struggle with "the old man." And this single fact, that the laws of our higher life cannot be obeyed by us without an effort at self-denial sometimes severe and painful, proves that our hereditary life is the opposite of heavenly life.

And the teaching of the Bible, too, agrees with our private experience and the experience and history of our race. The Scripture throughout recognizes man's hereditary state as a perverted, disorderly, fallen state. It represents Him as alienated from God, opposed to his laws, averse to doing his commandments; as spiritually corrupt, defiled, diseased throughout; as dead in trespasses and sins, and utterly unfit for the kingdom of heaven. Therefore the natural love of self must be denied, resisted and overcome. This old hereditary life must be forsaken or lost for the Lord's sake, that is, for the sake of that new and higher life which is his own— his very Self. Agreeable to his own words: " He that loseth his life for my sake, shall find it." (Matt. x. 39.) The natural heart must be re-created in the Divine image and likeness, or rather a new heart (or will) must be formed within and above the old one, before we can reach the heavenly state, or enter into the kingdom of heaven. Therefore the Lord says: " Except a man be born again [literally, *born from above*], he cannot see the kingdom of God." To be born from above, is to be born of Him who is above all, even the Most High. It is to be spiritually created anew in the image of our Divine Lord and Master. It is to receive from Him those sweet affections, and holy desires, and humble feelings, and noble purposes which belong to all heavenly states of mind, and which come down to us from God out of heaven. All who are thus " born from above," are, as Paul says, " a new creation. Old things are passed away;

behold all things are become new." (2 Cor. v. 17.) And by this inward spiritual renewal they become the true children of God. They receive a continual influx of his divine spirit—the spirit of gentleness, meekness, patience, love, forbearance, forgiveness, and heroic self-sacrifice for others' good. In their thoughts, dispositions and purposes, they resemble their Father in the heavens. They have their Father's name written in their foreheads. Thus Paul writes to the church at Ephesus: " That ye put off .. . . the old man which is corrupt according to the deceitful lusts, and be renewed in the spirit of your mind; and that ye put on the new man which after God is created in righteousness and true holiness." (iv. 22–24.)

In like manner Swedenborg, but more full and explicit:

"When man is regenerated, he becomes altogether another man, and is made new; therefore also when he is regencrated, he is said to be born again, and created anew. In this case, although his face is like what it was before, and also his speech, yet his mind is not like his former mind; for his mind when he is regenerated, is open towards heaven, and there dwells therein love to the Lord and charity towards his neighbor, together with faith. It is the mind which makes another and a new man. Change of state cannot be perceived in the body of man, but in his spirit, the body being only the covering of his spirit; and when it is put off, then his spirit appears, and this in altogether another form when he is regenerated; for it has then the form of love and charity in beauty inexpressible, instead of its pristine form, which was that of hatred and cruelty with a deformity also inexpressible. Hence it may be seen what a regenerate person is, or one that is born again, or created anew, viz., that he is altogether another and a new man."—A. C. 3212.

And so, conformably to this doctrine concerning the corrupt and anti-heavenly state of the natural heart, the Bible throughout teaches that a great work is to be done before we can enter the kingdom of heaven. It teaches that we must believe in, look to, and follow after the Lord Jesus Christ; "for without me," He says, "ye can do nothing." It teaches that we must learn and live according to the laws of the heavenly life which He has revealed;—must "hear the Word of God and *do* it," else we cannot be fit for an abode among the blessed. It insists on the necessity of repentance, self-denial, watchfulness and prayer. Its language is: "Except ye repent, ye shall all likewise perish." "Whosoever will come after me, let him deny himself." "What I say unto you I say unto all, Watch." "Pray without ceasing." It represents the life of those journeying heavenward, as a struggle, a warfare, a ceaseless conflict with the inclinations of the natural man, "the foes of our own household." It says: "Strive [literally, *agonize*] to enter in through the strait gate." "These [the multitude whom the seer of Patmos beheld 'arrayed in white robes'] are they who came out of great tribulation." And the Lord says: "If any man will come after me, let him deny himself, and take up his cross, and follow me. For whosoever will save his life, shall lose it; and whosoever will lose his life for my sake, shall find it." (Matt. xvi. 24, '5.)

Yes: Following in the footsteps of our Divine Master

—resisting and overcoming, through his ever-present divine aid, the evil inclinations of our hereditary nature, as He resisted and overcame the evils in his assumed humanity—this is the sure and the *only* sure way to heaven.   And this requires faith, courage, sacrifice, endurance, spiritual conflict and a willingness to give up our own selfish life for the Lord's sake—for the sake, that is, of that higher, purer, diviner life which He is at all times ready and longing to give, and which is Himself.   A man's life is his love; and *our* life is the life we receive by natural inheritance—the life of self-love and love of the world.   But this is not our *true* life. It is not properly human life.   True human or spiritual life is the Lord's own life in the soul of man.   It is the life of genuine charity—the living and active operation of a love that is quite the opposite of the love of self. This latter love must be denied and overcome before we can receive such love as the angels feel, and which is the Lord's own.   Thus we must lose *our* life for the Lord's sake, else we cannot find that which is our true and heavenly life.   Therefore He says that a man must *hate his own life*, else " he cannot be my disciple." (Luke xiv. 26.)

The apostle Paul also says : "We must through much tribulation enter into the kingdom of God."   And he exhorts us to " fight the good fight of faith "—pointing, plainly, to that spiritual warfare to be carried on within our own breasts by means of the truths of faith from the Word—a warfare against our natural proprium, or the ruling loves of the natural man.   And these truths which are the weapons of our warfare—the weapons wherewith we are to combat our pride, conceit, avarice, selfishness and all other hereditary evils—the same apostle elsewhere calls the "armour of God," and "the sword of the Spirit, which is the Word of God." (Eph. vi. 13, 17.)

The Lord also teaches that we are spiritually cleansed —are sanctified and saved, that is, brought out of a hellish and into a heavenly state, by means of the truth. "And for their sakes," He says, "I sanctify myself, that they also might be sanctified through the truth." "Sanctify them through thy truth; thy Word is truth." (John xvii. 17, 19.) It is the truth of God's Word which makes manifest our evils, and teaches us how to overcome them. It is the truth, therefore, by means of which we are spiritually washed and purified, and thus saved from sin and its consequences.

But the Bible, we shall be told, teaches that it is *the blood of Christ* which cleanseth from all sin. And so, indeed, it is. But what spiritual thing does the blood of Christ stand for or signify? It is the symbol of the precious and ever-living truth of the Word. This truth is the Lord's own life-blood which is forever being poured out for the purification and salvation of human souls. This, or the Lord operating through its instrumentality, can cleanse from sin, and clothe our souls in robes of righteousness. Hence that angelic throng which the Revelator beheld arrayed in white, are said to "have washed their robes and made them white in the blood of the Lamb."

But we are not spiritually cleansed, or brought into the heavenly state, by simply *understanding and believing*

9 *

the truth. Only by *doing* it—shunning as sins against God the indulgence of those dispositions and feelings which the truth condemns, can the nature of our ruling love be changed. By first *compelling ourselves* to yield obedience to the requirements of truth, we are brought at last into a state in which obedience is spontaneous and delightful. This is the heavenly state. And then our hearts are open to the influx of the Lord's love which is the life and soul of truth. We then eat his flesh and drink his blood, and He dwells in us and we in Him.

This, then, is the sure way to heaven; for it is the way to pass out of that low, carnal, selfish state in which we all are by inheritance, into that high, spiritual, un-selfish state in which the angels are. Nor is any other way possible—any other than this: first learning and then religiously *practicing* the revealed laws of the heavenly life. This is the teaching of Sacred Scripture as well as of enlightened reason and human experience. Accordingly we read:

"Not every one that saith unto me, Lord, Lord, shall enter into the kingdom of heaven; but he that *doeth* the will of my Father which is in heaven." (Matt. vii. 21.)

"Therefore whosoever heareth these sayings of mine and *doeth* them, I will liken him unto a wise man who built his house upon a rock. . . . And every one that doeth them *not*, shall be likened unto a foolish man who built his house upon the sand." (v. 24.)

Jesus saith: "And why call ye me, Lord, Lord, and *do* not the things which I say?" (Luke vi. 46.)

"And He answered and said unto them, My mother

and my brethren are these which hear the Word of God and *do* it." (Luke viii. 21.)

"He that hath my commandments and *keepeth* them, he it is that loveth me; and he that loveth me shall be loved of my Father, and I will love him, and will manifest myself to him." (John xiv. 21.)

"And the dead were judged out of those things which were written in the books, according to their *works*." (Rev. xx. 12.)

And so throughout the inspired Volume. Again and again are we told that it is only by obeying the voice of the Lord, following after Him, keeping his commandments, learning and *doing* the truth, that we can arrive at the heavenly state; and that, in the great Hereafter, every one will be judged according to his *works*.

"That a man is saved," says Swedenborg, "according to his works, the Lord also teaches in his parables, several of which imply that they who do good are accepted, and that they who do evil are rejected. (See Matt. xxi. 33–44; xxv. 1–12, 14–34. Luke xiii. 6; xix. 13–25; x. 30–37; xvi. 19–31.) . . . Nevertheless, there are many in Christian churches, who teach that faith alone is saving, and not any good of life or good works. They add, also, that evil of life or evil works do not condemn those who are justified by faith alone, because they are in God and in grace."—*Doc. of Life*, n. 2, 4.

But it is important to remember that the nature or quality of the works by which we are to be judged, depends on the kind of motive which entered into them as their prompting cause, or which moved us to do them. If the motive was evil or purely selfish, the works themselves were of the same nature, however good they may have been in their outward form. Accordingly Swedenborg says :

" But by the deeds and works according to which man is judged, are not meant such deeds and works as are merely exhibited in the external form, but such also as they are internally ; for every one knows that every deed and work proceeds from man's will and thought ; for if it were otherwise, his deed would be mere motion, like that of an automaton or image. Wherefore a deed or work in itself considered, is nothing but an effect which derives its soul and life from the will and thought, so that it is will and thought in effect, therefore will and thought in an external form. Hence it follows that such as are the will and thought which produce a deed or work, such also is the deed or work. If the thought and will be good, the deeds and works are good ; but if the thought and will be evil, the deeds and works are evil, although outwardly they may appear alike."—H. H. n. 472.

But our life's love cannot be speedily changed. We cannot quickly pass from hell to heaven, or from a supremely selfish which is an infernal state, to the opposite or unselfish state which is heavenly. This great change, like all orderly divine processes, is slow and gradual. Accordingly Swedenborg says :

" Man, when he is born, as to hereditary evils is a hell in the least form ; and also becomes a hell, so far as he takes from hereditary evils and superadds to them his own. Hence it is that the order of his life from nativity and from actual life, is opposite to the order of heaven ; for from the proprium he loves himself more than the Lord, and the world more than heaven ; when yet the life of heaven consists in loving the Lord above all things, and the neighbor as himself. Hence it is evident that the former life which is of hell, must be altogether destroyed; that is, evils and falsities must be removed, to the intent that new life, which is the life of heaven, may be implanted. This cannot in any wise be done hastily; for every evil being inrooted with its falsities, has connection with all evils and their falsities; and such evils and falsities are innumerable, and their connection is so manifold that it cannot be comprehended even by the angels, but only by the Lord. Hence it is evident, that the life of hell with man cannot be destroyed suddenly, for if suddenly he would altogether expire; and neither can the life of heaven be implanted suddenly, for if suddenly, he would also expire. There are thousands and thousands of arcana, of which scarcely one is known to man, whereby he is led of the Lord, when from the life of hell into the life of heaven. That this is so, has been given me to know from heaven; and it has been likewise confirmed by several things which came to the apperception. Inasmuch as man knows scarcely anything concerning these arcana, therefore many have fallen into errors concerning man's liberation from evils and falsities, or concerning the remission of sins, by believing that the life of hell with man can in a moment be transcribed into the life of heaven with him through mercy; when yet the whole act of regeneration is mercy, and no others are regenerated, but those who receive the mercy of the Lord by faith and life during their abode in the world."—A. C. n. 9336; see also n. 9334, 5398.

Now is not this teaching amply sustained by the testimony of reason, experience and the Volume of revelation? The upbuilding of the kingdom of heaven in the soul, is a truly divine work, yet one which cannot be performed without our voluntary coöperation. It should, therefore, bear some resemblance to the rest of the Creator's works.

And how does the Divine creative energy display itself throughout the material universe? Why, in every formative process it proceeds gradually. Nothing comes forth full-formed and complete all at once—no, nor very suddenly. All things endowed with life—trees, plants, animals, men—commence from something minute, and advance by slow degrees to their mature state. And trees and animals that are destined to live longest, are always slowest of growth and latest in arriving at maturity. All orderly divine processes are gradual. Our globe itself—so science teaches—was many ages in becoming fitted for the abode of man. The face of nature shorn of its verdure by November's frosts, is gradually renewed by Spring's warm sunshine. The tiny germ within the acorn is gradually developed into the sturdy oak. The infant advances by slow degrees to the full stature of manhood. Must not the new spiritual man, then, advance by a corresponding process to the full stature of angelhood? All analogy proves that a man's ruling love is never suddenly changed.

And the same doctrine agrees with and is confirmed by universal experience. For who does not know from experience that the uprooting of avarice and selfishness from the natural heart, and implanting therein the loves of heaven, is no sudden work? Conviction of sin and conversion (which is simply turning about and facing in the opposite direction) may be sudden. But who ever heard of a man's ruling love (which means his entire character) being suddenly changed from evil to good?

—or, of a person passing quickly from an infernal to a heavenly state, and remaining permanently in it? Paul's conversion while on his way to Damascus, was sudden. But were all his evil loves as suddenly subdued, and "the old man" or the natural proprium brought under complete subjection to the Divine? So far from it, we find him many years after his conversion, making this sad but frank confession: "I am carnal, sold under sin. . . . To will is present with me; but how to perform that which is good, I find not. For the good that I would, I do not; but the evil which I would not, that I do. . . . I find then a law, that, when I would do good, evil is present with me;" and he concludes with the exclamation "O wretched man that I am! Who shall deliver me from the body of this death?" (Rom. vii. 14–24.) Which shows that the apostle's state was yet many removes from that of heaven.

And the Scripture confirms the teachings of analogy and experience. Our Saviour as to his humanity, is our pattern. And we read that "He grew, and waxed strong in spirit;" that He "increased in wisdom and stature, and in favor with God and man" (Luke i. 80; ii. 52)—language which shows that the process of glorification, or the descent of the Divine Life into, and its union with, the human, was gradual. We are told also that "the kingdom of heaven is like a grain of mustard-seed . . . which indeed is the least of all seeds; but when it is grown it is the greatest among herbs, and becometh a tree, so that the birds of the air come and lodge in the branches thereof." (Matt. xiii. 32.) Again it is compared to seed which, when sown, springs up and unfolds gradually, "first the blade, then the ear, after that the full corn in the ear." (Mark iv. 28.) Such passages plainly teach that the heavenly life is acquired not suddenly, but by slow degrees, just as a plant or tree unfolds and matures; and that one proceeds according to the laws of divine order as surely as the other. And the Lord takes care that the seed-germs of the heavenly kingdom shall be early and securely stored up in the interiors of every little child.*

Only those, then, can go to heaven, who begin on earth (when of mature years) to develop and strengthen within themselves the life of heaven: Which is done through religious obedience to the laws of that life—by shunning all known evils as sins against God. No others, after they shall have left the material body, will have any desire to go there; nor could they breathe its pure atmosphere, nor endure its light and warmth. They would be as much out of their element in heaven, as a fish is out of his when taken from the water. They would find the sphere of heaven so suffocating as to cause them unutterable anguish. Accordingly Swedenborg says:

"Unless heaven be within a person, nothing of the heaven without him flows-in and is received. Many spirits entertain the opinion that heaven may be given to every one from immediate mercy; and because of

---

* "It would be impossible for any one to live as a man without a germ of innocence, charity and mercy, or something of a similar nature thence derived. . . . This germ man receives from the Lord during infancy and childhood, as may be seen from the states of infants and children. What he then receives is treasured within him, and is called in the Word a *Remnant* or *Remains*, which are of the Lord alone with man, and furnish him with the capacity of becoming truly man on his arrival at adult age." —A. C. n. 1050.

their belief, they have been taken up into heaven. But when they came there, because their interior life was opposite to that of the angels, they grew blind as to their intellectual faculties till they became like idiots, and were tortured as to their will faculties so that they behaved like madmen. In a word, they who go to heaven after living wicked lives, gasp there for breath, and writhe about like fishes taken from the water into the air, and like animals in the ether of an air-pump after the air has been exhausted. Hence it is evident that heaven is not without one, but within him."—H. H. n. 54. See also n. 400, 518, 525.

Look, now, at the practical tendency of this new doctrine. Accept it as true, then farewell to all reliance on the efficacy of a death-bed repentance. Farewell to the delusive hope of ever reaching heaven through mere belief, or *faith alone*. The doctrine shows us that no amount of prayers, or tears, or penitent confessions, or pious words uttered on the bed of death or in the felon's cell, can avail to change the ruling love. It reveals the necessity, first, of feeling and acknowledging our utter dependence on the Lord; and second, of yielding a voluntary and implicit obedience to the laws of his kingdom. Thus its tendency is to make people more eager to learn and more careful to obey the revealed laws of the angelic life. Every noble and righteous purpose cherished, every unselfish and brotherly act performed, every self-denying effort put forth in the name of the Lord and in acknowledged dependence on Him for the needed wisdom and strength, is a step on the way to heaven ;—something done towards recreating the soul in the Divine likeness, or building it up to " the measure of a man, that is, of the angel."

10

IX.

LIGHT AND HEAT IN HEAVEN.

AMONG the first questions which people are naturally inclined to ask about the heaven of angels, are such as the following : Have they light and heat there, as we have here ?   If so, what is their nature and origin ? Do they come from a sun, like the light and heat of this world ?   If the answer be, Yes, then what is the nature of that sun, and how does it differ from our own ?   Swedenborg ought to be able to answer these questions, if his claim to have enjoyed long and open intercourse with the angels be well-founded.   And he *has* answered them with all the fullness that we might expect.   Let us see what his answers are, and then subject them to a careful examination.   He says:

"The sun of this world does not appear in heaven, nor anything which exists from this sun, because all that is natural.   For nature commences from this sun, and whatsoever is produced by it is called natural.   But the spiritual in which heaven is, is above nature, and entirely distinct from the natural ; nor do they communicate with each other except by correspondences.

"But although the sun of the world does not appear in heaven, nor anything which exists from this sun, still there is a sun there ; and light and heat and all things which are in the world and a great many more, but not from a similar origin ; for the things which exist in heaven are spiritual, and those which exist in the world are natural.   The sun of heaven is the Lord ; the light there is divine truth, and the heat is divine good, both of which proceed from the Lord as a sun.   From that origin are all things which exist and appear in heaven."

"The Lord appears in heaven as a sun, because He is the divine love from which all spiritual things exist, as all natural things exist by means of the sun of this world. It is that love which shines as a sun. . . . He appears differently according to each individual's reception of Him; in one way, therefore, to those who receive Him in the good of love, and in another to those who receive Him in the good of faith. To those who receive Him in the good of love, He appears as a sun, fiery and flaming according to reception. These are in his celestial kingdom. But to those who receive Him in the good of faith, He appears as a moon, white and shining according to reception. These are in his spiritual kingdom."—H. H. n. 116–118.

"The light in heaven is so great as to exceed by many degrees the mid-day light of the world. I have often seen it, even in the evening and night. At first I wondered when I heard the angels say that the light of the world is little more than shade in comparison with the light of heaven. But since I have seen it, I can testify that it is so. Its whiteness and brilliancy surpass all description. The things seen by me in heaven, were seen in that light; thus more clearly and distinctly than things in the world.

"The light of heaven is not natural like that of the world, but spiritual; for it proceeds from the Lord as a sun, and that sun is divine love. That which proceeds from the Lord as a sun, is called in the heavens divine truth, although in its essence it is divine good united to divine truth. Hence the angels have light and heat; light from the divine truth, and heat from the divine good. From this consideration it is evident that the light and heat of heaven are not natural but spiritual from their origin."—Ibid. 126, '7.

"The degrees of spiritual heat may be understood

from those of light, for heat and light exist in equal degrees. As to the spiritual light in which the angels dwell, I have been permitted to see it with my own eyes; and among the angels of the higher heavens it is so bright and yet so glowing as to surpass description . . . even by the radiance of the natural sun. In a word, it exceeds a thousand-fold the noonday light of the world."—D. L. W. n. 182.

"The heat of heaven in its essence is love. It proceeds from the Lord as a sun, and is the divine love in Him and from Him. Hence it is evident that the heat of heaven is spiritual as well as its light; for it is from the same origin. The heat of heaven, like its light, is everywhere various. That in the celestial kingdom differs from that in the spiritual; and it differs also in every society. And not only does it differ in degree, but even in kind. It is more intense and pure in the Lord's celestial kingdom, because the angels there are more receptive of the divine good. It is less intense and pure in the Lord's spiritual kingdom, because the angels there are more receptive of divine truth. And it differs also in every society according to reception.

"There is heat also in the hells, but it is unclean. The heat in heaven is what is meant by sacred and celestial fire, and the heat of hell is what is meant by profane and infernal fire; and by both is meant love. Celestial fire means love to the Lord and love toward the neighbor, and every affection derived from these loves; and infernal fire means the love of self and the world, and every lust derived from these loves."—H. H. n. 133, '4. See also A. C. n. 1053, 2196, 2776, 3636, 4415.

Scores of passages similar to the foregoing, might be quoted from Swedenborg's writings. And he nowhere teaches anything at variance with this, though enjoying open intercourse with the angels, and daily writing of what he heard and saw in heaven, for a period of nearly thirty years. What evidence can be adduced in confirmation of these statements? is the next question;—for we should not accept the mere *ipse dixit* of any man on a subject of this nature.

First, it cannot be denied that there is an air of reasonableness and probability about the statements, which is utterly repugnant to the idea of delusion on the part of the author. There is also a directness and simplicity in the manner of the statements, which we all recognize as among the characteristics of a truthful revelation. And their reasonableness becomes more and more manifest, the closer they are examined,—another strong indication of their truth. For consider:—

Angels are human beings removed from the lower or primitive stage of existence, and advanced to a higher and more mature state. They are all in the human form. They possess the human faculties, but in a more perfected state than those of people on earth. They also have the human organs—eyes, ears, hands, feet, etc.,—the same as men. And wherever they are mentioned or referred to in the Bible, they are spoken of as in the human form; and in some places their faces, mouths, eyes, ears, and hands are particularly mentioned.

Now *eyes* imply the existence of some sort of light as the medium of their exercise or use, just as ears imply the existence of some sort of an atmosphere. If there were no such thing as light, eyes would be useless and we should not have them; for the Creator makes nothing without use as an end. He adds no useless appendage to any creature. And having eyes we could not see without some suitable medium—some kind of light. But *our* organs of sense are material, and therefore adapted to this material world. With our bodily eyes we see, and with our fleshly hands we handle, material things—and these alone. And the light and heat of this world, and the sun from which they emanate, being themselves natural, are adapted to our natural or fleshly organs.

But everything in the spiritual world is spiritual. The bodies of the angels are spiritual bodies; and we have Paul's testimony that "there is a natural body, and there is a spiritual body." (1 Cor. xv. 4.) And the organs of sense which the angels possess, must be suited to the spiritual things of their world, as our bodily organs are adapted to the material things of this world. The light and heat of heaven must therefore be spiritual, else they would not be suited to the nature of the angels, nor be in harmony or homogeneous with the things of their world.

And we know what spiritual light is. It is that which illumines the understanding—the light of divine or spiritual truth. When this light dawns upon us, it brings day to our mental world. The light of divine truth shows us the path in which we ought to walk—the path that leads to heaven. And we know, too, what spiritual heat is. It is that which warms us internally and spiritually; that which sets the soul aglow; that which we feel when the heart throbs with emotions of gratitude and love. Love is spiritual heat; and its effects in the moral or spiritual realm are such as correspond to the effects of the sun's heat in the material realm. It warms and quickens and vivifies.   Hence it is common to hear people who abound in love towards others, called *warm-hearted.*

And from what other source can spiritual light and heat proceed, than a spiritual sun?   And a spiritual sun must be a living sun.   And what can a living sun be, but the Lord Jehovah Himself?   What but the very sun in whose bright beams of truth and love the angels continually rejoice—the sun of the spiritual world?   And can there be any reasonable doubt that this sun is the incarnate Word—the Divine Man who, when on earth, declared: "I am the light of the world;" who is the Enlightener of all minds and the Quickener of all hearts; "in whom is life," and whose life "is the light of men"? (John i. 4, 9.)   The spiritual sun must be to the universe of souls, what the natural sun is to the realm of matter.

Consider again, that angels are human beings in an advanced stage;—men and women raised from this primary and rudimental to a higher or more interior state of existence.   And if advanced to a higher state, they should possess a keener insight and enjoy a wider range of vision than we do.   They ought therefore to dwell in light of superior brilliancy.   And so we might reasonably expect that the sun of heaven would be immensely brighter than the sun of this world.   We should expect it to surpass our sun in splendor by as many degrees as heaven is higher than earth, or as angels are superior to men.   Accordingly Swedenborg says:

"The light of heaven in which the angels dwell is, in

respect to the light of this world, as the light of the sun at noonday to that of a candle, which becomes invisible and as nothing when the sun rises."—A. C. 1053.

It cannot be denied, then, that the seer's disclosure on this subject, is altogether reasonable. Indeed we cannot conceive of an answer essentially different, that would at all satisfy the demands of reason.

Then there have been in different ages and countries many pious and trustworthy persons, whose spiritual eyes have been occasionally opened, and whose recorded experiences on such occasions agree entirely with Swedenborg's statements, and may be said therefore to furnish corroborative evidence of their truth. Cases like that, for example, recorded of the grandfather of Heinrich Jung Stilling in the latter's Autobiography (p. 22, Harper's edition); and that of Rev. Wm. Tenant of Freehold, New Jersey, who was apparently dead for several days, and after his resuscitation described what he saw while in that state; among other things "an ineffable glory"—a "*glory all unutterable.*" (See Memoir of Rev. Wm. Tenant.) Dr. Passavent says: "Persons recovering from deep swoons and trances, frequently describe themselves as having been in this region of light—this light of the spirit, if I may so call it—this palace of light in which it dwells, which will hereafter be its proper light; for the physical or solar light which serves us while in the flesh, will be no longer needed." (Quoted in Mrs. Crowe's *Night Side of Nature*, vol. ii., p. 163.) And Dr. H. Werner (Doctor of Philosophy, Stuttgard and Tübingen), in his *Guardian Spirits*, tells of a seeress with whom he was intimate, and who, in her state of trance, often spoke of seeing a bright Sun and of being in its light. On one occasion she says: "I see the Sun, and these beings quite different from men—much more pure and noble—are not in the Sun, . . . but I see them in the neighborhood of the Sun. O, if it were so fair, so glorious on the earth below, as here where there are no human passions, it were then good to live there. This whole life above consists of love. Everything that is and is done here, proceeds from love. This principle makes all the happiness that reigns here above." (p. 30, 'i, New York edition, 1847.)

Numerous facts like these are accessible, and from sources perfectly authentic. And while they harmonize with, and go to confirm the truth of, Swedenborg's statements, they at the same time find in his revealings their only rational and philosophical explanation.

And turning to the Bible we find still further confirmation of the truth of his statements. We find there a record of facts which it is impossible rationally to explain upon any other theory than that furnished by his pneumatology. Take, for example, the phenomenon recorded in Exodus (24th chapter), when Moses, Aaron, Nadab and Abihu were called to "come up unto the Lord." It is there said that "the glory of the Lord abode upon mount Sinai; . . . and the sight of the glory of the Lord was like devouring fire on the top of the mount in the eyes of the children of Israel." And this, too, although the Lord's glory was veiled by a cloud to the multitude who stood gazing at the foot of the mount. What must have been the appearance of that glory to Moses who went up into the mount and the cloud!   No wonder that when he came down, "the skin of his face shone" as the record says.

Then we read in the gospel by Matthew (17th chapter): "And after six days Jesus taketh with him Peter, James and John his brother, and bringeth them up into a high mountain apart, and was transfigured before them; and his face did shine as the sun, and his raiment was white as the light.   And behold there appeared unto them Moses and Elias talking with Him. . . . And as they came down from the mountain, Jesus charged them, saying, Tell the vision to no man until the Son of Man be risen again from the dead."   This is the way Jesus appeared to the disciples when their spiritual eyes were opened: "his face did shine as the sun."   That it was with their spiritual and not with their natural eyes that the disciples saw Jesus on that occasion, is evident; 1st, from the fact that they saw Moses and Elias at the same time; and these persons, being spirits and long time dwellers in the spiritual world, could not be seen by any eyes but those of the spirit; and 2d, from the Lord's own words, "Tell the vision to no man," etc.   A *vision* is a supernatural appearance—something seen with the spiritual and not with the natural eyes.

Again, the seer of Patmos tells us that, "being in the spirit on the Lord's day," he heard behind him a great voice, "saying: I am Alpha and Omega, the First and the Last."   And turning to see whence the voice came, he says: "I saw seven golden candlesticks; and in the midst of the seven candlesticks, one like unto the Son of Man . . . and his countenance *was as the sun* shineth in his strength." (Rev. i. 10, 13, 16.) To be "in the spirit," is to be in an exalted spiritual state—in a state to see as those do who are in the spiritual world, or who have their spiritual eyes opened.

Then there is the testimony of Paul in his memorable speech before king Agrippa (and repeated elsewhere), which perfectly agrees with, and finds a rational explanation in, Swedenborg's disclosures. "Whereupon," says the apostle, "as I was going to Damascus, with authority and commission from the chief priests, at mid-day, O king, I saw in the way a light from heaven *above the brightness of the sun*, shining round about me and them that journeyed with me. And when we were all fallen to the earth, I heard a voice speaking unto me, and saying in the Hebrew tongue, Saul, Saul, why persecutest thou me ? . . . And I said, Who art thou, Lord ? And He said, I am Jesus whom thou persecutest." (Acts xxvi. 12, 13.) Observe that the apostle beheld this dazzling brightness at *mid-day*, and says that it exceeded the brightness of the sun. The light was overpowering in its splendor It was more than he and his fellow travellers could endure; and they fell prostrate on the earth.

Now what was the nature of that light ? and to what realm did it belong, the natural or the spiritual ? Certainly not to the natural; for what light in the realm of nature is so overpowering as that was ? What natural light is above that of the sun at noonday ? And why not seen by all the people in that region round about, if it were merely natural light ? No: The light which Paul and his companions beheld on that occasion, was from the Sun of the spiritual world—their spiritual sight being suddenly and providentially opened to enable them to see it. And if the light of that Sun is, as Swedenborg says, "a thousand times greater than that of the sun of this world," no wonder that they all fell to the earth, and that Paul himself "could not see for the glory of that light" (Acts xxii. 11), and remained "three days without sight." (ix. 9.) Who could stand before such dazzling brightness, if it burst suddenly upon him? Observe further, that, within that overwhelming blaze was a *person*—the Lord Jesus Christ himself—from whom came the words in Hebrew, "Saul, Saul, why persecutest thou me?" Observe, also, that this great light burst upon them *suddenly*, and as suddenly vanished; and the apostle himself called it "a light from heaven."

And thus we find that remarkable experience of Paul, producing what is commonly called his miraculous conversion, to be in perfect agreement with Swedenborg's disclosures; and while furnishing additional confirmation of their truth, receiving from them at the same time an easy and philosophical explanation. And can you find in any of the old theologies—can you find *anywhere* else but in Swedenborg's pneumatology, a rational explanation of that memorable occurrence?

And that it is the Lord Jesus Christ or Jehovah God, who is the Sun of the spiritual world, is plain from many passages of Scripture. Thus the inspired Psalmist says: "Jehovah God is a sun and shield." "Jehovah covereth Himself with light as with a garment." And Isaiah says: "Jehovah shall be unto thee an everlasting light."

And the apostle John: "God is light," and "God is love"—for love is spiritual heat whence comes spiritual light. And of that city which the seer of Patmos beheld in vision "coming down from God out of heaven," it is said "the glory of God did lighten it, and the Lamb is the light thereof." And "there shall be no night there; . . . for the Lord God giveth them light." And the Lord when on earth proclaimed Himself "the light of the world." And John calls Him "the Word" which was "in the beginning with God, and is God"— "the true light which lighteth every man." He is the enlightener of all souls, the Sun of the moral universe.

Thus do reason, Scripture, the recorded experiences of gifted seers and of devout men in all ages, unite in attestation of the truth of Swedenborg's revelation concerning the Sun of the spiritual world, and the nature of the light and heat thence proceeding. And there is no conflict in the testimony rendered, but perfect agreement among all these witnesses. And the witnesses, we observe, are quite independent of each other. The conclusion is, therefore, inevitable. For what the Bible declares, and reason approves, and the experience of prophets and seers in all ages confirms, must be true beyond question.

Nor is the evidence exhausted yet. As we prosecute our inquiry into the laws and phenomena of the spiritual world, we shall find additional proof accumulating at every step. We shall find this central fact of the existence of a spiritual Sun, connecting itself as intimately with the other facts and phenomena of the spiritual world, as the fact of the natural sun's existence connects itself with the other facts and phenomena of our terrestrial world,—with the motion of the planets, the existence and color of the clouds, the verdure of the fields, the aspects of the landscape, the countless tints of the violet and the rose. These all presuppose and depend wholly upon the sun, and could not exist without it.

X.

PRACTICAL TENDENCY OF THIS DISCLOSURE.

GRANT that what Swedenborg tells us about the Sun in the angelic heavens be true, what then? Is the disclosure one of any practical value? Is it calculated to improve the character of those who accept it, or to quicken their endeavors after righteousness? For if it can be shown that the legitimate tendency of any revealed fact or law is good and wholesome, that it furnishes food or stimulus to the better part of our nature, and tends to exalt and ennoble the character of the believer, that is the strongest possible evidence of its truth. But if, on the other hand, its obvious tendency is pernicious—if it is calculated to exert a debasing influence on the character, you can have no stronger evidence that the alleged revelation is false. " For every tree is known by his own fruit; for of thorns men do not gather figs, nor of a bramble bush gather they grapes." (Luke vi. 44.) No more can the fruits of righteousness be the legitimate product of false teaching or a spurious revelation. By its obvious practical tendency, you may know whether the alleged revelation be true or false. Let us apply this test to Swedenborg's disclosures concerning the spiritual Sun.

It was said in the last chapter, and shown by extracts from the seer's writings, that the spiritual Sun does not appear the same to all the angels. Its appearance is always in correspondence with the state of the beholder. To those of the highest heaven, who receive the light of divine wisdom and the warmth of divine love in largest measure, the Lord appears most glorious even to their external vision. He appears as a sun warm and bright according to their internal reception of his light and life. To those of a lower heaven who receive his love and wisdom in an inferior degree, He appears less glorious —comparatively as a moon. While to those not in heaven, whose lives are not in harmony with its laws, and in whose hearts is none of God's unselfish love, but the supreme love of self instead, the sun of heaven does not appear at all. Their state is, therefore, one of comparative cold, darkness and night. Hence the meaning of that " outer darkness " into which the wicked are said to be cast; for they have shut the door of their souls against the Sun of righteousness, and therefore the myriads of interesting and beautiful things which that Sun reveals to the angels, are invisible to them.

Now the different angelic heavens are neither more nor less than different states of human life—all good, but some superior to others. And so, too, the different kinds and degrees of evil in the wicked, are what necessitate the different hells. The higher states of angelic life, are such as are in accord with the higher laws of the soul, or with the truths of the spiritual and celestial senses of the Word.

And, every man, when he passes into the spiritual world, takes his own character with him. He goes there precisely the same individual that he was internally while living in the flesh. His inner and spiritual life as to all its predominant characteristics, remains. And the process of forming this inner life, is a process of clarifying or obscuring the spiritual vision—of improving or impairing the soul's eyesight. It is a process by which we become qualified to enjoy the blessed light and warmth of the Sun of heaven, or incapacitated for beholding his face and rejoicing in his kindling beams.

Note what this process is, or the manner of its procedure. As to our spirits we are always in the spiritual world, though at present unconscious of the fact. And every law of the spirit's life—every ray of spiritual truth that we receive—is a beam from the spiritual Sun. And as we obey the truth we have learned, we come to experience a positive delight in it. The vital element in truth is the Lord's love; and it is this which causes the delight. By religious obedience to the truth, our hearts become warmed and expanded and more and more receptive of this vital element; the range of our spiritual vision·is extended, and we become receptive of more and still higher truth. With every act of self-denial prompted by religious principle, there comes as a rich reward an increased desire for more and higher truth, and an increased capacity for receiving it. And so by religiously *living* the truth, we come more and more into the light and love and joy of it. As saith the Lord: " He that *doeth* truth cometh to the light."

In this and in no other way can our souls be prepared for the light by which the angels see. If we seek and love and reverently follow the light of heavenly truth while here on earth, we shall be prepared to rejoice in the glad beams of heaven's Sun when we enter the other world. But if, on the contrary, we care nothing about it, take no delight in it, turn our thoughts away from it, and walk not according to it, we shall gradually incapacitate ourselves for receiving it. Every infringement of known spiritual laws, is an injury to the soul's eyesight. And if disobedience or neglect be persisted in, we shall be unable to bear the light of the spiritual Sun in the great Hereafter. We shall hate and flee from it, and choose instead the " outer darkness," as owls and bats shun the light of day, and prefer instead the shades of night. Agreeable to the Lord's own words: " He that doeth evil hateth the light, neither cometh to the light, lest his deeds should be reproved." And what darkness is so dreadful as that which results from the loss of the moral or spiritual eyesight!—the loss of all desire for the true light, and even of the capacity to receive or apprehend it! " If, therefore, the light that is in thee be darkness, how great is that darkness!" saith the Lord.

Thus the practical tendency of this disclosure is seen to be good and wholesome. For it teaches that our spiritual vision while we are yet in the flesh, is becoming dimmed or clarified according to our degree of af-

11 *

fection for the truth and our fidelity in obeying its be-
hests.   And it warns us not to forget or transgress the
Divine commands, under penalty of dimming or destroying our spirit's eyesight, and thus preparing ourselves for the " outer darkness."   Its tendency therefore
is, to make us watchful against the indulgence of any
known evil, and to stimulate our desire to learn and
practice the laws of the heavenly life; for it is in this
way only that we can become qualified to behold and
rejoice in the beams of heaven's bright Sun.

Then see how this disclosure concerning the nature
of heavenly light and heat, helps us in the interpretation
of the Bible; for there is, as we should expect, an intimate connection between the spiritual sense of the Word
as revealed through Swedenborg, and his disclosures concerning the spiritual world.

In its natural or literal sense the Bible appears to
treat much of natural things ;—of the earth and clouds,
winds and waters; of rocks, trees and mountains—sun,
moon and stars.   And it was once regarded as the very
highest authority in settling questions of natural science.
But latterly a great change in this respect has come
over the mind of Christendom.   Many of the beliefs
prevalent in the days of Galileo, have been discarded by
every religious sect.   Many of the deepest thinkers of
our day have reached the conclusion that the Bible was
never meant to teach us about natural but only about
spiritual things; that, rightly understood, it will be
found to treat exclusively of God, the soul and things
belonging to the soul's appropriate realm ; that it is, and
was meant to be, a revelation not of natural but of spir-

itual truth—truth suited to the wants of our higher nature, and is therefore to be spiritually interpreted. And
when it speaks in the letter of things belonging to the
natural realm, in its higher and true sense it speaks of
the corresponding things within or above nature—things
in the realm of spirit.

For example: When the Bible speaks of *man*, it
means the inner and real man—not the material and
perishable, but the spiritual and immortal part. When
it speaks of the resurrection, it means the resurrection
not of the material body, but of the spiritual—the real
individual temporarily enshrined in matter. When it
speaks of a second birth, it refers not to a natural or
carnal birth, but to the birth of the soul into the kingdom of heaven. When it speaks of heaven and hell, it
means no natural localities such as are referred to by
these terms taken in their natural sense, but certain
states of the soul—one, exalted and blissful, the other,
degraded and miserable. When it speaks of the coming of the Lord, it means no outward coming cogniza-
ble by the eye of sense, but an inward and spiritual
coming—a coming of his own truth and love to the understandings and hearts of men. When it speaks of
light and heat, it means truth and love which are spiritual light and heat to which the natural correspond.

If, then, it be true, as the deepest thinkers are everywhere beginning to see and acknowledge, that the Bible
was not given to teach us natural but spiritual truth, it
is clear enough that it must be spiritually interpreted.
Accordingly when it speaks of the sun and of light, we
are to understand that, in its higher and true sense, the

spiritual Sun and spiritual light are what is meant. Take a few texts for illustration. Can any one doubt that spiritual light, or divine truth which illumines the understanding, is what is meant in passages like the following ?

"Jesus said, I am the *light* of the world; he that followeth me shall not walk in darkness, but shall have the *light* of life."   "Yet a little while is the *light* with you. Walk while ye have the *light*, lest darkness come upon you." "While ye have the *light* believe in the *light*, that ye may be the children of light."   "I am come a *light* into the world, that whosoever believeth in me should not abide in darkness."   "*Light* is come into the world, but men love darkness rather than light because their deeds are evil."   "He [the incarnate Word] was the true *light* which lighteth every man that cometh into the world."   "God is *light*, and in Him is no darkness at all."

Yes : The light of divine truth which is spiritual, is what enlightens the souls of men while they tabernacle in the flesh.   But it cannot enlighten those who, because of their evil loves and their unwillingness to see and abandon them, shut their eyes against it.   "For every one that doeth evil, hateth the light, neither cometh to the light, lest his deeds should be reproved."

But spiritual light must emanate from a spiritual luminary, as surely as natural light must come from some natural luminary.   And what can that luminary be but the Lord Himself who is the enlightener of all minds, and who, we are assured by Swedenborg, appears before the eyes of the angels in greater or less brilliancy according to their states of receptivity of his wisdom and love—his appearance being in exact correspondence with the states of the beholders. To the highest angels whose love is purest and most ardent, He appears as a sun of indescribable brilliancy; and to those in lower states, or whose love is less intense, He appears comparatively as a moon. Therefore when the Bible speaks of the sun and moon, we are to think of something above the natural luminaries so named—of the spiritual sun and moon to which the natural correspond.

This will help us to understand the meaning of a passage of Scripture which, being literally interpreted, has been the occasion of considerable excitement and alarm at different periods of the church. We refer to that in Matthew (ch. xxiv.—repeated in Mark xiii. and Luke xxi.), where, after foretelling the fearful trials—the wars, famines, pestilences, etc. (all spiritual, according to the true interpretation), which the church would be called to encounter before the Lord's second appearing, it is added, as if this were the last crowning event in the grand drama : " Immediately after the tribulation of those days, the sun shall be darkened, and the moon shall not give her light, and the stars shall fall from heaven. . . . And then shall appear the sign of the Son of Man in heaven."

Christians have generally given to this prophetic announcement a sensuous interpretation. But here as everywhere else in his Word, the Lord refers to spiritual things. He is speaking not of the natural sun, moon, and stars, but of the spiritual things to which these natural luminaries correspond. And since we are, as to our spirits, now and always in the spiritual world, therefore we are ever under the influence of the spiritual Sun. We receive from it all our spiritual light and warmth. But its light does not appear to our outward sense as light (as it does to the eyes of angels), but manifests itself by a certain internal illumination—that kind of enlightenment which spiritual truth, when received, furnishes to the understanding. Nor is its heat sensibly perceived by us as heat, but manifests itself by a certain warmth of feeling, or a kindling in the heart of the emotion of love—love of whatever is just, sincere, good and true. Thus do the beams of the spiritual Sun reach and affect the spirits of people yet in the flesh. But when may that Sun be said to be darkened?

The natural sun always shines with undiminished splendor. Yet he undergoes *apparent* changes. Sometimes he is wholly or partially eclipsed. Sometimes he is obscured by the vapor and smoke in the earth's atmosphere. He sinks beneath the horizon, and his face is hidden from our view. And in familiar language all such changes are predicated of the sun itself. When suffering an eclipse, we say the sun is darkened. Seen through mist, dust, or smoke, we say the sun is pale, dim, or red. When his face appears in the east, we say he is *rising ;* and when, again, he approaches the western horizon, we say he is *going down.* All such language, we know, expresses not the absolute but only the apparent truth. For the sun itself does not change. His apparent changes in respect to light, heat, and diurnal motion, are all caused by our atmospheric conditions and contents, and the motion of the earth on its axis.

Carrying this thought along with us (and it is one of great importance to every Bible student), we can understand why changes are predicated of the spiritual Sun (the Lord), when in strictness of language that Sun is unchangeable. We can see that all apparent changes in Him are purely subjective—caused by changes in the states of recipient subjects. To the angels of the highest heaven the Lord appears as a sun, because they receive his love in the greatest fulness—his appearance being in correspondence with their state of life. Therefore when the principle of charity or true neighborly love ceases to be living and operative in the church, then, in relation to the church, the Sun of heaven is darkened.

And to the angels of a lower heaven who receive the Lord's love in an inferior degree, but yet are in the truths of faith, He appears comparatively as a moon. Accordingly when the Word is misunderstood and falsified by the church, when faith is in eclipse and falsities are taught and accepted for truths, then, in relation to the church, the moon does not give her light. And when the knowledges of genuine good and truth have so far faded out from the minds of professing Christians that they no longer know what spiritual good and spiritual truth are, then, in relation to the church, the stars have fallen from heaven.

Now look at Christendom as it was prior to the memorable year 1757. Its character stands recorded on the page of history. Look at it—and what do we see? That celestial principle of love to the Lord and the neighbor which shone conspicuously in the early days of the church, making her members of one heart and mind and binding them all together in the bonds of a beautiful brotherhood—that principle had died out or departed from the church. And there was no vital faith in the divinity of the Lord, the divinity of the Word, or in a life after death. The Scripture had become falsified on every fundamental doctrine, and spiritual darkness brooded over all Christendom. Even the knowledges of spiritual good and truth were lost to the great body of the church. As fixed and guiding principles they were no more. They had fallen from their heavenly places in men's minds. And thus was fulfilled *in relation to the church*—really and perfectly fulfilled according to its spiritual and true meaning—this prophetic declaration: "The sun shall be darkened, and the moon shall not give her light, and the stars shall fall from heaven."

But at this juncture—amid the general darkness that enveloped the church—amid the clouds of ignorance and error and doubt and denial which had extinguished in the minds of nominal Christians all the heavenly luminaries, a glorious light breaks forth to rejoice and save a sinking world. From within or above the cloud of the letter—out from the living soul of Scripture—out from that world where angels dwell, long clouded and obscured, the spiritual Sun pours kindling beams on a benighted church. And *thus* the Lord of life appears all glorious in the clouds, agreeable to his own prophetic declaration: "And then shall ye see the Son of Man coming in the clouds, with power and great glory."

And mark the signs of this Second Coming—the consequences of this newly risen Sun. Mark how its piercing beams are dispelling the old darkness !—how they have already pervaded with their light and life nearly every department of human thought ! Under their quickening influence the human intellect has everywhere burst its old swathing-bands, and leaped forth with unprecedented vigor. And on the natural plane what a magnificent harvest already begins to wave ! Science, literature, philosophy, art, industry, politics, morals and religion have all begun to feel the influence of the Second Coming. Old things are everywhere passing away, and all things are being made new. All the forms of human thought prevalent a century ago, are changed or changing. Old religious dogmas, old systems of philosophy, old forms of government, old methods of education, old theories of medicine, old industrial processes, old ideas on all subjects, are being continually summoned to judgment. And one by one they are beginning to retire before the waxing light of truth, as creatures of the night retire before the opening day. In the general enlightenment and progress of mankind during the last hundred years, on the natural plane of thought and action, do we not witness something like a fulfillment of the prophecy ? " For as the lightning cometh out of the east, and shineth even unto the west, so shall also the coming of the Son of Man be."

We thus see that the great Swede's disclosure concerning light and heat in heaven, and their origin, while perfectly reasonable in itself, accords well with the teachings of Scripture, is most beneficent in its practical tendency, and helps us to a truer and more rational interpretation of some portions of the written Word. Candid and thoughtful minds will not reject the concurrent testimony of all these witnesses.

XI.

ENVIRONMENT IN HEAVEN, AND WHAT DETERMINES IT.

HAVE the angels an outward or phenomenal world as people on earth have? If so, what is its general character or aspect, and what determines it? Since they possess the human organs, eyes to see and hands to handle things, we should expect there would be objects to be seen and handled. We cannot conceive of their existing as human beings without an earth to stand and walk upon; nor can we conceive of their being in a blissful state with no kind of objective world, and compelled to gaze forever on mere emptiness. But what answer does Swedenborg give to the above questions? Briefly this:

That the angels live upon a substantial earth (not material), and are surrounded by innumerable objects that are far more beautiful and perfect than any that exist on earth—but all spiritual. And their senses being far more acute than ours, and the light in which they dwell far more brilliant, they see the objects in their world with greater distinctness than we see those in ours. And the law which determines the aspect of their outward world, is the same as that according to which the Sacred Scripture is written—the same law that always governs in the descent of the Divine love and wisdom to ultimates—the law of correspondence between the internal and external, or between cause and effect. Spirit tends forever to clothe itself in correspondential forms. It cannot become clothed in any other. God cannot speak or reveal Himself to finite beings, except according to correspondence. He cannot create, and so exhibit his love and wisdom to the senses of men, except according to the same law. And the objects which appear in heaven, exist there by virtue of an influx from the Divine into the minds of the angels, and through them into their outward or phenomenal world. The character of their outer is therefore determined by that of their inner world. The former is the visible representation of the latter. The things which greet their senses are the creations, and therefore the correspondential forms, of their own affections and thoughts. Thus their outward world corresponds in all respects to the world within them. Every active principle in their minds is pictorially represented to the outward sense, and under a form perfectly correspondent. The objects round about them, therefore, are so many mirrors, as it were, reflecting with mathematical precision the world of thought, affection and purpose within them. But we will give Swedenborg's report on this subject in his own language.   The following extracts contain the substance of it :

"The nature of the objects which appear to the angels in heaven cannot be described in few words.   For the most part they are like the things on earth, but in form more perfect and in number more abundant.   That such things exist in heaven, is evident from those seen by the prophets [as by Ezekiel, Chap. xl.–xlviii.; by Daniel, Chap. vii.–xii.; by John, Rev., from first to last chapter].   They saw such things when they were in the spirit and heaven was opened to them ; and heaven is said to be opened when the interior sight which is that of a man's spirit, is opened.   For the things in heaven cannot be seen with the bodily eyes, but with the eyes of the spirit."—H. H. n. 171.

"Whenever it has been granted me to be in company with angels, the things of heaven have appeared to me exactly like those in the world,—so perceptibly indeed, that I knew not but that I was in the world, and in the palace of a king there. . . . Since all things which correspond to the interiors [of the angels] also represent them, therefore they are called REPRESENTATIVES.   And since they vary according to the state of the interiors with the angels, therefore they are called APPEARANCES ; although the objects which appear before their eyes, and which are perceived by their senses, appear and are perceived as much to the life as those on earth appear to man ; nay, much more clearly, distinctly and perceptibly. The appearances thence existing in the heavens are called *real* appearances, because they really exist.

"To illustrate the nature and quality of the objects which appear to the angels according to correspondences, I will here adduce a single instance.   To those who are in intelligence there appear gardens and paradises full of trees and flowers of every kind.   The trees are planted in the most beautiful order, and so interwoven as to form arbors with entrances of verdant fret-work, and walks around them,—all of such beauty as no language can describe. . . . There are also species of trees and flowers there, such as were never seen and could not exist in the world. On the trees also are fruits according to the good of love in which the intelligent are principled. Such things are seen by them, because a garden and paradise and also fruit trees and flowers correspond to intelligence and wisdom.

"The paradisiacal scenery of heaven is stupendous. There are paradisiacal gardens presented to view, of an immense extent, consisting of all sorts of trees, of a beauty and pleasantness exceeding every idea of human thought, which yet appear in so living a manner before their external sight, that they not only see them in the gross, but also perceive every single object much more vividly than the bodily sight does when exercised on similar objects here on earth."—A. C. n. 1622.

" Representatives are presented in the other life according to states of the interiors with spirits, for they are correspondences. Around spirits who are in truths from good, appear the most beautiful representatives, namely, houses and palaces glittering with gold and precious stones, also gardens and paradises of ineffable beauty; all these from correspondence. But around those who are in truths not from good, there appear nothing but craggy places, rocks, and bogs, and sometimes shrubberies, but unpleasant and barren; these also are from correspondence. But around those who are in falsities from evil, there appear fens, privies and other offensive objects: the reason of which is, that all representatives in the other life are external things figured according to the states of the interiors; for thus the spiritual world presents itself visible there."—Ibid. n. 10,194.

" The visible objects which are in heaven correspond

12 *

to the interiors of the angels, or to those things which belong to their faith and love, and thence to their intelligence and wisdom." Some "live in elevated places which appear like mountains, . . . and in a vernal atmosphere. There are presented before them, as it were, fields, harvests and vineyards. Everything in their houses glistens as if made of precious stones; . . others dwell in gardens where appear beds of flowers and grass-plats beautifully arranged, and rows of trees round about, together with porticos and walks. The trees and flowers are varied every day. The view of the whole in general presents delights to their minds, and the varieties in particular continually renew them. And because these objects correspond to things divine, and those who behold them are in the knowledge of correspondences, they are perpetually replenished with new knowledges whereby their spiritual rational faculty is perfected."— H. H. n. 489.

"Substances in the spiritual world appear as if they were material, but still they are not. And since they are not material, therefore they are not constant, being correspondences of the affections of the angels, and permanent with their affections, and disappearing with them."—D. W., § VIII. See also A. E. n. 650, 1211, '12, '18, '26.

Such is the uniform teaching of Swedenborg concerning the objective world in heaven, and its determining cause. And can we conceive of anything more reasonable? It satisfies the best instincts and deepest longings of our nature—yes, and the intuitions of our highest reason also. For what is more reasonable than that the outer world of those in the realms of bliss, should be in complete correspondence with their inner world?—a true

pictorial representation of their noble and beautiful souls?
The flowers of love that are ever opening in their hearts,
the fruits of charity they are ever busy in bringing forth,
the green and living things of intelligence which are
constantly springing up within them—why should not
these go forth and embody themselves or *appear* under
corresponding forms of beauty and loveliness? Why
should not the fragrance, verdure and bloom of the outward angelic world, be in perfect correspondence with
the fragrance, beauty and bloom of angelic minds?

Almost every one has an instinctive perception that
there exists an intimate relation between the beautiful
and the good—a relation so intimate that the former is
the divinely ordained representative of the latter. We
all feel an instinctive repugnance to connecting innocence
and virtue with dismal scenes or unsightly objects, for
we recognize their native disagreement, or unsuitableness
to each other; while inward evil and outward ugliness
seem naturally to belong together. Thus Milton, in
portraying the beautiful scenery round about Adam and
Eve in the days of their innocence, has but uttered the
universal sentiment of mankind; and his utterance, therefore, meets with a ready response from the universal
human heart. Every one feels that a place less beautiful than that sweet Garden which the great poet has so
finely pictured, would not have agreed with the innocence
and purity of the couple he describes. So universal is
the perception that the good and the beautiful belong
together, and that the Creator designed the one to be
the visible image of the other. Considering the purity
and innocence of the denizens of heaven, what, then,

might we reasonably expect would be the character of their surroundings?

Then the light in which the angels dwell, and which is said to be a thousand-fold brighter than that of our sun, is another consideration in favor of the truth of Swedenborg's disclosures on this subject. For if they are in a state to bear a thousand-fold brighter light than people on earth enjoy, then the objects they behold around them ought to be a thousand times more numerous and beautiful than are seen here on earth. Besides, we know that the most exalted and enlightened minds always see with other eyes than those of the ignorant and depraved. The former, on account of their superior purity and enlightenment, behold a world of beauty which is quite hidden from the latter. All the ways and works of God are surpassingly beautiful; but light and the right kind of eyes are needed to enable the beholder to discern their beauty. By virtue, therefore, of their superior light and better eyesight, the angels ought to see round about them precisely such a beautiful world as Swedenborg has described.

And the Bible adds its testimony also to that of reason, experience, and the best instincts of our nature. Read the description of the Garden in which man is said to have been placed at the time of his creation, and where "the Lord God caused to grow every tree that is pleasant to the sight and good for food." For although that Garden and all its beautiful belongings are not to be literally interpreted—although they are to be taken as the representatives of the internal states of the most ancient people in the days of their innocence and integrity—the account serves our purpose none the less for all that. For the beautiful surroundings of the angels are but the outward representatives of their internal states —their affections and thoughts—and are in perfect correspondence with them.

And because the Scripture is composed according to the same great law that determines the aspect of the objective world in the Hereafter, therefore the Lord's spiritual kingdom—the regenerate human soul, viewed singly or collectively—is described in the Bible by the various precious metals, innocent animals, and beautiful objects in nature; as by gold and silver; by sheep, lambs and doves; by mountains and hills and well-watered gardens; by vineyards and oliveyards, cedar-trees and the trees of lign-aloes; by a good land, "a land of water-brooks, and fountains that spring out of valleys and hills"; "a land of vines and fig-trees and pomegranates." These and other like things are often mentioned in the Word where the Lord's kingdom—the regenerate human heart —is treated of. And we cannot suppose such things were selected without a sufficient reason. They are a part of God's own Word; and when the Divine speaks or acts, it is ever according to the highest reason and perfect divine order. And the reason why such things are mentioned in the Word when the states of the regenerate are treated of, is, that they are the correspondential forms of those heavenly principles which the Lord establishes in the hearts of all whom He creates anew in his own image and likeness. And these principles, in becoming embodied under the various beautiful forms which appear in heaven, are only assuming their own appropriate vestments,—the very forms which the Creator Himself has ordained for them.

Let us now look at the law which, according to Swedenborg, determines the whole character or aspect of the objective world in the Hereafter. If it is not susceptible of a complete demonstration, we hope at least to furnish strong presumptive evidence of its truth.

This law, as already stated, is that of correspondence, which means a relation similar to that existing between the soul and the body. It is in the nature of every spiritual principle to go forth and embody itself under some outward form. And the form *must* correspond to the living principle that enters into, creates and sustains it. We see this tendency of the human spirit constantly manifested here on earth; for even here the affections of every man are forever seeking embodiment, and they first create for themselves certain correspondential forms in the thought of the understanding. Thus their forms exist mentally, or in the world within man, before they attain a visible and tangible existence in the world without him. They are visible to the mental before they are seen by the bodily eye. This is true of everything that man creates—temples, houses, gardens, machinery, pictures, statuary, furniture, clothing, and the like. These things are the offspring of some desire or love with which they correspond as body with soul; and they all existed as objects of thought in man's spiritual world (his mind), before they existed as objects of sight in the natural world. There is nothing made by the hand of man which was not, in all its parts, visible to the eye of the mind before it was visible to the eye of sense; and nothing which does not correspond to the love that gave it birth, as effect corresponds to cause, or body to soul. Thus all the things in this natural world which are products of human ingenuity, are correspondences of the affections and thoughts of men. They are visible representative forms of certain invisible mental states which they body forth and to which they correspond. And the changes which are continually taking place in that portion of the outward world which is subject to man's control, keep pace with men's internal or mental changes to which they correspond, and without which no outward changes could occur.

Every individual on earth strives to create around himself (and succeeds if he has the means and opportunity) an outward or objective world which is in exact correspondence with his inner or mental world—that is, so far as relates to *the natural degree of his mind.* He impresses himself, as to this degree, on whatever he makes or causes to be made. His own mind, his coarseness or his culture, his refined taste or the absence of it, is visibly stamped on all around him,—on the house he builds, the furniture he orders, the pictures he buys, the trees he plants, and the flowers he cultivates. If his means and opportunity are ample, all his surroundings will, after a while, be a certain representative image of himself; they will be in exact correspondence with his external or natural mind, and therefore a true expression of the natural affections and thoughts in which they originated. So true is this, and so well understood generally, that almost any careful observer can tell at a glance, by his visible surroundings, the man of culture and refinement from one of low breeding and depraved tastes.

And as with individuals, so with communities or men in larger form. Every community, so far as its means will permit, creates an outer in correspondence with its inner world—that is, with its own prevailing mental character. Let a man travel through South Africa or Patagonia, and then visit the towns and villages of New England or Old England, and although he might not converse with one of the inhabitants, but only look at their environment, he would see the difference in the mental condition of the people of those countries as plainly as if their affections and thoughts were all written in a book.

But it is to be observed that the world which people create round about them here, being external and natural, is in correspondence not with their internal and spiritual, but with their external and natural thoughts and affections. And if there exists this correspondence between the natural mind and the world which this mind creates round about itself in the realm of nature—if we see everywhere a strong tendency in natural affections and thoughts to go forth and embody themselves under corresponding natural forms—then it is reasonable to conclude that this law of correspondence must be the very law that determines the character or aspect of the objective world in heaven. What other conceivable law is there, to which the rational mind so readily yields assent?

Furthermore, every one knows how much the outward aspect of all things on earth depends on the mental state of the beholder. The outer is ever taking on the com-

plexion of the inner world, even here. There are times
when a dismal pall seems spread over all creation ; when
all around us seems like a desert; when the sweetest
flowers are undelightful, and the laughter of children has
no music to our ears, and the faces of dearest friends no
beauty to our eyes ;—times when the loveliest scenes in
nature—the brightest sunshine and the verdant earth—
have for us no cheerful smile, but rather an indignant
frown. And are not these the times when the heart is
cold and desolate and sad ? when darkness and gloom
brood over our inner world ? But when the sunshine
returns to the soul, when the heart glows with affection,
and hope is bright and buoyant, and the world within
us becomes lighted up with a sweet and serene joy, how
changed is the aspect of the world without ! Nature no
longer mourns or frowns, but greets us everywhere with
benignant smiles. The very air seems balmy, as if laden
with the perfume of flowers. The faces of friends beam
with unwonted lustre. There is music in the rain's dull
drizzle, and in the wind's low sigh. The aspect of the
whole outward world is changed, and that which seemed
so sombre and frowning but a little while ago, is now
radiant with beauty and with smiles.

Such is the controling power which our inner or subjective exerts over our outer or objective world, even
here on earth. Such the manifest tendency of the soul
to stamp its own moods or complexion on all its surroundings ;—to color and shape the outward in complete
correspondence with itself. Men of the deepest insight
have ever seen and acknowledged this law. It is well
expressed by one of our own poets, who sings:

> " It is the soul's prerogative—its fate
>   To shape the outward to its own estate.
>   If right itself, then all around is well;
>   If wrong, it makes of all without a hell.
>
>   .   .   .   .   .   .
>
>   Turn where thou wilt, thyself in all things see
>   Reflected back.—
>
>   .   .   .   .   .   .
>
>   Who has no inward beauty, none perceives,
>   Though all around is beautiful.—
>
>   .   .   .   .   .   .
>
>   Soul ! fearful is thy power, which thus transforms
>   All things into thy likeness."

If such be the power of the soul here on earth, to
"transform all things into its likeness," what should result when it is released from its material clog and earthly
limitations, and brought consciously into a world, the
substances of which being altogether spiritual, are plastic
to its every breath ?   What but the very thing declared
in the passages cited near the commencement of this
chapter ?   We submit that the only rational conclusion
to be drawn from the brief argument we have here presented, is, that there is just such an outward or objective
world in heaven as Swedenborg has described, the character or aspect of which is determined by the great and
universal law that he has revealed—the law according to
which the Sacred Scripture is written, and creation has
proceeded from the beginning, and spirit in all worlds
forever seeks to embody itself—the law of correspondence.

And let it be added in conclusion (and this is further
evidence of its truth) that the doctrine is not purely
speculative, as might at first be supposed, but one of

great practical value. It offers us a heaven that is not a realm of unsubstantial shadows, but one of substantial realities. It shows us myriads of human beings, once denizens of earth, now advanced to a more perfect state, with faculties improved, and all the senses become far more acute, and an external world of indescribable beauty. And by revealing the underlying and determining cause of its wondrous beauty—the pure and unselfish loves in the hearts of the angels—it acquaints us with this momentous fact: that our objective world in the Hereafter will be a complete representative of our inner selves, in exact correspondence with our own characters or ruling loves; beautiful beyond conception if these are noble and unselfish, but dreary and dismal if they are mean and selfish. It shows us that, since we take our characters with us into the other world and can take nothing else, therefore every one will take with him his own heaven or—his own hell; for both these kingdoms are within men's souls; and the heaven or the hell that will be visible round about us in the Hereafter, will be the correspondential image of that which has been formed within us here.

Thus the doctrine settles forever—and upon a basis as substantial as the soul itself—the question in regard to our entrance into heaven, showing the utter impossibility of admission from immediate mercy. It teaches with clearness and impressiveness the solemn truth, that each one is making while here on earth, his garden or his wilderness, his paradise or his desert, for the ages to come;—is building for himself a beautiful palace or a gloomy prison-house that is to endure forever. What teaching can be more solemn than this? What more practical, or more potent in benign influence when clearly understood and cordially accepted?

XII.

SOCIETIES IN HEAVEN.

ARE the angels endowed with social affections kindred to those of men? and have they an opportunity to exercise them? Do they all dwell in one society, or are there many societies? And if arranged into societies, what is the law that governs in the arrangement? What answer does Swedenborg give to these inquiries?—for he must have known how the case is, if his claim to open intercourse with the heavenly world be well founded. But we will first consider the subject in the light of reason.

It was shown in the early part of this work that the angels are all from the human race. They are human in their form and nature—men and women in an advanced or thoroughly regenerate state. Therefore they must possess social qualities; and social qualities imply social relations, or the existence of societies. For man is a social being. He was created to live in society; and he cannot be happy without intercourse with his fellows. In a perfectly isolated state, what would there be to call forth his affections or to give exercise to his varied powers? The faculties of each soul have a definite relation to other souls, as truly as the eye has to light, the ear to air, the tongue to flavors, and the nose to odors. Which proves that man was created for society, as plainly as our bodily senses, by their very constitution, presuppose the existence of light, air, flavors and odors, to which they bear a fixed and definite relation.

Besides, we know that people are not happy when deprived of all intercourse with their fellows. And for this obvious reason : that they are gifted with affections which crave the fellowship of kindred minds, and they cannot be happy without the opportunity to exercise these affections. We can hardly conceive of a severer sentence than that which condemns a human being to solitary confinement for a long time. Cases have occurred where such isolation has caused an utter wreck of the mental faculties, reducing the individual to a state of. lunacy.

Unless, therefore, all the native and strong appetencies of the soul are to be extinguished in the Hereafter—unless our mental constitution is to be entirely changed, we must then as now desire association with others. And to possess this innate social inclination, this hunger of the heart for society, and at the same time to be denied the possibility of social intercourse, would render us supremely miserable. Much of our happiness in this world, comes from the exercise of our social feelings—from the interchange of thought with kindred minds, and the doing of kindly deeds for others. From all of which the conclusion is inevitable, that the angels must possess a social nature ; and if heaven is a happy state, they must have ample opportunity for its exercise. And this involves the necessity of social intercourse and social relations.

13*

But do all the angels live in one and the same society? This seems highly improbable. It would not be in accordance with the Divine order and arrangements as revealed in this lower world. Here, all things are distributed into series or societies. They are beautifully grouped; yet the groups exist and work together in admirable harmony.

There are groups of suns and systems in the immensity of space; and groups of planets in the several systems. And on the earth trees and flowers are usually grouped, one variety flourishing in one locality, and a different one in another. So, too, birds, animals, insects and fishes are commonly found in groups. And every muscle in our bodies consists of a group of similar fibres, and every crystal in the bosom of the earth, of a group of lesser crystals.

It is evidently God's plan, therefore, to arrange things of a similar nature into groups or societies. And we may reasonably conclude that man, for whose behoof all other things were created, would not form an exception to this general plan. We should expect that heaven would be typified by the things of earth that are in order; and that the angels would be distributed into many different but concordant societies.

But a still stronger argument may be drawn from the known diversity in human character. This diversity depends not merely upon a difference in education, habits, and outward circumstances, but equally upon a difference in the native constitution of men's minds. No two minds are ever constituted precisely alike. No two things in the universe are exactly alike—no two pebbles on the beach, no two leaves on a tree, no two feathers on a bird, no two hairs on the head of man or body of beast. And the reason is, that the Creator, being Himself infinite, delights in variety. And the diversity existing among men in the original constitution of their minds as well as in their features and complexion, is similar to that observable throughout the created universe. Sometimes this diversity is slight, as among people of the same tribe or nationality ; sometimes scarcely discernible, as among those of the same family. Again,—as among people of different races, the Malay and the American, the African and the Caucasian,—the diversity is very wide. And these people are just as different in their mental characteristics as in their physical constitution.

Now this known diversity of character is the distributing social force among people in this world, whereby they are arranged into different groups or societies. In general, different races and nationalities do not incline to associate. But Africans prefer the society of Africans; Chinamen the society of Chinese ; English, French, Germans, Italians, etc., the society of those of their own nation. And for this obvious reason : that people of the same nation are usually most alike in their tastes, habits and feelings ; and people everywhere prefer the society of those who are most like themselves.

And among people of the same country we find many different societies, resulting from diversity of character and that implanted inclination which leads men to prefer the society of kindred minds. Every one has his circle of intimate friends, in whose society he finds himself most free and happy. And these are usually people of a character near akin to his own—of similar tastes, habits, manners, feelings and purposes. It is this similarity of character which draws them together, and renders their society mutually agreeable. Hence we find those who are deeply absorbed in any particular subject —as temperance, peace, abolition, moral reform, and the like—anxious to make the acquaintance and enjoy the society of persons known to be interested in the same subject.

And where religion has taken a strong hold on the mind of a community, especially if doctrine or ritual is more thought of than the spirit and life of religion, there you will find those of similar beliefs and ecclesiastical preferences, drawn into the same society. They associate under the prompting influence of that implanted instinct which attracts each one to his like. Thus Methodists prefer to associate with Methodists, Baptists with Baptists, Friends with Friends, Catholics with Catholics, and so on. And there is nothing wrong in this. Each one, in choosing the society of those most like himself, is but yielding to a law of his nature—the law of spiritual affinity. The wrong comes when, through a narrow and mistaken view of the subject, people look upon those of a society or creed different from their own, as therefore inferior to or less righteous than themselves, and assume toward them an unfriendly attitude.

We have an illustration of the same law in all voluntary associations; for the evil as well as the good are drawn together by mutual affinity. Thus profligates prefer the society of profligates, gamblers the society of gamblers, thieves the society of thieves; and tipplers, burglars, pirates, and the like, the society of those of like character. The law is universal. Everywhere like ones have an affinity for each other; and by the force of such affinity they are drawn and held together. And it is only in the society of like ones that they feel quite confent and at home. They are then free and feel at home, because they feel at liberty to act out themselves —to speak as they think, and do as they desire.

And the same great law is observable everywhere throughout the domains of animated nature. Beasts, birds, fishes and insects are found grouped according to this same law. Those of the same species are found in the same group, because of their mutual affinity. They love to be together. Nor does this law cease to operate . even in the lower kingdoms of nature. Every tree is but a group of homogeneous fibres, and every simple mineral a group of homogeneous atoms which are drawn and held together by force of mutual attraction. There can be no doubt, therefore, about the universality of this law; and if universal, it must exist in heaven as well as on earth.

But setting aside the argument from analogy, is not the wide diversity observable among men, viewed in connection with the fact that every one takes his own character with him into the other world, sufficient of itself to prove the distribution of the heavenly inhabi- tants into many distinct societies? And from what we know of the law that governs in human associations on earth, we may infer the law that governs in angelic as- sociations in heaven. It is the law of spiritual affinity. In heaven as on earth, those nearest alike in character must love to be together, and feel happiest and most at home in each other's society. As natural attraction, therefore, is the law in the natural world, that arranges in distinct groups objects most nearly related, so spiritual attraction determined by the spiritual relationship and consequent affinity of spirits, *ought* to be the law in the spiritual world that distributes both good and evil spirits into many distinct societies.

And precisely this is what has been revealed through Swedenborg on the subject. He says that the angels are distributed into innumerable societies, some of them consisting of myriads and others of thousands. And there is nothing forced or arbitrary in this arrangement. . Every one goes in freedom to the society he loves and is nearest akin to. The law that governs in all angelic associations, he says, is the law of spiritual affinity. Through the constant operation and force of this law, angels of like character are drawn together and held together in the same society. To cite his own words:

"The angels do not all dwell together in one place, but are distinguished into larger and smaller societies according to the differences of the good of love and faith in which they are. They who are in similar good form one society. Goods in the heavens are of infinite variety, and every angel is such in character as is his own good. Those of like character are brought together as it were spontaneously; for with their like they are as with their own [relations] and at home; but with others, as with strangers and abroad. When they are with their like they are also in their freedom, and thence in every delight of life.

" All who are in similar good also know each other —although they had never met before—just as men in the world know their kindred, relations and friends. The reason is, that in the other life there are no kindreds, relationships and friendships but such as are spiritual, that is, of love and faith. I have several times been permitted to see this, when I have been in the spirit, withdrawn as it were from the body, and thus in company with angels. On such occasions I have seen some who seemed as if I had known them from infancy. But others seemed wholly unknown to me. They who seemed as if known from infancy, were those who were in a state similar to the state of my spirit; but they who were unknown, were in a dissimilar state."—H. H. n. 41-46; also A. R. n. 611.

"The universal heaven is distinguished into societies according to the differences of the love of good, and every spirit who is elevated into heaven and becomes an angel, is conveyed to that society which is distinguished by his ruling love. On his arrival there, he is as though he were at home, and living in the house where he was born. The angel perceives this, and is there consociated with those like himself. When he departs thence, and goes to some other place, he is always sensible of a certain inward resistance, attended with a desire to return to his like, and thus to his ruling love. It is in this way that consociations in heaven are effected. The like occurs in hell, where also they are consociated according to loves which are the opposite of the loves of heaven."—Ibid. n. 479.

All good people, we know, are not quite congenial, and would not be happy in each other's society. Their good is of a different quality; and there are many kinds and degrees of good even in heaven, some of which are widely different from others. "As all in heaven," says Swedenborg, "are distinguished according to goods, it may be clearly seen how manifold and various good is; for it is so various that there is no instance of one being in like good with another; yea, if myriads of myriads should be multiplied to eternity, the good of one would not be like that of another, just as the face of one is never like the face of another. Good also in the heavens forms the faces of the angels."—A. C. n. 7236.

And as there are countless degrees of good in heaven, so there is, according to Swedenborg, an endless variety there. And this variety adds greatly to its perfection. It is this which necessitates the distribution of the angels into many distinct societies; for only those who are in a similar kind and degree of good, have a strong affection for each other. There may be a thousand persons —all good; but their good may be so different both in kind and in degree, that they feel no strong attraction toward each other, and would not, if left in perfect freedom, choose each other's society. Being spiritually unlike, they would prefer to live apart; for they are spiritually remote from each other. As Swedenborg says:

"The angelic societies in the heavens are also distant from each other according to the general and specific differences of their goods. For distances in the spiritual world are from no other origin than from a difference in the states of the interiors; consequently, in the heavens, from a difference in the states of love. Those are far apart who differ much, and those are near who differ little. Similarity brings them together."—H. H. n. 42.

"All in heaven are consociated according to spiritual affinities, which are those of good and truth in their order. So is it in the whole heaven, so in every society, and so in every house.   Hence it is that the angels who are in similar good and truth, know each other like those related by consanguinity and affinity on earth, just as if they had been acquainted from infancy."—H. H. n. 205.

We are told, also, that there is a similarity of expression—a strong family likeness—among those of the same society ; for the affections are there clearly revealed in the face, which is their representative image.   No one in heaven has a face that does not correspond to and faithfully express his prevailing affections.

" All who belong to the same angelic society, resemble each other in general, but not in particular. . . . It is well known that every race of people have some general resemblance in the face and eyes, whereby they are known and distinguished from other races ; and the distinction between families is still more marked.   But it is more perfect in the heavens, because there all the interior affections appear and shine forth from the face, for the face in heaven is the external and representative form of those affections.   No one in heaven is permitted to have a face that is not in correspondence with his affections."—Ibid. n. 47.

The reasonableness of all this is too obvious to need any argument.   And these disclosures accord with the teachings of Scripture as well as with the intuitions of reason.   The " many mansions " in the Father's house of which the Divine Saviour spake, clearly point to the many angelic societies resulting from the endless diversity of good and truth in heaven.   Besides, the word translated *heaven* is usually found in the plural (heavens), both in the original Hebrew and Greek of the Bible— another circumstance indicative of the fact that there are

14

many heavens, or many different states, all of which are good and heavenly, necessitating therefore many different angelic societies; for every such society is a heaven in a less form. The apostle Paul, too, speaks of being " caught up to the *third* heaven " on one occasion,—a fact revealing a diversity of state among the angels, and the consequent plurality of the heavenly societies.

Moreover, there are just as strong reasons for the division of the whole angelic heaven into distinct societies, as there are for the division of all the inhabitants of the spiritual world into the two classes of good and evil ; or for the Scripture doctrine of a heaven of angels and a hell of devils. For the many different societies both in heaven and in hell, result from the operation of the same law that produces the two grand divisions of spirits whereof the Bible so often speaks—the law of spiritual affinity. This law is not arbitrary, nor of man's inventing, but has its foundation in the very constitution of the human soul, and is as fixed as the law of chemical affinity. It is by virtue of this law that angels of like character are drawn together and held together in the same society. For every one in the other world yields to his attractions, and goes whithersoever his ruling love leads him ; and this invariably leads him to the society of those who are most like himself. There he is as if with his own kindred—they *are* his spiritual kindred. There he is in freedom, is contented and happy. There, and there only, does he feel quite at home.

And here we have another display of the Lord's boundless wisdom and love in providing a home in his own house for every one who has learned to love the good and the true in however humble a degree. The African and the Arab, the Hindu and the Turk, the Anglo-Saxon and the Indian—every one of whatever color, clime, or creed, who has religiously followed the light vouchsafed him, will find there a congenial home in the society of kindred spirits. He will be among his spiritual kith and kin, and have no desire to be elsewhere, being in just the society that is suited to him, and that he most covets. But the heaven of the Mahometan will not be that of the Christian, nor will all the good from Christian lands dwell together, but every one in his own heaven—every one in the society of those he loves best, and in happiness proportioned to the kind and degree of his goodness. All who have an affinity for the society of the just, will find a congenial home in some one of the " many mansions " in the realms above.

Then look at the practical tendency of this doctrine. It is plain to see how it discountenances that narrow and exclusive spirit which would have us believe there is but one kind and degree of goodness, but one acceptable or saving creed, and but one denomination or church through which an entrance into heaven can be effected. It inculcates the beautiful truth which all the best people in Christendom are beginning to see and acknowledge, that the church on earth—though one in spirit, like the societies in heaven—must needs consist of an endless variety. It deals a fatal blow, therefore, to the old sectarianism which has so long disfigured and misrepresented the Christian religion; and shows that it is a part of the beautiful economy of God, avouched by everything in heaven as well as on earth, that people's minds should differ not less widely than their faces; and that this very diversity, giving rise to different denominations or churches, will add to the beauty, strength and perfection of the whole, when all shall become animated by the Divine Master's spirit.

The catholic spirit of the New Theology, by which as well as by its doctrines it is so broadly distinguished from the Old, and which is well illustrated by the diversity in the heavenly societies, may be further seen from passages like the following, in which the writings of Swedenborg abound.

"When love to the Lord and charity toward the neighbor, that is, the good of life, are made the essentials with all and with each individual, then churches, how many soever they may be, make one; and each is then one in the kingdom of the Lord. This is also the case in respect to heaven where there are innumerable societies, all different from each other; but still they constitute one heaven, because all are principled in love to the Lord and charity toward the neighbor [though in different degrees]."—A. C. n. 2982.

"The varieties and differences of doctrinals [in the various churches] are innumerable. . . But notwithstanding there are so many varieties and differences, still they together form one church when all acknowledge charity as the essential of the church; or, what is the same, when they have respect to life as the end of doctrine; that is, when they inquire how a man of the church *lives*, and not so much what are his sentiments; for every one in the other life is gifted with a lot from the Lord according to the good of his life, not according to the truth of doctrine separate from this good."—Ibid. n. 3241.

"The Lord's spiritual kingdom in the heavens is various according to what appertains to faith, insomuch that there is not one society, nor even one in a society, who, in those things which relate to the truth of faith, is entirely agreed with others as to his ideas. Nevertheless the Lord's spiritual kingdom in the heavens is one, because all account charity as principal; for charity constitutes the spiritual church, and not faith, unless you say that faith is charity. Whoever is principled in charity, loves his neighbor, and with regard to his dissenting from him in matters of belief, this he excuses, provided only that he lives in goods and truths. He does not even condemn the well-disposed Gentiles, although they are ignorant of the Lord, and know not any truth of faith; for he who lives in charity, that is, in good, receives such truths from the Lord as suit with his good; and good Gentiles receive such truths as in another life may be bended into truths of faith."—A. C. n. 3267.

"Let this truth be received as a principle, that love to the Lord and charity towards our neighbor are the essentials on which hang all the law, and concerning which all the prophets speak, and thus that they are the essentials of all doctrine and of all worship, then all heresies would vanish, and out of many churches would be formed one church, however they might differ as to doctrines and rituals. . . Then all would be governed as one man by the Lord, being like the members and organs of our body, which, although diverse in their forms and functions, have nevertheless relation to one heart on which they all depend both in general and in particular, be their respective forms ever so various. In this case, too, every one would say of another, in whatsoever doctrine or in whatsoever external worship he was principled, This is my brother; I see that he worships the Lord, and that he is a good man."—Ibid. n. 2385.

"Let numbers be multiplied even to thousands and tens of thousands, if they are all principled in charity or mutual love, they all have one end, namely, the common good, the kingdom of the Lord, and the Lord himself. In which case the varieties in matters of doctrine and worship, are like the varieties of the senses and viscera in man, which contribute to the perfection of the whole. For then the Lord, by means of charity, enters into and operates upon all, with a difference of manner according to the particular temper of each; and thus arranges all and every one into order, as in heaven so on earth. And thus the will of the Lord is done on earth as it is in heaven, according to what He himself teaches."—A. C. n. 1285.

XIII.

THE HUMAN FORM OF HEAVEN.

SWEDENBORG tells us repeatedly that heaven is in the human form.   Not only every angel and every society of angels, but the entire angelic heaven, he says, is in this form; so that the angels, viewed collectively, appear before the Lord as one man.   To cite a single passage:

"The entire heaven resembles one man, who is therefore also called the GRAND MAN (*Maximus Homo*).   And what is wonderful and hitherto unknown, all the parts of the human body correspond to societies in heaven. Wherefore it has been occasionally said that some of those societies belong to the province of the head, some to that of the eye, others to that of the breast, and so on."—A. C. n. 2853.   See also n. 684, 1276, 2996, '8, 3021, 3061.

This, we are aware, has an odd sound to the ears of most people when they hear it for the first time. Perhaps there are few things in the seer's writings which appear more arbitrary or fanciful—or, to some minds, more ridiculous. It is usually one of the first things which an opponent of his teachings seizes upon and flouts. It is often referred to as sufficient evidence in itself of the wild and fantastic character of his teachings. Thus the Rev. Dr. Pond, in his " Swedenborgianism Reviewed," after devoting two or three pages to a statement of the doctrine, adds,—.

" To my own apprehension, the whole account is supremely ridiculous ; being destitute alike of sense and decency, and worthy only of contempt."—p. 196.

Let us see, then, if the doctrine be either ridiculous or unreasonable. But first let us endeavor to learn what the author meant that we should understand by the expression, *Maximus Homo.*

When Swedenborg says that heaven is in the human form, he uses the word *form* in the sense in which we use it when speaking of civil, social, or ecclesiastical affairs. We speak of a form of government; but when such expression is used, no one thinks of any visible shape, but of the nature and adjustment of the various parts composing the government. A person who reads and understands the organic law of the state, sees therein its form of government. We speak, also, of the form of society in a particular age or nation ; and by this is meant the nature and relation of its several parts—the nature and arrangement of its social, industrial, commercial, educational, artistic, moral and religious elements. Again, we speak of the form of a church, or of church polity; and by this we mean the order, relation, subordination, etc., of its various functionaries, the mode of their appointment, and their respective duties.

When it is said, therefore, that heaven is in the human form, the meaning is that it is in human order; that all the innumerable societies of which it consists, are so arranged and adjusted as to express most perfectly the truly human principles which constitute the essential spirit and life of heaven. In other words, the relation, mutual dependence, and intercommunication of the societies composing the whole angelic heaven, and the uses they respectively perform, correspond to those existing among the various organs of the human body, and to their respective uses. One is a perfect representative image of the other.

Accordingly, Swedenborg often speaks of the angelic societies as located in different organs of the Grand Man; of some as in the head, some in the heart, some in the spleen, some in the liver; and of others, again, as in the eye, ear, knee, or foot. And his meaning is, that such societies correspond to these bodily organs; that is to say, their relation to the other societies of heaven and the special functions which they perform in the Grand Man, correspond to the relation existing among such bodily organs, and to their respective uses in the human body.

"It has also," he says, "been given me to know what particular angelic societies belong to each particular province of the body, also what are their qualities; as,

for instance, what and of what quality belong to the province of the heart; what and of what quality to the province of the lungs; what and of what quality to that of the liver; also what and of what quality to the different sensories, as the eye, the ear, the tongue, and so on."
—A. C. n. 2998.

It thus becomes plain what he means when he says that heaven is in the human form. It is a spiritual and not a natural idea which he is endeavoring to express. And when we shall have fairly grasped his meaning, and duly considered the subject, we shall see that he could have employed no other terms which would express so fully and with such precision the beautiful and orderly arrangement of the whole angelic heaven, and the harmonious relation of its innumerable and diverse societies.

But let us push our inquiry a little further, that we may see more clearly the ground and origin as well as the truth of this disclosure.

Everything that exists must exist in some form. And the forms of all things will be found to correspond to their essential nature, or to the kind of life that determines their forms. The form always corresponds to the essence. The ox, the eagle, the lion, the dove, each has a form suited to its needs, or correspondent to its own peculiar life. It follows that the higher and nobler the life, the more beautiful and perfect will be the form; otherwise there would be no correspondence of one with the other.

If we look at the lowest creatures in the animal kingdom, we find them closely allied to vegetables, consisting of few parts, and these comparatively simple in their structure. Their forms are inferior, and their wants and capacities correspondingly limited. As we ascend the scale of animated nature, we find a gradual increase of wants; powers more varied; faculties enlarged and multiplied. And corresponding to this increase of desires and enlargement and multiplication of faculties, we find the forms of life also becoming more complex. We find them rising above the earth, provided with the means of locomotion, and simulating, in degrees more or less remote, the human form; until at length we arrive at man, the last link in the great chain connecting all below him with all above. Created to stand erect, with his feet upon the earth and his face toward heaven, he alone is capable of looking above himself, and of intelligently reciprocating or giving back the love and wisdom which flow from God. In man, therefore, the circle of life is complete. In a state of order he is the image and likeness of his Maker. He is the complex, therefore, of all the powers and gifts of other creatures, with the two human faculties—liberty and rationality—superadded.

Now it is because human life is the highest and noblest kind of life—because human wants are more numerous, and the human faculties more. enlarged, exalted, and varied than those of any other creature, that the human form through whose instrumentality alone these faculties can manifest themselves, is the very perfection of all forms. God himself, who is the perfection of all that is human, is in this form. He is a perfect Divine Man. In Him everything truly human exists in infinite fulness, variety and perfection. Therefore when He manifested Himself on earth to the eye of sense, He appeared in the human form. And when in more ancient times He filled the body of an angel with his own Divine life, and thus became manifest to the spiritual senses of his chosen seers as "the angel of Jehovah," his form was always the human.

And it is a Divinely-revealed truth that man was created in the image and likeness of God. His form, therefore, is one capable of receiving and expressing, in a finite degree, something of that truly human life which flows from the Divine Humanity. This life when received, becomes in man the life of love to the Lord and charity toward the neighbor. And this is the essential life of heaven. Other creatures below man may receive and enjoy lower degrees of life; but he alone can receive and enjoy this higher or heavenly life, because he alone is in the human form. And the more we receive of this life, the more truly human we become in our thoughts, feelings, dispositions and purposes; and the more faithfully do we express through our human form—by our looks, words and actions—the love and wisdom which are the essential constituents of true humanity. For the most beautiful and perfect human form is that which best expresses the purest and most exalted human love.

And as it is with a single individual, so with a society or community—with men in the aggregate. The more of true human life each member of a community receives, or the more each one suffers himself to be governed by the highest good and truth, the more orderly, industrious, united, healthy and happy is that community. The more truly human does it become in its form, organization and activities. It appoints its wisest men to preside over its interests, because every one is aiming to subject himself to the government of the highest good and truth. And so the form or order of that community becomes more and more human. All its corporate acts express more and more faithfully the human thoughts and feelings with which the minds of its individual members are imbued. Such community is in the human form, therefore, just so far as the individual minds composing it are truly human. It is the tendency of true human life, wherever it exists, to mould the collective as well as the individual man into a corresponding human form.

But a consideration of the wonderful mechanism of the human body, and of the mutual dependence of its various parts, will furnish the best idea of the human form, and reveal most clearly the order of heaven. For as the body in its entireness corresponds to the soul, so its different parts correspond to the various faculties and functions of the soul, or to the goods and truths of heaven in their various orders and degrees. Therefore the bodily organs correspond to the various societies of which the whole angelic heaven is composed, and which are the living embodiment of these goods and truths.

On a careful survey of the human system, we find it composed of numerous parts which are all different from each other. Its structure is the most complex of any object in the universe. There is no other created thing which consists of so many parts; yet no two of these parts are found to be precisely alike. Some of them differ widely both in form and function. But, notwithstanding the endless number and diversity of parts, they are all mutually dependent, mutually adapted to each other's wants, and work together in admirable harmony. Every organ however minute, has its post assigned it, and its appropriate work given it to do The brain, heart, liver, pleura, the lungs, pancreas, and abdominal viscera—how different are these from each other in their form and structure! How different also in their functions, or in the work given them to do! Yet how admirably do they harmonize! What entire unanimity among these numerous and diverse parts! What perfect concert of action!—all the more perfect because of their diversity. With what beautiful brotherly love do they all work together, and what tender regard has each for the welfare of all the rest! If one is out of order, all the others are more or less uncomfortable. If one suffers, all the rest sympathize and suffer with it. It is a law—and herein we have a beautiful illustration of the great law of brotherhood—that each shall discharge its appropriate function, not apart from the others and for the sake of itself alone, but in harmony with and for the welfare of all the rest. And the more faithfully it labors to do this, the more does it promote its own health and strength, as well as the health and strength of the other members. The welfare of each is linked indissolubly with that of all the others. One life pervades them all, and each receives and enjoys that life in proportion as it respects and faithfully works for the good of the whole. The moment one ceases to do its work, or appropriates more than its share of the juices elaborated, or more than it needs to fit it for the performance of its appointed use, that moment comes disease—disease to itself and disease to all the rest. And if it persevere in

15

this abnormal course, sooner or later death ensues. Such is the law, fixed and unalterable. There is no escape from it. And what a striking exemplification does it furnish of the great law of spiritual life, the law of neighborly love!—yes, and the sure consequence of a persistent violation of this law.

Although one life pervades all the bodily organs, they do not all receive it alike. Their receptivity is as various as their forms. Some receive it in a higher degree than others, and perform more important and varied functions, and may therefore be said to be of a higher grade. And so there are gradations of rank among the members of the body. No one is entirely independent of the rest. No one is so high that it can dispense with the services of the most humble, and no one so low that it cannot do something to promote the health and strength of the highest. The head needs the foot, and the heart the hand, no less than the foot needs the head or the hand the heart. Even the hair and nails and the coarse cuticle on the soles of the feet have their use, and add to the beauty, completeness and perfection of the whole.

Behold, here, then, in the human body, a representative image of heaven!—the most perfect image of order, harmony, unity, freedom, mutual dependence and brotherly love! The relation of the bodily organs to each other, and the uses they respectively perform, are as the relation existing among the angelic societies, and their respective uses; because heaven as a whole and in each of its parts, is in the human form. And notwithstanding there are in heaven as in the human body gradations of rank and office, notwithstanding some there have more important functions to perform than others, there is no pride or disdain on the one hand, nor envy or humiliation on the other, any more than among the different members of the body. Notwithstanding there exist authority and obedience, there is nothing like tyranny on the one hand or slavishness on the other. There is the most perfect freedom coupled with unspeakable bliss; for every one acts as his ruling love prompts, but he loves nothing which is not good and true. Be his office high or low, he does precisely that which he is qualified to do best, and in the doing of which he finds a pure delight. Conscious that he could not be so useful or happy in any other sphere, he has no desire to be anywhere or anything else than he is. Whatever there is, therefore, of exaltation or subordination, of authority or obedience there, neither is felt or thought of as such, any more than in the human body.

From what has been said, we trust that Swedenborg's meaning, when he says that heaven is in the human form, will be sufficiently plain. And although the heavenly societies are innumerable, and all different from each other, yet there exists the most perfect union among them—a union corresponding to, and beautifully symbolized by, that among the different organs of the human body. And herein is revealed the true nature of that union among Christians on earth, to which the Lord refers when He speaks of his disciples being made "perfect in one." It is a union of parts that are as different as are the different members of the human body; parts animated, nevertheless, by one and the same life, as in the case of the bodily organs; for the essential life of all in heaven, is the life of love to the Lord and the neighbor.

It cannot be denied that the human form is the most perfect of all forms. And if the Lord's disciples (and surely those composing the heavenly societies are to be reckoned as such) are "made perfect in one," then must the whole heaven of angels be in the human form; and the doctrine of the Grand Man as revealed through Swedenborg, must be true. For under any other form than the human, or arranged in any other order than that of the different parts of the human body, the heavenly societies could not be said to be "perfected into one;" since their arrangement would be less beautiful and orderly and their union less perfect than it might be.

Then the testimony of the great Apostle to the Gentiles might be cited in corroboration of the truth of this doctrine. Writing to the Church at Rome, he says: "For as we have many members in one body, and all members have not the same office, so we, being many, are one body in Christ." (Rom. xii. 4, 5.) Again to the Corinthian Church: "For the body is not one member, but many; and ye are the body of Christ, and members in particular." He further says there is no schism among the bodily members, and there ought not, therefore, to be any in the body of Christ; that the various parts or members of this body (the church), "should have the same care one for another."

Now the church on earth ought to be, and so far as

it is a true and living church it will be, an image of heaven. And Paul, in the passages referred to, plainly teaches that the church of Christ is in the human form; that its various parts or members, in their mutual relation and dependence, correspond to the different parts of the human body. And if many persons on earth—all of them disciples of the Lord—are " one body in Christ, and every one members one of another," should not the same be true in heaven? Should not the diversity be even greater there than in the church on earth, and the harmony and union at the same time more complete? and the form or order of heaven, therefore, more perfectly human than that of the church?

What, now, are the practical considerations suggested by this disclosure?—for it has important practical bearings. What is its legitimate tendency? Plainly to enlarge and liberalize the mind that accepts it, and to impart to the affections something of that breadth and expansiveness which characterize the Lord's all-encircling love. It shows us that there are innumerable kinds and degrees of good and truth in heaven, all derived from the infinity of the Divine Goodness; endless diversity of character and state even among the angels, and consequently a place somewhere in the abodes of the blessed, for every one who has within him anything of the life of heaven, however humble in quality or limited in degree. It is opposed, therefore, to everything like narrowness, bigotry, sectarianism, or exclusiveness. It encourages us to look chiefly at the essential things of religion,—the spirit and the life of heaven,—and to regard as of comparatively small consequence whatever does

15 *

not lead to or in some way promote these. It rebukes the natural disposition to make ourselves the standards of all excellence, and to judge the character of others by our own peculiar views and feelings; and does not allow us to depreciate another's good because it differs from our own in kind or in degree. It teaches us that good people are not all alike; that, although so different sometimes as to be quite uncongenial to each other, they may, nevertheless, belong to the great body of Christ,—may dwell, as to their spirits, in the same Heavenly Father's house, although in different apartments.

The doctrine further teaches that the most perfect union, harmony, peace and good-fellowship are compatible with great diversity of character, rank, occupation and office; that this diversity, indeed, renders the union and harmony all the more perfect when the different parts in the social body are duly adjusted, and one life pervades them all. It shows us that gradations of rank and character may exist without pride, disdain, or tyranny on the one hand, or envy, jealousy, or humiliation on the other; and that these very gradations furnish wider scope for the infinitely diversified powers of man, and multiply and strengthen the ties that bind the human race together. Its tendency is to make us regard as honorable every position and occupation in life which is useful; to lead every one to desire and seek just that sphere of usefulness which his gifts of body and mind best qualify him to fill; and whether that sphere be high or low—in the head or foot, the eye or hand of the social body—to work there contentedly and faithfully, forever thankful that he is a man.

Let this doctrine be generally accepted and devoutly believed, and what a change would speedily be wrought by it in nearly all existing churches! How quickly would bigotry, intolerance, and belittling sectarianism —all doleful creatures of the night—take their departure, as owls and bats retire at the approach of dawn! For all agree that the Church on earth ought to be, and in a state of true order *will* be, somewhat like the church in heaven. All Christians, indeed, pray for this. Accepting, therefore, the new doctrine of the human form of heaven — the doctrine of endless diversity coupled with completest harmony and unity — they would no longer aim at perfect uniformity in things pertaining to the church, for they would see that no such uniformity exists in heaven. They would see that perfect agreement in doctrine or ritual (save in two or three fundamentals) is neither to be expected nor desired; that variety everywhere—in the spiritual no less than in the natural realm—is the Divine order. And seeing this, they would allow and encourage the utmost freedom of thought and inquiry on religious or doctrinal questions, not deprecating but cordially welcoming whatever diversity might result from such freedom. Prejudice against new ideas, or against writings said to contain them, would everywhere be condemned and frowned upon as a hindrance to religious progress.

Thus would bigotry and intolerance be banished from the churches, and in their place would come a grand catholicity, broad and beautiful as that in heaven. Instead of antagonistic sects warring against, fretting and weakening each other, we should have, out of many and diverse communions, one harmonious and united Church; not one in doctrine, discipline and form of external worship, but one in spirit,—one in the real and practical acknowledgment of the Lord and his Word,— a Church all the more beautiful and perfect, because of the endless diversity among its component parts.

It cannot be denied, therefore, that this doctrine of the human form of heaven, is good and wholesome in its practical tendency. And what stronger evidence of its truth could any one desire than this? No such beneficent results could flow legitimately from a doctrine which is itself false. "Of a bramble-bush men do not gather grapes," "neither can a corrupt tree bring forth good fruit."

XIV.

A HEAVEN FOR THE NON-CHRISTIAN WORLD.

IT will not be denied that, since the memorable year 1757—the alleged date of the last General Judgment —the human race, especially throughout Christendom, has enjoyed a steadily increasing degree of enlightenment on religious as well as on all other subjects. The new angelic heaven has been pressing with continually augmenting force upon all minds—pressing in every direction like a subtle and elastic atmosphere. And under the influence of this pressure, a gradual change in theologic thought has been going on in the minds of individuals and churches. The theology of Swedenborg's day has undergone important modifications, and the change is still in progress. The theology of the present time as it exists in the popular mind (however it may remain unaltered in the creeds) is quite different from that of the last generation. Hence it is not uncommon to meet with persons nowadays, who disbelieve and reject many of the doctrines set forth in the very creeds they have subscribed. And others who still profess loyalty to the "standards," are found giving to their creed a very different interpretation from that clearly intended by its original framers.

This is one of the hopeful signs of our times:—A green and tender leaf on the fig-tree, which proclaims a spiritual summer nigh. In the fluctuation and modification of religious beliefs which we see going on around us, there is abundant cause for joy and hope. It is because the fountains of the great deep in men's minds are breaking up, and the windows of heaven are opening, and increasing light from out the new angelic heavens is bursting upon the world, that such things are coming to pass. It is, moreover, a verification of what Swedenborg foresaw and predicted more than a century ago.

" In consequence and by means of the Last Judgment," he says, " the communication between heaven and the world, or between the Lord and the church, has been restored.

" The state of the world and of the church before the Last Judgment was as evening and night, but after it as morning and day.

" After the Last Judgment was accomplished, there was joy in heaven, and such light in the world of spirits as was not there before. . . A similar light also arose in men in the world, giving them new enlightenment."—Contin. L. J. 11, 13, 30.

Now, because of the changes in religious thought here referred to, it is difficult to say what is the present prevailing belief among Christians respecting the condition of the non-Christian world in the Hereafter. But the general belief in Swedenborg's day was, that all the heathen (unless converted to Christianity before dying) must perish everlastingly. Archbishop Cranmer says: "If we should have heathen parents, and die without baptism, we should be damned everlastingly." And Noel's catechism, regarded as high authority in the Church of England, says: "Without the church [meaning outside of the church professing the Christian religion] there can be nothing but damnation and death." This was the declared doctrine also of the Council of Trent, was held by the Roman Catholic Church, and believed, too, by Luther and Calvin. The latter says: "Without her bosom [that is, outside the pale of the Christian Church] no remission of sins or salvation is to be hoped for."—*Ed. Harold Browne's Expn. of* 39 *Articles*, p. 447, *N. Y. Ed.* 1865.

Then, if we read attentively the letters from foreign missionaries and the reports of Missionary Societies, or note the expressions used in prayers and sermons at meetings held in aid of the cause of foreign missions, we cannot fail to see that the belief is still clung to by Protestant Christians, that the myriads in the heathen world, unless converted to Christianity, are all doomed to hell. Besides, this belief is a strictly logical inference from some of the doctrines of the former Christian church regarded as fundamental and essential, such as the doctrine of vicarious atonement, and justification and salvation by faith alone.

The evidence, therefore, is abundant and undeniable, that the general and well-nigh universal belief both of Roman Catholic and Protestant Christians prior to Swedenborg's time, was, that all of the non-Christian or Gentile world who die unconverted to Christianity, must inevitably be lost, and forever suffer the torments of the damned.

We need not stop to show the unreasonableness and cruelty of such a doctrine; nor how it mars the beauty of the Divine character, and militates against every right conception of God's love and justice. This must be sufficiently apparent to all. To suppose that God would permit hundreds of millions of human beings to be born in regions where He knew they would live and die without any belief in the Gospel of our Lord, or any knowledge even of the existence of such a Gospel, and that He would provide no means for the salvation of these innumerable hosts; and to suppose, further, that they are all to be doomed to eternal hell torments for not believing doctrines which they never had the opportunity of learning, were a supposition so extreme in its unreasonableness, that we can only wonder it should ever have been entertained for a moment by any sane people. The belief is too absurd and revolting to merit a serious refutation. Talk about Swedenborg's madness! Why, if he had ever taught anything half so absurd and monstrous as this old dogma, once so generally accepted among Christians, there would indeed have been good ground for such imputation.

Let us now hear the New Church doctrine on this subject, as revealed through the illumined Swede. And if you consider the general darkness of the period in which he lived as compared with our own times, you can the more easily judge whether his claim to have written under a special Divine illumination, be or be not well founded.

" It is a common opinion that those who are born out of the church, who are called Heathen or Gentiles, cannot be saved, because they have not the Word and are therefore ignorant of the Lord, without whom there can be no salvation. Nevertheless it may be known that they also are saved, from these considerations alone: that the mercy of the Lord is universal, that is, extended toward every individual ; that they are born men as well as those within the church, who are respectively few ; and that it is no fault of theirs that they are ignorant of the Lord.

" Every person who thinks from enlightened reason, may see that no man is born for hell ; for the Lord is love itself, and it is agreeable to his love that all be saved. Therefore also He has provided that all shall have some kind of religion, and thereby be in the acknowledgment of a Divine, and in the enjoyment of interior life: for to live according to religion is to live interiorly. For then man looks up to a Divine ; and as far as he looks up to a Divine he does not esteem the world, but removes himself from it, consequently from the life of the world, which is exterior life.

" That Gentiles are saved as well as Christians, may be known to those who understand what it is that makes heaven in man. For heaven is in man ; and those who have heaven in themselves enter heaven after death. It is heaven in man to acknowledge a Divine and be led by Him.

"It is known that Gentiles live a moral life as well as Christians, and that many of them live better than Christians. Men live a moral life either for the sake of the Divine, or from a regard to the opinion of the world. The moral life which is lived for the sake of the Divine is spiritual life. Both appear alike in the external form, but in the internal they are altogether different. One saves man; the other does not. For he who lives a moral life from a regard to the opinions of the world, is led by himself. But let this be illustrated by an example.

"I have often been instructed that Gentiles who have led a moral life, have lived in obedience and subordination, and in mutual charity according to their religion, and have thence received something of conscience, are accepted in the other life, and are there instructed with anxious care by angels in the goods and truths of faith; and that, while under instruction, they behave themselves modestly, intelligently and wisely, and willingly receive truths and are imbued with them. Besides, they have formed to themselves no principles of the false contrary to the truths of faith, which are to be shaken off, much less scandals against the Lord,—like many Christians who cherish no other idea of Him than that of a common man."—H. H. n. 318–321.

"The mercy of the Lord is infinite, and does not suffer itself to be confined to the small number within the church, but extends itself to all throughout the world. For those who are born out of the church, and are thereby in ignorance as to matters of faith, are not blamable on that account; nor are they ever condemned for not having faith toward the Lord, because they are not aware of his existence. What considerate person can suppose the greatest part of mankind must perish eternally, because they were not born in that quarter of the globe denominated Europe, which respectively contains so few? Or that the Lord would permit so great a multitude of human beings to be brought into existence to perish in eternal death? This would be alike contrary to the Divine nature and to mercy. Besides, those who are out of the church and are called Gentiles, live a much more moral life than those within the church, and far more easily embrace the doctrine of a true faith. This is very evident from the state of souls in another life; for the worst of all are those who come from the so-called Christian world, bearing mortal hatred both against their neighbor and the Lord, and being more addicted to adultery than any other people on the face of the earth."— A. C. 1032.

This, remember, comes professedly as a revelation on the subject we are considering. And what shall we say of it? That it is unreasonable?—senseless?—indicative of some strange hallucination on the part of the seer? On the contrary, it is so perfectly in accord with the dictates of reason and common sense, that the rejection of it, or even a doubt about its truth, would seem to indicate a mental condition closely allied to insanity. Since God is love, He can never forsake any portion of the children of men. He can never be indifferent to their welfare. He can never cease his efforts to save and bless them. If He should, that moment He would lose or lay aside his most distinguishing attribute: He would cease to be Infinite Love. For it is in the very nature of this love to be " long-suffering," " plenteous in mercy and truth," " not willing that any should perish, but that all should come to repentance." And it is in the nature of Divine Wisdom to adapt its teachings to mankind in their various stages of development and of moral disorder. When, therefore, man perverts the highest truths, and extinguishes in himself their light and life, then truths of a lower order are given him—truths better suited to his lower and perverse state ; and Infinite Love seeks to secure his obedience to these. And when, through the perversion of these, he sinks to a still lower or more external state, then truths of a yet lower degree are mercifully vouchsafed him.

Thus the Lord, in the plenitude of his wisdom and love, forever adapts his truth to the states of all finite minds. Evermore does He impart to all his human offspring as much and as pure truth as they are able to receive. And when they fall into states to profane the highest truths, then these are mercifully taken from them ; or what is equivalent, their eyes are veiled, as it were, so that they may not see or acknowledge them to be truths. As it is written : " He hath blinded their eyes and hardened their heart ; that they should not see with their eyes, nor understand with their heart, and be converted, and I should heal them." (John xii. 40.)

This is as true of nations as it is of individuals. Hence no nation has ever been left without a religion of some sort, nor without some religious truth. And the form which religion takes in any age or country, and the character and amount of religious truth which is acknowledged, will depend on the general state of the people, and be suited to their state. And more and higher truth will be given them so soon as they are prepared to receive it.

None of the heathen nations, therefore, are left wholly

destitute of religious truth.   With all the errors and ab-
surdities in the Mahometan and Pagan religions, there
are to be found many important truths, many wholesome
precepts, many laws of heavenly charity.   And all who
obey these laws from a principle of religion, are thereby
saved from the evils they forbid.   And not only this,
but fidelity to the little truth they know, prepares them
for the reception of more and higher truth when they
enter the other world.   A person may be born amid
such surroundings that he will be brought up in great
ignorance and even in the belief of great errors, and yet
be preserved in a state of child-like innocence.   And as
this is a state receptive of wisdom, such person will
readily receive instruction in the world of spirits, and
be there fitted for the kingdom of heaven in the way that
children are.   We may thus see how it is possible for
people in the non-Christian nations, to be finally admitted into heaven, notwithstanding the many errors they
imbibed on earth.   Indeed they may, on account of their
greater innocence and simplicity, receive instruction in
the other world more readily than many Christians.

"Occasionally," says Swedenborg, "it has been granted me to converse with Christians in another life concerning the state and lot of the Gentiles out of the church,
that they receive the truths and goods of faith more easily
than Christians who have not lived according to the
Lord's precepts; and that Christians think cruelly concerning them in supposing that all who are out of the
church are damned, and this in consequence of a received
canon, that out of the Lord there is no salvation; and
that this is true, but that the Gentiles who have lived in
mutual charity, and have done what is just and equitable

from a kind of conscience, in another life receive faith and acknowledge the Lord more easily than they who are within the church and have not lived in such charity; also that Christians are in a false principle in supposing that they alone have heaven, because they have the book of the Word written on paper but not in their hearts; and that they know the Lord, and yet do not believe Him Divine as to his Human, yea, acknowledge Him only as a common man as to his other essence which they call the human nature; and on this account when they are left to themselves and their knowledges, do not even adore Him; and therefore they are the people who are out of the Lord, for whom there is no salvation."— A. C. n. 4190.

"All the good of charity even among the Gentiles, is seed from the Lord; for although they have not the good of faith as those within the Church (where the Word is) may have, yet they are nevertheless capable of receiving it. Such Gentiles as have lived in charity in the world, as they are wont to do, embrace and receive the true faith or the faith of charity, much more readily than Christians, when they are instructed therein by angels in another life."—Ibid. n. 932. See also n. 1032, 9256; A. E. n. 1180; D. P. 330.

It is as true of Pagan as of Christian nations, that they have more truth than they are careful to obey. In every nation upon earth men's beliefs are better than their practice. The religious code of Pagans as well as of Christians is far better than the general character of the people. He who walks according to the light vouchsafed him, does all that the Lord requires of him. No one can be held accountable for disobeying truth of which he is ignorant, especially if his ignorance be no fault of his. Therefore a wrong which a man does

16*

ignorantly, is not a sin. Sin implies a knowledge of the law transgressed. It consists in disobedience to known and acknowledged truth. If we ignorantly transgress, we feel very different from what we should if we did the same act with a full knowledge at the time that we were violating a divine law. Is it reasonable, then, that those born in Pagan lands should be forever doomed to darkness and woe, because of their non-obedience to truth which they never heard of?

No: God is a Being infinitely wise and just. And all that *such* a Being can require of individuals or nations, be they Jews, Mahometans, Pagans or Christians, is, that they live according to the light they have. And all who do so live, will finally be received into heaven; for by their religious obedience to the few truths they know they are prepared to receive more and purer truths in the world of spirits.

Such, briefly, is the doctrine revealed through Swedenborg on this subject; a doctrine that fully accords with our highest conception of the Divine character and attributes, as well as with the dictates of reason and common sense.

And not less clearly does the doctrine agree with the teachings as well as with the entire spirit of Holy Scripture. The Word of God simply requires us to walk according to the light that is given. "While ye *have* light, believe in the light, that ye may be the children of light," saith the Lord (John xii. 36). And we really believe in the light, only when we walk according to it (H. H. 351; A. C. 4239; A. R. 67; A. E. 346). "Walk while ye *have* the light." Those to whom the light of the Gospel has not come, cannot walk according to it, and are not, therefore, to be judged by it. For what is it that brings, or on whom is pronounced, the sentence of condemnation? The Lord answers: "This is the condemnation, that light is come into the world, and men loved darkness rather than light, because their deeds were evil." (John iii. 19.) From which it is plain that there can be no condemnation where the light has not come; for condemnation consists in a rejection of the light when offered. Neither is sin imputed to those who err through ignorance; for the Lord further says: "If I had not come and spoken unto them, *they had not had sin.*" (John xv. 22.) And that, in the day of final adjudication every one will be held accountable for only that measure of truth which has been vouchsafed him, is plain from these words of the Lord: "And that servant who knew his Lord's will, and prepared not, neither did according to his will, shall be beaten with many stripes. But he that knew not, and did commit things worthy of stripes, shall be beaten with few stripes. For unto whomsoever much is given, of him shall much be required; and to whom men have committed much, of him will they ask the more." (Luke xii. 47, 48.) Equally conclusive, too, is the apostle's testimony, and clearly teaching the very same doctrine: "Of a truth," he says, "I perceive that God is no respecter of persons; but *in every nation* he that feareth Him and worketh righteousness, is accepted with Him." (Acts x. 34, 35.) Which is virtually saying that there are some righteous and God-fearing people in every nation, and that all such will be saved.

And so we find the teaching of the Bible to agree with that of Swedenborg on this subject; and the testimony of both to be in complete accord with the whole spirit of the Christian religion as well as with the verdict of enlightened reason.

And not only does Swedenborg teach that the heathen *may* be saved, but he says that more of them actually *are* saved than of those who profess the Christian religion; and he tells us why.

"It is a very common thing with those who have conceived an opinion respecting any truth of faith, to judge of others that they cannot be saved but by believing as they do, which nevertheless the Lord forbids, Matt. vii. 1, 2. Accordingly it has been made known to me by much experience that persons of every religion are saved, if so be, by a life of charity, they have received remains of good and of apparent truth. . . The life of charity consists in man's thinking well of others, and desiring good to others, and perceiving joy in himself at the salvation of others. But they have not the life of charity, who are not willing that any should be saved but such as believe as they themselves do, and especially if they are indignant that it should be otherwise. This may appear from this single circumstance, that more are saved from the Gentiles than from among the Christians; for such of the Gentiles as have thought well of their neighbor, and lived in good-will to him, receive the truths of faith in another life better than they who are called Christians, and acknowledge the Lord more gladly than Christians do; for nothing is more delightful and happy to the angels, than to instruct those who come from earth into another life."— A. C. n. 2284; also, 1059.

This, we doubt not, will have a strange sound to the

ears of many who have been educated in the old theologies, and who hear it now for the first time. But is it not both reasonable and Scriptural? Does it not accord with these words of the Lord? "And I say unto you that many shall come from the east and west, and shall sit down with Abraham and Isaac and Jacob in the kingdom of heaven. But the children of the kingdom shall be cast out into the outer darkness." (Matt. viii. 11, 12. See also Luke xiii 24–31.) By "the children of the kingdom" are plainly meant those who have the Word, and who imagine (as did the Jews) that, for this reason alone, they would be saved in preference to those who have it not (as in the case of the Gentiles), and who have not therefore eaten and drunk in the Lord's presence, nor heard his voice in their streets. And by the "many" who would come from the four quarters and find a welcome, while "the children of the kingdom" would be thrust into the outer darkness, are as plainly meant the Gentiles—the non-Christian peoples who have not the written Word.

And not only does Swedenborg teach that fewer are saved from among Christians than from among the Gentiles, but that the worst of all the devils in hell are from the Christian nations. "This I can aver," he says, "that they who come into the other life from the Christian world, are the worst of all, hating their neighbor, hating the faith, and denying the Lord; for in the other life the heart speaks, and not the lips merely. Besides, they are more given to adultery than the rest of mankind." —A. C. 1885 ; also 1032.

But while the worst of the devils go from Christian

countries, so likewise do the best of the angels. Those from among Christians who go to heaven, rise to a higher state than do the good from among Gentiles, while those who are lost sink to a deeper hell. How can it be otherwise? For Christians, being in possession of the Word, have a greater amount of truth than the Gentiles, and truth of a higher order and a purer quality. And the higher and purer the truth, the higher the state to which those will rise who receive and live according to it. The truths of the Christian religion are deeper and more heart-searching than those of any other religion. Therefore strict obedience to these truths must bring the richest reward—must develop the highest and noblest life. And on the other hand they who know but disobey these truths, commit greater sin than those can who are ignorant of them. They sin against greater light. They become more wicked; therefore they sink to a deeper hell,—are beaten with more stripes. This is in accordance with the universal law, that the better a thing is, the worse are the consequences resulting from its abuse. What Swedenborg says, therefore, about the worst of the devils being from Christian countries, is altogether reasonable.

His statement on this point, too, is corroborated by well-established historical facts. For it is matter of history that scenes of the most dismal horror which the sun ever shone upon, have been enacted in Christian lands; that the blackest crimes which the page of history records, have been perpetrated within the bounds of Christendom. Can there be any doubt, then, that the very worst spirits in the other world, are from Christian lands?

Such is the doctrine revealed through Swedenborg concerning the state of the Heathen in the great Hereafter,—very different, we see, from that hitherto believed and taught in the Christian church. A doctrine truly catholic in its spirit, wholesome in its tendency, boundless as God's love in its embrace, and in complete agreement with Holy Scripture and enlightened reason. It assures us that the Lord has left none of his intelligent creatures without sufficient light, if they follow it, to guide them to the realms of bliss. It declares that people of every nation and creed, be they civilized or barbarous, may be saved and are saved so far as they live according to the truths they know; and, furthermore, that the worst of all the devils in hell are from Christian countries; and that those who live under the noonday light of the Gospel, may be lost and *are* lost if they walk not according to that light.

Thus the new doctrine affirms this momentous truth—a truth often reiterated in the writings of the great seer, and which deserves to be engraven indelibly on every heart—that entrance into the kingdom of heaven depends not upon what people *know*, but upon how they *live;* not upon the character or amount of the truth they believe, but upon the motive and measure of their obedience to its requirements; not upon the brilliancy of the light that illumines their pathway, but upon their fidelity and sincerity in following the light. Therefore "while ye have the light, believe in the light, that ye may be the children of light," saith the Lord. And the only genuine and saving belief, is that which avails to the renovation of the heart and life; for " with the heart man believeth unto righteousness." And Swedenborg often says that a genuine belief, or belief in the Lord, involves obedience to the Divine precepts, and can have no existence without it. To cite a single passage:

"By believing in the Lord, man has conjunction with Him, and by conjunction, salvation. To believe in Him, is to have confidence that He will save; and because no one can have such confidence but he who *leads a good life*, therefore this also is meant by believing in Him." —A. R. 67. See also T. C. R. n. 151; A. C. 896, 9239; A. E. 349.

XV.

ARE EARTHLY RELATIONSHIPS CONTINUED IN HEAVEN?

HAVING ascertained the law that determines all associations in the Hereafter, an interesting question arises: Are the ties of natural consanguinity continued in heaven? In other words, Will those who have sustained on earth the relation of parents and children, brothers and sisters, husbands and wives, dwell together (supposing they all become regenerate) in the same angelic society, and maintain a similar relation toward each other in heaven to that they bore on earth? Or will these natural relationships cease with the death of the body, and new relationships take their place?

There is something surpassingly beautiful—something, indeed, holy—in the ties that bind kindred and friends together on earth. Every one recognizes the beauty and sacredness of these ties. The links in that chain of love formed by the members of a happy family, how golden and precious! The affection between brothers and sisters, how cordial and sincere! The love of children for their parents, how sweet and confiding! The love of parents for their children, how deep and tender! The affection between husband and wife, how beautiful and holy!

These natural relationships image more faithfully than anything else can, the higher and enduring spiritual relationships which exist in heaven. The relation of the children to each other, affords the truest type of the fraternal relation existing between the members of an angelic society. The relation of children to their parents —their affection for them, their dependence upon them, and their obedience to the parents' every wish and word —furnishes the best idea of the relation of the angels to the Lord, of their affection for, their dependence upon, and their obedience to, the Heavenly Father. The relation of the parents to the children—their tender love and ceaseless care for them, their consideration for their weakness, their patience with their faults, and their thoughtful provision for all their wants, what a beautiful image is this of the relation of the Lord to the angels, of his infinite love and ceaseless care for them, and his bountiful provision for all their wants!

Thus does a loving, well-ordered and happy family furnish the truest picture of heaven, of anything known on earth. Such a family is itself a heaven in miniature. Accordingly we find that, in the written Word (which, in its true sense, treats altogether of spiritual things) the terms which are employed in all languages to express the most intimate and tender earthly relationships, are used to express the relationships existing in heaven, and among heavenly-minded people on earth. Thus God, in respect to the inmost, paternal, heaven-begetting principle of his nature—Divine Love—is called the Heavenly Father. And in his relation to the church, or to those whose hearts have become wedded to Him by love and obedience, He is called Bridegroom and Husband. And those thus wedded (which is the case with all who have in themselves the heavenly marriage of good and truth) are called Mother, Wife and Bride. And the angels and regenerate men—all who are born of this heavenly Father and Mother, that is, born again, "born from above" —are called children. They are God's children, begotten of Him in his own image and likeness; and viewed in their relation to each other, they are brethren, and are so called in Scripture. Thus Jesus says to his disciples: "One is your Father—God; and all ye are brethren."

Here, as in other passages of Scripture, we are taught that there are spiritual relationships to which the natural correspond, and of which they are the representative image. And as spiritual things are superior to the natural whereby they are shadowed forth,—the spiritual sense of the Word superior to the natural sense,—the spiritual world superior to the natural world,—the soul or spirit of man superior to the body,—therefore spiritual relationships are, and must needs be, superior to the natural. They are more interior, more enduring, more perfect and blissful.

Now, when the natural body dies, man passes (in a

spiritual body) out of the 'natural, and comes consciously into the spiritual realm. He leaves behind him all natural things; or, what is equivalent, he passes into a realm where these things are no longer seen or thought of. He leaves the natural body; but straightway finds himself in the enjoyment of superior faculties belonging to a superior kind of body, which has always been within the natural—a body that is spiritual and substantial. He leaves the natural world; but immediately enters, or has opened up to his consciousness, another world in which all things are more real and substantial, but spiritual in their nature. He leaves the natural or literal sense of the Scripture, that is, he no longer sees or thinks of this sense; but he comes into the perception and understanding of a vastly higher and more important sense, viz., the spiritual. He leaves the natural memory, that is, the memory of merely natural facts,—or, what is the same, this memory becomes quiescent; but a new, more interior and enduring memory is then developed, viz., the spiritual.

Now the logical inference from all this is, that natural relationships terminate when the body dies, and new and higher relationships are then established; and that these new relationships rest upon higher or more interior ground, and are determined by people's spiritual resemblance or proximity to each other. The members of the same family on earth are said to be closely related; and they are so naturally. But this is simply a flesh and blood relationship—often nothing more; and as such, we should expect it to cease when the body dies. For members of the same family are often quite different in character. Some are passionate and others calm, some bright and others dull, some deceitful and others frank—born, too, of the same parents, and subjected to the same nurture and discipline. Naturally, therefore, they are as near akin as they can be, and in their faces they may resemble each other. But spiritually viewed, there is little or no resemblance between them; they are wholly unlike, and have no moral or spiritual affinity. And in view of the law that governs in every association of spirits, it is plain that they would have no desire to dwell together in the spiritual world. Their spheres would be mutually repulsive, and their society mutually disagreeable.

The conclusion, therefore, seems irresistible, that the natural relationships of this world will not be continued in the world beyond; but that new relationships based upon interior and spiritual resemblances, will be established there. The legitimate deductions of reason bring us to this conclusion. Now let us see how far Swedenborg's disclosures accord with these deductions.

" Consociations in the other life are comparatively like relationships on earth, in that there is an acknowledgment as of parents, children, brethren, kinsfolk and connections; according to such differences is their love. The differences are indefinite, and the communicative perceptions so exquisite as to admit of no description,—no respect whatever being had to parents, children, kinsfolk, and connections on earth, nor to any personal considerations of quality or character, consequently not to dignities, riches, and the like, but only to the differences of mutual love and faith, the faculty of receiving which each had obtained from the Lord during his abode in the world."—A. C. n. 685.

" That the truths of the church are called brethren, is manifest from this, that the sons of Jacob represented the truths of the church in the complex. That in ancient times they were called brethren from spiritual affinity, is because the new birth or regeneration made consanguinities and affinities in a degree superior to the natural birth; and because the former derive their origin from one Father, namely, from the Lord. Hence it is, that men after death who come into heaven, do not any longer acknowledge any brother, nor even mother or father, except from good and truth; according to these they enter there into new fraternities or brotherhoods. Hence it is, that they who were of the church called each other brethren."—A. C. n. 6758.

" That in the spiritual world or heaven, there are no other consanguinities and affinities, except of love to the Lord and neighborly love, or, what is the same thing, of good, was made manifest to me from this consideration: that all the societies which constitute heaven and which are innumerable, are most distinct from each other, according to the degrees and differences of love and of faith thence derived; also from this circumstance, that they mutually know each other, not from any affinity which had existed in the life of the body, but solely from a principle of good and truth thence derived. A father does not know a son or a daughter, nor a brother a brother or sister, nor indeed a husband a wife, unless they have been principled in like good. They meet, indeed, on their first coming into another life, but they are soon dissociated, inasmuch as essential good, or love and charity, determines every one to his particular society and enrolls him in it. In the society in which every one is enrolled, consanguinity commences; and thence proceed affinities even to the circumferential parts."—Ibid. n. 3815.

" In another life, all are consociated according to affec-

17 *

tions, and they who are consociated constitute a brother-hood; not that they call themselves brethren, but that they are brethren by conjunction. Essential good and truth in another life make what is called on earth consanguinity and relationship; wherefore they correspond. For goods and truths considered in themselves do not acknowledge any other father but the Lord, for they are from Him alone. Hence all are in brotherhood who are in goods and truths. Nevertheless there are degrees according to the quality of goods and truths. These degrees are signified in the Word by brethren, sisters, sons-in-law, daughters-in-law, grandsons, granddaughters, and by several names of families. On earth, however, they are so named in respect to common parents, however they differ in affections; but in another life such brotherhood and relationship is dissipated, and they all come into other brotherhoods, unless on earth they have been in similar good. At first, indeed, they generally meet, but in a short time are disjoined; for gain in that life does not consociate, but, as was said, affection, the quality of which then appears as in clear day."—A. C. n. 4121.

Here as elsewhere it will be seen that Swedenborg is perfectly consistent. And his revealings accord, too, with the verdict of enlightened reason and sound philosophy. Had he told anything essentially different, its want of agreement with his other teachings, as well as with reason and philosophy, would have been at once apparent. It also would have lacked—what it now clearly has—the undeniable support of Scripture. For the Bible tells of other and higher relationships than those of flesh and blood. It declares that before a man can enter the kingdom of heaven, he must be born again —"not of blood, nor of the will of the flesh, nor of the will of man, but of God"—thus clearly teaching us that there is a higher and nobler kind of birth than that into the realm of nature. The first birth is natural, the second is spiritual. "Howbeit," says the apostle, "that was not first which is spiritual, but that which is natural; and afterward that which is spiritual." (1 Cor. xv. 46.)

That which is first in the order of importance, is always last in the order of time. The fruit comes *after* and never *before* the flower. The development of the heavenly is always subsequent to that of the earthly or corporeal life. The angel is formed out of, and therefore subsequent to, the man. Consequently those relationships which are spiritual in their nature, or which result from regeneration, must be superior to those resulting from natural generation. They must be akin to the relationships existing in heaven. Accordingly the Lord desires that we shall all become his children—children of the Heavenly Father—his spiritual children, of course. And He tells us how we can become such, or what we must do; and among other things, that we must be willing, if need be, to sunder the ties of natural kindred,—be willing to forsake father, mother, brothers, sisters, wife, children, and whatsoever is dearest to the natural man, for his sake. He counsels his disciples to call no man their father upon earth; adding: "for One is your Father which is in heaven; and all ye are brethren." And at another time, "stretching forth his hand toward his disciples, He said: Behold my mother and my brethren! For whosoever shall do the will of my Father which is in heaven, the same is my brother and sister and mother." (Matt. xii. 49, 50.)

Who cannot see that in all such passages it is a spiritual relationship to which our Lord refers ?—a relationship resulting from the new spiritual birth, and grounded in spiritual faith and love? Such is the only kind of relationship (and this should be conclusive of the whole question) which He ever recognizes as belonging to his kingdom in the heavens. And what other relationship should we expect—what other, indeed, can there be—in a kingdom that is purely spiritual?

XVI.

MEETING AND RECOGNITION OF FRIENDS IN THE HEREAFTER.

IN view of what has been said in the foregoing chapter, questions like the following will naturally arise: Shall we not, then, meet our earthly friends in the spiritual world? Shall we not recognize them and be recognized by them in return? Will not the mother meet her darling child, and know and love it as her own? Will not husbands and wives, brothers and sisters, meet there in tender and loving embrace, and remember and renew the relation they sustained in the natural world? Is not the desire for such reunions in the Hereafter, among the implanted instincts of our nature? And in seasons of sore bereavement do we not derive support and solace from the belief that this natural and deep desire of our hearts will be granted?

Most assuredly. And there is no reason to doubt

that it will be granted. Every implanted instinct of our nature will have its demands satisfied in the spiritual world. Every one will, therefore, be permitted to see and recognize the friends he has known and loved on earth, and to remain in their company so long as may be mutually agreeable. But such meeting and mutual recognition in the Hereafter, take place in the intermediate state or world of spirits, where all souls go immediately after the death of the body. This is neither heaven nor hell, but a realm or state between the two, like the world in which we are now living, and having communication with both. This is the realm or state in which they find themselves immediately after leaving the body, for bodily death effects no change whatever in the character. They are, when they first awake to consciousness, in a state precisely similar to that in which they were before death. The same external thoughts or affections, the same natural or external memory, the same natural desires and feelings are still alive and active. Hence the reason why everything on a person's entrance into the other world, appears there precisely as it did here; for in that world everything without corresponds to the individual's own state—to the thoughts and feelings within him. So long, therefore, as he continues in the same external state in which he was before death, will he see around him objects similar to those by which he was surrounded on earth, —so similar, indeed, that it is often hard for a person to be quickly convinced that he has actually passed through the gate of death. And he will have precisely the same face as before; for the face in the other world corresponds to the mental state, or to the thoughts and affections that are present and active.

It is in the world of spirits, therefore, where all are in the same mental state in which they were when on earth, and therefore look just the same, that friends and natural relatives meet and converse, and share each other's society so long as their intercourse proves mutually agreeable. If some have died many years before, and gone to their final home, either in the upper or the nether realms according as their real character may have been heavenly or infernal, they are, through the Divine mercy, temporarily remitted into the world of spirits; that is, they are brought into the same state of exterior memory, thought and affection in which they were when in the flesh; consequently their faces appear just the same as they did in this world. In this state of their exteriors it may be mutually agreeable to remain in each other's company for a considerable time. But if they are spiritually and internally unlike, the dissimilarity will shortly reveal itself, and they will not long be happy in each other's society. As the interiors of each become more and more manifest to the other, they will feel a mutual repulsion, and will desire to separate. And when they shall have come fully into the state of their interiors, the quality of which determines the kind of society they are fitted for, then whatever disagrees with their ruling loves is removed from their exteriors; their external memory which enabled them when on earth to recall their relationship and all belonging to it, becomes closed or quiescent; and their faces take on an expression corresponding to the character of their interiors. And when their interiors are fully laid open, if their characters or loves are different, they will not only be disinclined to remain together, but will appear as strangers to each other. Their natural memory being lost or closed, they will no longer remember their former friendship or relationship; nay, they will not know that they have ever seen each other before, though they may have dwelt for years beneath the same roof, and sustained the most intimate of earthly relations. Their faces, too, will appear unfamiliar, being no longer such as they had been in the world, but so changed as to be the images of their ruling loves.

In the intermediate state or world of spirits, therefore, where all, being still in externals, appear as they did on earth, friends and natural relatives meet and recognize each other, and remain together as long as they desire. But when their natural memory and affections have faded or become quiescent, and they have entered into the state of their interiors, then natural relatives cease to be remembered or thought of; and if their characters are essentially unlike, they will no longer desire to remain together, having no affinity for each other.

"Those who have friends and acquaintances in the life of the body, all meet and converse together in the world of spirits, when they desire it; especially wives and husbands, and also brothers and sisters. I have seen a father conversing with six sons whom he recognized; and many others conversing with their relations and friends; but as their characters were dissimilar in consequence of their life in the world, after a short time they separated. But they who pass from the world of spirits into heaven or hell, afterwards see each other no more, nor do they know anything about each other, unless they are of similar disposition from similar loves. They see each other in the world of spirits, and not in heaven nor in hell, because they who are in the world of spirits are brought into states similar to those which they had experienced in the life of the body, being led from one into another; but afterwards, all are brought into a permanent state similar to that of their ruling love; and in that state one knows another only from similitude of love; for similitude conjoins, and dissimilitude separates."—H. H. n. 427; see also A. R. 153.

In accordance with what is here taught is the following, which tells us why those who have been closely related on earth, will ultimately be as strangers to each other in the world beyond, if there be no internal likeness—no spiritual relationship between them.

"When the spirit of man first enters the world of spirits, which takes place shortly after his resuscitation, he has a similar face and similar tone of voice to what he had in the world, because he is then in the state of his exteriors, and his interiors are not yet disclosed. This is the first state of man after death. But afterwards his face is changed and becomes entirely different, assuming the likeness of his ruling affection or love in which the interiors of his mind were in the world, and in which his spirit was in the body. . . . I have seen some spirits shortly after their arrival from the world, and knew them by their face and speech; but when I saw them afterwards, I did not know them. They who were principled in good affections appeared with beautiful faces, but they who were principled in evil affections, with faces deformed; for the spirit of man, viewed in itself, is nothing but his affection whereof the face is the external form. The reason also why the face is changed, is because in the other life no one is allowed to counterfeit affections which are not properly his own, nor, consequently, to put on looks which are contrary to his real love. All in the spiritual world, therefore, whoever they may be, are brought into such a state as to speak as they think, and to express by their faces and gestures the inclinations of their will. Hence the faces of all become the forms and images of their affections. And hence it is that all who have known each other in the world, know each other also in the world of spirits, but not in heaven nor in hell."—H. H. n. 457.

It must not be inferred, however, from what has been said, that natural relationships are necessarily incompatible with spiritual; or that those who have been closely related on earth, cannot also be internally related, and so dwell together forever. On the contrary, we are taught that those who have been near and dear to each other in the flesh—members of the same family on earth—may, if they become regenerated, become still nearer and dearer to each other in heaven, and forever dwell together in the same angelic society. We are taught that marriages *may* take place in this world upon a deep spiritual ground—that is, between parties who are the spiritual complements of each other. Where this is the case, the union is a truly conjugial one—is at once both spiritual and natural. And because it is a union of souls as well as of bodies, therefore the death of the body will not dissolve it. They will remain united forever, being the complements of each other. And their union in heaven will be more full and complete, and attended with delights as far superior to those that accompany marriage here below, as heaven is superior to earth or angels superior to men. This, however, only when there is a union of souls between the parties. If the union is merely external, and the two have no spiritual affinity, it will not be renewed or continued in the Hereafter.

The same remarks are applicable to other earthly relationships. They may be, and sometimes are, continued in heaven, with their pleasures refined, their joys exalted, and their delights immensely increased. This, too, is what the great seer teaches.

"Certain souls," he says, "who were with me [on one occasion], were let into a state of innocence, from which they conversed with me through spirits ; and they confessed that it was a state of such joy and gladness that the human understanding could form no conception of it, for it was their very inmosts which were affected. . . They were with those who had been their parents, grandparents, and ancestors, that is, with their entire family for two centuries back. They were admitted together with them into that heaven, and their joy was such as cannot possibly be described."—Spl. D. 832, '4.

Such is Swedenborg's teaching concerning the meeting and recognition of friends in the Hereafter, and the continuance or cessation of natural relationships. Does it sound like the ravings of a madman or the utterances of a fanatic? Stretch your imagination to the utmost, and see if you can conceive of any different view that is at once so rational, philosophical, and scriptural as this.

The doctrine here disclosed is one that fully meets the demands of our reason as well as of our God-implanted desires and instincts. It satisfies the cravings of even the strongest natural affection. It permits the bereaved wife or husband to indulge the fond hope of meeting in the Hereafter the beloved companion gone before. It gives to all who are bound by the ties of natural consanguinity, the comforting assurance that when death snatches from their embrace some dearly loved one—a parent, child, brother, sister, husband, or wife—the separation will be but for a season ;—that they may confidently rely on a blissful reunion in the spiritual realm. What solace there is in such assurance! What balm to bereaved affection! What support in seasons of deepest sorrow!

And while the doctrine deals so tenderly with the natural affections, while it ministers all the comfort which the heart is capable of receiving in times of sore bereavement, it at the same time discloses a more exalted and heavenly state of affection than the natural, and a higher and holier relationship than that between members of the same family on earth. It teaches that the truest and holiest brotherhood, that of which the natural is but a faint image, exists between those who have been "born from above "—" born of the Spirit "— and have become children of the Heavenly Father. It teaches that natural relationships cease in the spiritual realm, and are succeeded by higher and holier relationships ; that natural kindred, when they come fully into the state of their interiors, will (if they are spiritually far asunder) no longer see or know each other, and will lose all remembrance of their earthly relationship. It thus furnishes a rational and philosophical solution of a problem that has hitherto embarrassed theologians, and been a trouble to many pious minds. For it shows us that

those who enter heaven will never have their peace dis
turbed by the harrowing thought that some of their near
kindred in the flesh are in the nether realms; for although this may be true, they will know nothing of it,
having no recollection of their natural kindred. And
if their states are very unlike, they would not recognize
them should they see them. Their voices would sound
unfamiliar, and their faces would be as the faces of
strangers. Though kindred in the flesh, they are kindred no longer; for the flesh and all its belongings have
been laid aside.

Thus does the spiritual in all things transcend the
natural. Thus do the tenderest earthly relationships,
having fulfilled their appointed use on earth, fade and
die out from the memory and the affections in the great
Hereafter; and in their stead spring up those higher
and nobler spiritual relationships, determined not by the
accident of natural birth, but by the new birth from
Above, and the consequent proximity or likeness to the
Heavenly Father.

Such is the doctrine as revealed for the New Church
on this subject. While it accords with the spirit of holy
Scripture and with all we know of the Divine character
and attributes, it agrees also with the highest spiritual
philosophy, and satisfies the sternest demands of the
understanding and the intensest longings of the heart.

XVII.

PERSONAL APPEARANCE OF THE ANGELS.

WHEN a traveler in a foreign land writes an account of his travels, he is expected to describe the personal appearance of the people he visits, as well their character, manners and customs. Without such description his narrative would be incomplete and unsatisfactory. So natural, indeed, is it for people to inquire about the personal appearance of those whom they know only from the lips or pen of another, that a novelist would never think of dismissing one of his heroes without gratifying his readers on this point. If he should, they would be disappointed, and would not fail to note the omission as a conspicuous defect in the story.

Now, Swedenborg professes to have enjoyed open intercourse with the denizens of the spiritual world for a period of nearly thirty years. He claims to have daily seen and conversed with both angels and devils during this long period. If this is true, we should expect him to say something about the personal appearance of the people he saw there—to tell us how they look, whether beautiful or ugly. And this he has not failed to do. He says that the inhabitants of heaven are all in the human form, and beautiful beyond the power of language to describe. And he has told us why they are so beautiful. Their figures and faces, he says, are the very images of the spirit that animates and moulds them. They are the correspondential forms of their elevated thoughts, sweet affections and noble purposes. For Mind is the controling power throughout the universe; and so entire and absolute is its sway in the spiritual world, that the minds of all, both in heaven and in hell, mould their bodies into forms exactly correspondent to their essential nature. The face of every one there, is the image of the spirit within him. The appearance of the outer proclaims with undeviating certainty the character of the inner man; for there the body and the soul are in such perfect correspondence that the former is the exact image of the latter. We will cite the seer's own language on this subject:

"The human form of every man after death is the more beautiful, the more interiorly he had loved divine truths and lived according to them; for the interiors of every one are opened and formed according to his love and life; wherefore the more interior is the affection, the more conformable it is to heaven, and hence the more beautiful is the face. . . . All perfection increases toward the interiors, and decreases toward the exteriors; and as perfection increases and decreases, so likewise does beauty. I have seen the faces of angels of the third heaven, which were so beautiful that no painter, with all his art, could ever impart to colors such animation as to equal a thousandth part of the brightness and life which appeared in their faces."—H. H. n. 459.

"Beauty derived only from the truth of faith, is like the beauty of a painted or sculptured face; but the beauty derived from the affection of truth which is from good, is like the beauty of a living face animated by celestial love; for such as is the quality of the love, or of the affection beaming from the form of the face, such is the beauty. Hence it is that the angels appear of ineffable beauty. From their faces beams forth the good of love by the truth of faith, which not only appears before the sight, but is also perceived by the spheres thence derived. The reason why this is the source and origin of beauty is, that the universal heaven is a GRAND MAN, and corresponds to all even the most minute things appertaining to man. He, therefore, who is principled in the good of love and thence in the truth of faith, is in the form of heaven, consequently in the beauty in which heaven is, where the Divine of the Lord is all in all. Hence also it is, that those who are in hell, since they are contrary to good and truth, are in horrible deformity, and in the light of heaven they appear not as men but as monsters."—A. C. n. 5199.

" The understanding of man is nothing else but the will unfolded and formed, so that its quality may appear visibly. Hence it is evident whence beauty is, viz., of the interior man, that it is from the good of the will by the truth of faith. The truth of faith itself presents beauty in the external form, but the good of the will sets it in and forms it. Hence it is that the angels of heaven are of ineffable beauty, for they are as it were loves and charities in form ; wherefore when they appear in their beauty, they affect the inmost principles. With them the good of love from the Lord shines forth through the truth of faith, and as it penetrates it affects."—Ibid. n. 4985 ; also n. 3212.

" When the angels present themselves visible, all their interior affections appear clearly from the face, and thence shine forth, so that the face is their external form and representative image. To have any other face than that of their respective affections, is not allowed to any in heaven. They who feign any other face, are cast out from the society. Hence it is manifest that the face corresponds to all the interiors in general, both to the affections and the thoughts thereof, or to those things which are of the will and understanding with man. Hence also in the Word by face and faces are signified the affections."—Ibid. n. 4796.

"Evil spirits may also be known from their faces, for all their lusts or evil affections are inscribed on their faces; and it may likewise be known from their faces with what hells they communicate; for there are very many hells all distinct according to the genera and species of the lusts of evil. In general their faces, when seen in the light of heaven, are almost without life, being ghastly like those of dead bodies, in some cases black, and in some monstrous; for they are the forms of hatred, cruelty, deceit and hypocrisy; but in their own light among themselves, they appear otherwise from fantasy."—A. C. n. 4798.

Many more passages similar to these might be cited; and however the phraseology or form of expression may vary, their substance will be found invariably the same.

And here, as on other subjects, the seer's assertions address themselves to our rational intuitions, and meet with a ready response from every enlightened and un-prejudiced mind. For every one sees that, if the character of the angels is as pure and exalted as he tells us it is, their personal appearance cannot be other than he has so often described it. If their interiors are purer, their souls more beautiful, than those of men—if they are wiser, nobler, more loving and unselfish, then we should expect them to be more beautiful in form and aspect. This is so reasonable that a child sees the utter absurdity of any doctrine essentially different. For a child sees that it is impossible for such exalted human excellence as that to which the angels have attained, to exist under hideous and repulsive forms; and it has an equally clear and instinctive perception that these latter are the appropriate forms of wicked spirits or demons.

All men are physiognomists to some extent, even without knowing it; for every one forms some idea of the character of others from the features and expression of their faces. And the idea they form would seldom fail of being correct, were it not that people often act the hypocrite, and make their faces lie as they do their lips and actions.

And what is thought to constitute the most exalted human beauty here on earth? What sort of a face do people of high culture and a truly Christian spirit commonly regard as most beautiful? Is it not that combination of features and that expression which reveals the most and the highest order of *mind?*—that which expresses the noblest qualities of heart in union the most exalted powers of intellect?—that which seems in the highest degree instinct with the divine attributes of wisdom and love? To a cultivated mind that face, and that only, is beautiful, which reveals a beautiful soul; and it is beautiful just in the degree that it expresses the thoughts, feelings, aspirations and hopes of such a soul. A person's face speaks as plainly as his lips, and often more truthfully. For many a time does the face reveal thoughts and feelings which the lips vainly strive to conceal. The looks often contradict the words. And if the graces of heaven—humility, meekness, resignation, courage, benevolence, gratitude, hope, love, trust—really dwell in the heart, they will to some extent reveal themselves in the countenance even in this world. And those who have any just appreciation of the spirit of true religion, will call that countenance most beautiful which expresses the largest measure of these heavenly graces.

It is the quality of the spiritual and invisible part, then —the peculiar characteristics of mind and heart which the face discloses—that makes all the difference among people on earth in respect to beauty. And among cultivated Christian people that face will always be thought most beautiful, which expresses most of the higher and nobler qualities of humanity. There is no beauty in the human countenance apart from the mental beauty—the lofty thoughts, the sweet affections, the tender sympathies, the noble purpose which it reveals. This is confessed by all the great masters in literature. Thus Milton says of Adam and Eve while in their primitive innocence:

> "———— For in their looks divine
> The image of their glorious Maker shone,
> Truth, wisdom, sanctitude, severe and pure."

And Spenser, with the insight of a true poet, and clearly recognizing the influence of the soul upon the body even to the extent disclosed in Swedenborg's pneumatology, sings:

> "———— Every spirit, as it is most pure,
> And hath in it the more of heavenly light,
> So it the fairer body doth procure
> To habit in :   .   .   .   .   .
> For of the soul the body form doth take,
> For soul is form and doth the body make."

And in a like strain sing Addison and Young, Shakspeare and Goethe, Byron and Coleridge, and all the great masters in this art.

Every one knows, too, that a good artist is able to express all the passions and emotions of the heart in the faces of the figures he paints or carves: and can express them with such precision that people of some discern-

ment will read them the moment they look at the picture
or statue. Ask any distinguished sculptor to embody in
a bust certain well-defined mental or moral qualities, and
he will do it with such fidelity that every close observer
of human nature will read in that bust the very qualities
you described, almost as easily as if they were printed
in a book. This were impossible but for the correspondence existing between the face and the passions and emotions of the heart ;—a correspondence so exact and perfect, too, that where no willful deception is practiced, the
former may be taken as the representative image of the
latter.

Then look at the faces of little children—those young
immortals so guileless and innocent, so late from their
Maker's hand, with the impress of heaven so fresh upon
them—and how legibly can you see recorded there the
feelings of their hearts! How unmistakably do their
laughing faces tell of the exuberant life, the overflowing
joy and gladness within their little bosoms! And when
they experience disappointment, sorrow, vexation or
shame, how faithfully are these emotions imprinted on
their faces, and how quickly, too! And the same is true
of adults in the degree that they have retained the innocence and simplicity of childhood, or become as little
children by regeneration. When joy and gladness fill
their hearts, their faces are sure to reveal the fact. The
sunshine within streams out from their eyes, and sheds
its radiance over the whole countenance. Again, when
sorrow comes, when cares oppress and fears disturb and
gloomy thoughts becloud the soul, their faces proclaim
this inward change as clearly as the moving shadow on

the landscape proclaims the floating cloud between it and the sun.   This, indeed, is true of every one to some extent.   It is only with those who have lost the simplicity of childhood, and learned to practice the arts of deception, that the face ceases to be a true index of the mind;—fails to reveal by its changes the sunshine or gloom, the joy or sorrow, the peace or unrest that exists within.

And not only does the face reveal the transitory feelings, the changes of mental state, as from joy to sorrow, but it registers with fidelity those states which have become fixed and abiding.   Let a person harbor for any considerable time melancholy thoughts and dark forebodings; let him indulge in poignant grief, in anxious fears or bitter repinings; let him encourage by indulgence the growth of an inordinate love of the world, a mean and miserly spirit, or a sour and misanthropic temper, and how surely will this confirmed habit of his soul imprint itself upon his countenance!   Or let him, on the other hand, exercise the spirit of self-denial, let him repose calmly and trustingly on the Divine Providence, let him cultivate a cheerful and resigned disposition, cherish noble and unselfish aims, exercise himself habitually in kind and philanthropic deeds, and thus open his soul more and more to the influx of the Lord's unselfish love; and let this be continued for a series of years, and the heavenly quality of his inner man will be legibly inscribed upon his countenance.   You will see the angel shining through.   The light of heaven will sparkle in his eye, and the warmth of heaven will tinge his cheek with a lustre all its own; and this, too, in spite of the wrinkles that usually accompany declining years.

There is, then, abundant evidence right around us of the truth of what Swedenborg says as to the personal appearance of people in the other world, and of the great law that determines it. For we all know that there is a strong and continual tendency in whatever passion or principle is allowed to govern a man, to mould the countenance into a form correspondent with itself. We know that heavenly love deep-seated in the heart, has ever a tendency to light up the countenance with a heavenly radiance. And we know, too, that the tendency of all infernal principles is equally strong in this respect. All evil feelings long indulged, all sad and sickening thoughts, all dark and gloomy views of God, religion and human life, are perpetually operating, so long as they are entertained, to shape the outward corporeal part into complete correspondence with themselves;—perpetually working to divest the visage of its properly human expression, and imprint thereon the deformity of hell. If it is true that "a man's wisdom maketh his face to shine," it is equally true that a wicked heart will in time mould the countenance into an exact image of its wickedness.

It is certain, then—nothing, indeed, can be more so— that the human countenance was intended by the Creator to be the perfect image of the heart's affections. The face was plainly meant to be the mirror of the soul. And the nearer men approach to the innocence and simplicity of childhood, and the less disguises they wear, the less occasion do they have for concealment, and the more truly do their faces as well as their words express the thoughts and feelings of their hearts. How, then, should we expect it would be in heaven where innocence, simplicity, purity and love reign triumphant?—where all are willing to be seen in the light, and no one desires to express by his looks a single emotion that he does not feel? Should not the faces of the angels express with mathematical exactness the unselfish love that dwells within their bosoms? And if so, how surpassingly beautiful must they be! How easy to believe, therefore, what Swedenborg so often declares, that their beauty is beyond the power of art to picture or of human language to describe! Otherwise there would not be a perfect correspondence between their internals and externals, and the face in heaven would not be the mirror of the soul.

The face, then, being intended by the Creator to faithfully express the feelings and dispositions of the heart, corresponds to the interiors of the mind, or to the ruling love. This love, therefore, is what is meant by the *face* in Sacred Scripture when spiritually interpreted. Accordingly the Psalmist prays: "God be merciful to us and bless us, and cause his *face* to shine upon us." (LXVII. 1: LXXX. 3.) The inmost and very *esse* of the Lord, is pure, unselfish love. And when there is an influx of this love into our hearts, and we feel it as our own, then the Lord's face shines upon us, and we are saved—delivered from the love of self which is altogether infernal. And so the Psalmist again prays: "O God, cause thy *face* to shine, and we shall be saved." Deliverance from the dominion of self-love, and reception of the Lord's own love instead, is the only true salvation. Again, in Isaiah: "Your iniquities have separated between you and your God, and your sins have hid his *face* from you." Self-love is the very opposite of the Lord's; and they who are ruled by it, are in a sinful state, and have no conception of the Lord's love. His *face* is therefore hid from them. Again the Psalmist says: " Thy *face*, Lord, will I seek." We seek the Lord's face, when, through obedience to the laws of the heavenly life which He has revealed, we open our hearts to the reception of his own life, that is, his unselfish love. Again : " Blessed is the people that know the joyful sound; they shall walk, O Lord, in the light of thy countenance." The light of the Lord's countenance is the light of truth proceeding from his divine love, as light proceeds from and is the visible manifestation of heat in the natural world.

And hundreds of similar illustrations from Scripture might be added; all of which go to show the intimate connection of the spiritual sense of the Word, with the facts, phenomena and laws of the spiritual world; and how a knowledge of these latter may help us in the right understanding and interpretation of the former.

What, now, is the practical lesson to be drawn from the subject as here presented ?

It may be seen from what has been said, that beauty is the mark which God has set on goodness. The external beauty of the angels is but the type, or correspondential form, of their beautiful souls. Their pure and unselfish love exerts a potent influence over their bodily organism, moulding every feature into a form of corresponding grace and loveliness. Yes: it is love—love from the Lord, and therefore kindred to his own—that makes their faces so lovely. And this angelic beauty we are all made capable of attaining in some measure. But the only way of attaining it, is by strict and religious obedience to the revealed laws of the angelic life,—precisely as bodily health and vigor are attained and preserved by strict conformity to the laws of health. Encouraging and strengthening by exercise the growth of angelic dispositions, is the sure way of ultimately attaining to angelic beauty. Our bodies in the Hereafter will be just what we, by our volitions and conduct here, choose to make them—moulded into forms exactly correspondent to the dispositions we cherish and the feelings we habitually indulge—perfect images of our ruling loves: beautiful and symmetrical if we are careful to strengthen and confirm the principles that beautify the soul, but ugly and deformed if we encourage the growth of the opposite principles.

To conclude. It is a solemn and impressive fact, that within each of our material frames is a spiritual and immortal body, receiving its daily and hourly sustenance from the spiritual world; a body which lives and grows upon the food of angels, or the food of devils. And every year—yea, every day—this immortal body is approximating the exquisite symmetry and grace of heaven, or assuming more and more the hideous deformity of hell: and this, according to the prevailing tenor of our daily lives,—according to the dispositions we habitually cherish, and the motives from which we uniformly act. For here, in the flesh, our immortal part is daily and hourly taking on its enduring shape. Here it is continually developing—every feature and lineament—in exact correspondence with the nature of the principles we allow to govern us; that is, with the love that reigns and rules in our hearts, the central fire and moulding force of our immortal being.

XVIII.

REJUVENESCENCE AND GROWTH IN HEAVEN.

WHOEVER thinks of existence in heaven as a reality, can hardly help asking, Do people grow old there as they do here on earth? And is their age written on their faces, as it is on the faces of men? And do those who leave this world far advanced in years, and who enter the society of the blessed, forever retain the withered form and furrowed cheeks which they had at the time they left this world? There is really but one question involved in these interrogatories, and that is one concerning the age or *apparent* age of the denizens of heaven. Do they appear young or old? What is Swedenborg's answer to this question?

Before adducing his testimony, we will consider how the question *ought* to be answered. What is the verdict of reason on the subject, and what the inevitable conclusion to be drawn from the teaching of the last chapter?

If what has been said concerning the beauty of the angels is to be accepted as true, it follows that they do not grow old; or, at least, that age does not plow such furrows in their faces as it does in the faces of men. For we all recognize something comparatively unbeautiful in the wasted cheek, the lustreless eye, and the furrowed brow of old age. The faces and forms of men and women at ninety—however pure and innocent the lives they have led—would rarely be thought beautiful. They seldom—never, indeed—at that age realize our highest conception of the human form. What, then, might we expect would be the appearance of those who have been in heaven thousands of years, if Time laid his palsying hand on the bodies of angels as it does on those of men? Why, they would be divested of every vestige of human comeliness. Their features and forms would hardly be recognized as human, so shriveled and wasted would they be. And if those who die at an advanced age and go to heaven, are forever to bear about them the same decrepid form and furrowed cheeks which marked their declining years on earth, then would it, indeed, be a calamity to live "to a good old age" on earth. Unless the aged saint is to lose in heaven his wrinkles and his decrepitude, and return to the vigor and freshness of his earlier years, who would wish to remain on earth beyond the age of twenty?

What has been said, therefore, of the beauty of the angels, if true, is conclusive evidence that they do not apparently grow old in heaven; and that the good who die at an advanced age, must there rejuvenate—must return to the beauty and buoyancy of their "golden prime."

Besides, in this world all the usual signs of old age, are so many signs of a decaying process—signs that corporeal dissolution has already commenced; for what is decay but a gradual dying? But there is no death in heaven, consequently no decay. Therefore there can be no deterioration there of any of the powers of body or of mind ;—no blunting of the senses, no wasting of the form, none of the visible signs which in this world proclaim the coming on of decrepid old age.

Moreover, time cannot properly be predicated of that which is spiritual; consequently it cannot be predicated of the spiritual world, or of spiritual beings. We cannot say, nor even think, that God is old; nor that He is older now than He was ten thousand years ago, or younger than He will be ten thousand years hence. We cannot predicate age of love or wisdom or any of the Divine attributes. Nor can age be predicated of absolute Life. And God is the only absolute Life, and the infinite Fountain of life to angels and men. And Life itself is forever young and vigorous, forever fresh and new. And since the angels are continually becoming more and more perfect—continually being conjoined more closely with the Lord—continually receiving fresh increments of life from the One only Fountain of life, therefore they must be always advancing towards a state of ever-increasing vigor, bloom and beauty.

Such is the undeniable testimony of reason on this subject. Such is the conclusion logically deduced from known and admitted truths, and from premises already established. And this is precisely what Swedenborg has reported from personal observation, after long and open intercourse with the heaven of angels. Let the following suffice for illustration :

" Such as are principled in mutual love, are continually advancing in heaven to the spring-time of their youth;

and the more thousands of years they pass, they attain to a more joyous and delightful spring ; and so continue on to eternity, with fresh increments of blessedness according to their respective proficiencies and gradations of mutual love, charity and faith.   Those of the female sex who had departed this life broken with the infirmities of old age, having lived in faith towards the Lord, in charity towards their neighbor, and in conjugial love with their husbands, after a succession of ages appear to advance towards the bloom of youth, with a beauty surpassing all description ; for goodness and charity form their own image in such persons, and express their delights and beauties in every feature of their faces, insomuch that they become real forms of charity.   Certain spirits that beheld them were astonished at the sight. Such is the form of charity, which in heaven is represented to the life ; for it is charity that portrays it, and is portrayed in it, and that in a manner so expressive, that the whole angel, more particularly as to the face, appears as charity itself in a personal form of exquisite beauty affecting the soul of the spectator with something of the same grace ; by the beauty of that form, the truths of faith are exhibited in an image, and are also thereby rendered perceptible.   Those who have lived in faith toward the Lord, that is, in a faith grounded in charity, become such forms or such beauties in another life.   All the angels are such forms with an infinite variety ; and of these heaven is composed."—A. C. n. 553.

Every candid mind must admit that this is altogether reasonable.   And not only so, but any different view would at once appear unreasonable.   And the rejuvenating process in the other world, though it may proceed more rapidly than the aging process in this, proceeds according to a law no less fixed or intelligible.   The Divine wisdom and beneficence are alike reflected in both processes, and the reasonableness of the former is as clearly discernible as that of the latter. The spiritual organism being perfectly plastic to the influent life, as that life becomes sweeter and richer, and its influx more copious, the inevitable result must be a growing perfection of the human form, and a steady increase of human beauty.

Another question closely allied to the one we have just considered, is: Do those who die in infancy or childhood continue to grow in the other world, as they would have done had they remained longer in this? Or do they continue forever the same in stature as when they departed this life? Does Swedenborg answer this question? If so, how?

How would enlightened reason answer it? we again ask. Is it reasonable to suppose that an infant dying before it is able to walk, will remain to all eternity of the same infantile form, and be forever carried in some sweet mother's arms and dandled on some maternal knee? Is it probable—nay, is it conceivable that the all-wise and loving Father would permit an immortal soul to be thus prematurely arrested in its growth, and by an incident over which that soul had no control, and was therefore powerless to prevent? For we cannot conceive of the spirit of a little child developing into the grand, capacious, wise and loving soul of a full-grown angel, without a corresponding change or development of that spiritual organism which constitutes its body in the spiritual realm. The idea is repugnant to all our conceptions as well as our knowledge of the laws of divine order. As easily can we conceive of the luscious qualities of the full-grown and ripened peach or orange existing in the germ of that fruit soon as the flower has fallen ; or of these qualities becoming fully developed there, without a corresponding growth and development of the germ itself.　Far more reasonable is it to believe that the Lord has made provision for the growth of the spiritual body after the material has been sloughed off, that the soul may not be arrested in its development by the mere incident of bodily death.　The body grows on earth to the full stature of manhood by the steady accretion of material substance ; what should hinder its growth in heaven to the full stature of angelhood by a similar accretion of spiritual substance ?　The spiritual body while yet in the flesh, grows with the material,—indeed it is the growth of the spiritual which causes that of the material ; what then is to hinder its continued growth after it leaves the flesh ?　It is not natural but spiritual substance that feeds the soul while in the natural body ; and will it not have the same food, and the same means of growth therefore, after this body dies ?

It is clear enough, then, what the verdict of reason is on this subject.　Now listen to the testimony of him whose spiritual eyes and ears were opened, and who was able, therefore, to testify " from things seen and heard."

" Many persons may imagine that infants remain such in heaven, and exist as infants among the angels.　They who do not know what constitutes an angel, may have confirmed themselves in this opinion from the images sometimes seen in churches where angels are exhibited as infants.　But the case is altogether otherwise.　Intelligence and wisdom constitute an angel ; and so long as infants have not intelligence and wisdom, they are not angels, although they are with angels. But when they become intelligent and wise, then for the first time they become angels. Yea,—a thing that I have wondered at, —they then no longer appear as infants, but as adults; for they are then no longer of an infantile genius, but of a more mature angelic genius.' Intelligence and wisdom produce this effect. As infants are perfected in intelligence and wisdom, they appear more mature, thus as youths and young men, because intelligence and wisdom are real spiritual nourishment. For this reason the things which nourish their minds nourish their bodies also,—and this from correspondence; for the form of the body is but the external form of the interiors.

" It is to be observed that infants in heaven do not advance in age beyond the period of early manhood; and there they stop forever [*i. e.* so far as apparent progress in *age* is concerned]. That I might be assured of this, it was granted me to converse with some who were educated as infants in heaven, and who had grown up there; with some also when they were infants, and afterwards with the same when they had become young men; and I heard from them the progress of their life from one age to another."—H. H. n. 340.

And so we find that, on this as on other subjects, Swedenborg's revealings " from things heard and seen " are in perfect agreement with the intuitions of the highest reason, and with all that is known of the wisdom and dealings of Providence and of the laws of divine order. It is impossible to conceive of any different view of the subject, which will so completely satisfy the demands of sober reason and an enlightened understanding.

In view of such sublime revealings, what a precious boon is heaven !—yet a boon which all are made capable of attaining, and which it is the Lord's ceaseless desire and effort to help us to attain.   There flows forever the stream of the water of life, and forever increases in crystal clearness.   There the fountains of wisdom are ever fresh, and the flame of love burns with ever-increasing fervor. There beauty never fades, but ever grows more fresh and fair.   There none grow old, but all rejuvenate;—all who have passed on earth their manhood's prime, are forever advancing towards younger, yet still riper life.   Old age puts off its wrinkles there, and returns to the vigor and bloom of early manhood.   There joys never decay, and the warm current of bounding life gushes forth with perennial freshness.   And the simple yet all-sufficient reason is, that the angels are forever becoming more and more receptive of the Divine Life—forever drawing nearer and nearer, or becoming more and more like, Him who is the one eternal Source of all wisdom, beauty, life and joy.

XIX.

HOUSES AND HOMES IN HEAVEN.

ONE of the definitions which a distinguished lexi-cographer has given of heaven, is, " the home of the blessed."   And all good people, when they think of heaven, think of it as a HOME,—their *eternal* home. When they look forward to the time of their decease, they think and speak of it as the time when they hope to be taken home.   And when a righteous man closes his earthly pilgrimage, his neighbors say: " The good man has gone home." And they mean by this no more nor less than that he has gone to heaven.

Indeed, there is heavenly meaning and heavenly music in this monosyllable,—HOME. There is meaning in it which the universal human mind perceives, and music which the universal human heart feels. Home is the hallowed spot to which our fondest affections cling; the centre of our strongest attachments, our sweetest remembrances, our brightest hopes, our purest joys. Everything dear to the heart of a good man, everything most serene and peaceful in life, everything pleasant or even tolerable in death, clusters around this word. The soldier in the camp, the sailor on the seas, the traveler in foreign lands,—how does his eye kindle and his pulse quicken at the bare mention of this word! As sings the poet :

> "Who that in distant lands has chanced to roam,
> Ne'er thrilled with pleasure at the name of home?"

"Very often," says Dr. Sears, "when the eyes are closing in death, and this world is shutting off the light from the departing soul, the last wish which is made audible, is, ' to go home.' The words break out sometimes through the cloud of delirium ; but it is the soul's deepest and most central want, groping after its object, haply soon to find it as the clogs of earth clear away, and she springs up on the line of swift affection, as the bee with unerring precision shoots through the dusk of evening to her cell."—*Foregleams of Immortality*, p. 128.

Yes : Among all the deep wants of our nature, among the strong yearnings of every good man's heart, none are deeper or stronger than the want of, and the yearn-

20

ing for, a peaceful and happy home. To say of any man that he is *homeless*, is to picture him as forlorn and desolate, an exile and a wanderer, not yet having reached the goal of his earthly hopes.

Now, God has implanted no deep want in the human breast without providing for its gratification. As a wise and beneficent Being, he *must* provide for the ultimate satisfaction of every desire which his own boundless love has placed within us. And this universal desire for a home, is one which belongs to the soul's nature. It is rooted in our spiritual constitution,—so deeply rooted, too, that we may be sure it will not perish with the death of the body. And when we consider that this desire increases rather than diminishes in strength as we advance in the regenerate life, or approximate the heavenly state, how can we resist the conclusion that it will exist in heaven also, and be even stronger there than here?

And if this universal desire for a home goes with us into the other world (as it must, if it belongs to our spiritual constitution), we may be sure that the Lord, in the plenitude of his love and wisdom, will not fail to provide for its gratification in heaven. For the angels would be unhappy, and heaven would be no heaven to them, if, endowed with an intense longing for a home, the means and opportunity of satisfying this thirst were denied them.

The conclusion, therefore, is forced upon us, that there are and must be homes in heaven, as there are in all the best and happiest portions of earth.

But the moment we think of the angels as having *homes*, we think of them as dwelling in *houses*,—so intimately is the idea of home associated in our minds with *some* kind of habitation. We cannot even think of human homes without human habitations of some sort; and they are no more possible in heaven than on earth.

True, the first use of houses here, is defense against the storms and shelter from the cold and heat. But this, though it be their primary, is by no means their highest, use. A house everywhere stands as the representative image of home. It is the symbol of those home-born, home-bred, and home-felt joys which constitute "that best portion of a good man's life." Suppose there were no inclement skies, no chilling frosts, nor scorching heat, nor drenching rains, nor pitiless blasts, nor anything, indeed, to make houses necessary to bodily comfort, does it follow that human beings would then need and have no houses? By no means; for so long as the love of home lives in the hearts of good men and women, so long will some kind of habitation be sought and had as the symbol of that love. Human beings, and especially those who have made much progress in regeneration, will have houses as the sanctuaries of those pure domestic joys which are more than half the solace and sunshine and fragrance of life.

Therefore houses, though not needed in heaven as a defense against cold and storms, are needed for their higher spiritual uses. And as sure as there dwells in the hearts of angels the love of home (and we cannot think of them as existing without this love), so sure is it that they must have houses.

Moreover, the outward or phenomenal heaven would lose half its beauty if there were no houses. Picture to yourself the loveliest rural scene imaginable—fields and forests, trees and lawns, gardens and flowers, singing-birds and gurgling brooks, fleecy clouds and azure skies—and the picture would be clearly defective or incomplete without human habitations. The presence of beautiful houses as the symbols of life's sweetest joys, would be indispensable to the completeness of the scene. The æsthetic element of our nature demands this.

It is because the love of home is so deeply implanted in the human heart, that we always feel the need of a house as its symbol to complete the beauty of any landscape. Heaven, therefore, without human habitations would be lacking in one important element of beauty. It would not be our conception of the celestial realms. Besides, some of the deepest, tenderest, and best feelings of the heart—feelings which can be developed and kept alive only in the sanctuary of home—could not be visibly represented in heaven without houses. Therefore these feelings could not live—could, indeed, have no existence—in heaven; for every living thing in the hearts of the angels, is pictured there under visible and correspondential forms. This is the law which underlies and determines all the phenomena of the other world—the law of correspondence.

That there should be houses in heaven, therefore, seems altogether reasonable; and not only reasonable, but, if the inner is visibly pictured in the outer world there, there *must* be houses. The great law that determines the whole aspect of the phenomenal world in the Hereafter, necessitates this conclusion. And through the operation of this same law, the habitations of the angels ought also to be very beautiful; for these, like all their other surroundings, being the normal outbirth or true expression of their interior states, should be in exact correspondence with those states; that is, in correspondence with their prevailing thoughts, feelings, dispositions and motives—in short, with their ruling loves.

Such is the clear verdict of reason on this subject. Such the conclusion reached by fair and logical argument based upon certain known principles and deeply implanted instincts of our better nature. And now let us see how far the disclosures made through Swedenborg agree with this conclusion; for, if true, they should not be in conflict with reason. The following extracts are pertinent:

"Since there are societies in heaven, and the angels live as men, therefore they have habitations, and these likewise various according to each one's state of life; magnificent for those in a state of superior dignity, and less magnificent for those in an inferior condition. . . I have been present with the angels in their habitations, which are precisely like those on earth called houses, but more beautiful. They contain halls, parlors and bed-chambers in great numbers; also courts, and round about them, gardens, fields and shrubberies. Where the angels live in societies, their habitations are contiguous, close to each other, and arranged in the form of a city, with streets, alleys and public squares, exactly like the cities on earth. It has also been granted me to walk through them, and occasionally to enter the houses. This occurred in a state of full wakefulness, when my interior sight was opened."—H. H. n. 183, 184.

20*

"All the angels have their own habitations, which are magnificent. I have occasionally seen them, and admired them, and have there conversed with the occupants. They are so distinct and conspicuous that nothing can be more so. The houses on earth are scarcely anything in comparison. Indeed, the angels say that such things on earth are dead and not real; but that their own are alive and true, because they are from the Lord. Their architecture is such as to be the ground and source of the architectural art, with an indefinite variety. The angels have assured me that, if they could have all the palaces on earth, they would not exchange their own for them. What is of stone and mortar and wood is to them dead; but what is from the Lord, or from essential life and light, this, they say, is alive— and the more so, as they enjoy it with all the fulness of sense. For the things in heaven are perfectly adapted to the senses of spirits and angels; while things seen in the light of this solar world are altogether invisible to them.

"The walls of the habitations of angelic spirits are constructed with much variety, and are adorned also with flowers, and wreaths of flowers wonderfully composed, beside many other ornaments, which are varied in an orderly succession. At one time they appear in a clear light; at another time, in a light less clear; but always with interior delight. Their houses are also changed into more and more beautiful ones, as the spirits become more perfect in character."—A. C. n. 1626–1630.

"I have seen the palaces of heaven, which were magnificent beyond description. Their upper parts shone refulgent as if of pure gold, and their lower parts as if of precious stones. Some were more splendid than others; and the splendor without was equalled by the magnificence within. The apartments were ornamented with decorations which no words can adequately describe.

"I have also been informed that not only the palaces and houses, but the minutest particulars both within and without them, correspond to the interior things in the angels of the Lord; that the house itself in general corresponds to their good, and the various things within it to the various particulars of which their good is composed."—H. H. n. 185, 186.

Now all this is seen to be in perfect agreement with the laws of the spiritual world as unfolded by the same author. It is precisely what might have been logically inferred, if the ruling loves of heaven and the law that determines the phenomenal world there, be what he so often tells us they are. Everything he has said about the habitations of the angels, is found to be in perfect harmony with all his other disclosures, and to follow by strict logical sequence from his fundamental principles. So that what has been revealed through him on this subject is seen to have the merit of perfect consistency; and it is not less reasonable than consistent.

The houses in heaven, we are told, correspond to the character or internal state of those who live in them. They are the visible representatives of the ruling loves of their occupants. And so exact is the correspondence that no angel can dwell permanently in any other house than his own; for no other would be in correspondence with his state of life. His house is, in fact, a normal outbirth from his own state, built up or created from it and in correspondence with it.

As the angels are all in states of love akin to the Lord's own,—all in bright, cheerful, affectionate, happy states,

—therefore their houses are all very beautiful. But there are countless *degrees* and *kinds* of good in which the angels are, and a consequent endless diversity of state among them, just as there are among good men and women on earth. And accordingly their habitations, although they are all beautiful, are all somewhat different, corresponding to their different kinds and degrees of good. There is the same endless diversity in the heavenly habitations that there is in the character of their occupants;—the same, indeed, that characterizes the face of the whole habitable earth and every part of the material universe.

In the spiritual world every one's own state determines not only the character of his habitation, but his place of abode and all his surroundings. And he can feel perfectly at home nowhere but in the midst of surroundings which are in correspondence with his inner life. This is both reasonable and probable. The same law is operative among men on earth, and with close approximation to the same results. The character of every one does, in time, reveal itself to some extent in his earthly surroundings; and there is ever a strong tendency in this direction. If possessed of ample means, and left to act in perfect freedom, each one chooses a location and builds and furnishes a house corresponding to his idea of beauty, comfort and convenience. Give to some people the most magnificent habitation filled and surrounded with everything beautiful, and leave them to do with it as they please, and how long will it be before that palatial residence will be changed to a loathsome den ? Of a nature (inherited or acquired) akin to that of certain animals, they will, erelong, convert the loveliest habitation into a squalid stye. Place them where you will, amid whatever scenes of beauty or magnificence, and they cannot fail in time to stamp their own character on all their surroundings. And on the other hand, place people of refinement and culture in the humblest cabin, and will they not in time so beautify and adorn that cabin, that it will reveal to the intelligent observer something of their refined and cultivated tastes? And the reason is obvious; for every kind of life is delighted with, and therefore seeks, that and *only* that which corresponds with its own nature.

And the same great law that fashions the habitations and the whole outward aspect of heaven, is (as might be expected, if true) no less operative or potential in hell. Character (good or bad) shapes each one's house and all his surroundings in the other world, in complete correspondence with itself. And while the heavenly abodes are all inconceivably bright and beautiful, those of the nether regions are correspondingly dark and loathsome. Says Swedenborg:

"All those who are in evil, and have confirmed themselves in falsities against the truths of the church, and especially those who have rejected the Word, [in the other world] shun the light of heaven, and betake themselves to subterranean places and clefts of the rocks, and hide there. And they seek such retreats because they have loved falsities and hated truths; for such caverns and clefts of rocks and darkness correspond to falsities, and light corresponds to truth. . . They who have been sordidly avaricious dwell in huts and love swinish filth [such things being in correspondence with their state of life]."—H. H. n. 488.

Now, it is every one's ruling love which determines his real character or state. And a house being the place of one's residence, corresponds to his state. Each one's dominant love, therefore, fashions his spiritual house. For this love is the heart's home-centre. It is where the individual lives spiritually. It is the point towards which his soul perpetually gravitates, as surely as a ball suspended in the air forever gravitates towards the centre of the earth, or as the heart of a mother who loves her children and her household duties, perpetually gravitates towards her home whenever she is absent from it. Every one's thoughts and purposes are shaped and directed by his ruling love. If this be the love of wealth, of reputation, of preferment, of power, he will be continually meditating plans by which to obtain what his heart longs for. Or if it be the love of the Lord and the neighbor—the love of truth, justice, sincerity, uprightness, and of enlightening, improving and blessing his fellow-men, then will his thoughts centre on these things, and be chiefly occupied with plans for promoting them. So obviously true is it that each one's ruling love is the determining force within him. This is his heart's centre,—the point towards which his whole being gravitates and around which it perpetually revolves. This is his spiritual dwelling-place, his habitation, his *home.* And this, therefore, is what every one's house in the Hereafter represents or images to the outward eye.

And since the law which determines the phenomenal world in the spiritual realm, is the very same as that which determines the letter of the Word,—that is, the law of correspondence, which is none other than the relation of cause and effect,—therefore Swedenborg's descriptions of the phenomena of the other world, and his unfoldings of the internal sense of the Word, ought not only to harmonize, but mutually to confirm and illustrate each other. And this they are found to do in a manner so remarkable and striking as clearly to demonstrate the truth of both. It is, as we have often remarked, one of those verifications of the truth of his statements, such as no human ingenuity, however subtle, could have possibly contrived and in all cases made to tally.

Take the case of houses in heaven, and their correspondence and significance. The Psalmist says, "One thing have I desired of the Lord, that will I seek after, that I may dwell in the house of the Lord all the days of my life, to behold the beauty of the Lord and to inquire in his temple" (xxvii. 4). Is this to be understood literally? If so, one can hardly conceive of a more unreasonable desire than is here expressed. But, understood in its spiritual sense, the thing which the Psalmist here longs for above all else, is worthy the intense longing and supreme effort of every human being. For "the *house* of the Lord," interpreted by the rule of correspondence, means the will or life of the Lord,—his pure and unselfish love. To dwell in this house is to dwell in Him, or in that disinterested love which is from Him and is Himself—a love which pours itself forth liberally as the ever-bountiful sun,—a love which never seeks its own, but always the good of others. To dwell in this love is to have this love dwelling and operative in us. As saith the beloved disciple, "God is love, and he that dwelleth in love dwelleth in God and God in him." Is there anything so much to be desired as this? It is the noblest, highest, happiest state which a human being can attain to. It is the truly human state; yea, it is the heavenly state.

Interpreting the Psalmist's language spiritually, therefore, or by the rule of correspondence, we see that the thing he desired and resolved to seek above all else, is the thing worthy of every one's supreme affection and best endeavor. It is, indeed, what every regenerating soul *must* desire and seek after as the supreme good.

Again, after saying, "The Lord is my Shepherd: I shall not therefore want," the same inspired writer exclaims, "Surely goodness and mercy shall follow me all the days of my life, and I shall dwell in the house of the Lord forever." (xxiii. 6.) What sort of a house can here be meant? the thoughtful inquirer will again ask. Not any temporary, earthly, or material structure, but that spiritual, heavenly and eternal habitation which is the Lord's own,—that sweet and all-embracing love which is himself, his own essential life,—that "house not made with hands, eternal in the heavens." And every one comes into and evermore abides in this house, who, through self-denial and inward conflict, and obedience to the known laws of the Lord, comes into a state of disinterested neighborly love. So that this language of the Psalmist, in its spiritual sense, is seen to be, like all inspired language, of universal application. Every soul that takes the Lord for his shepherd and guide, and faithfully follows Him, may be sure of the abundant and continued influx of his goodness and mercy, and may confidently say, " I shall dwell in the house of the Lord forever."

And so of other passages in the Word which speak of " the Father's house," " the house of the Lord," " the house of the God of Jacob," etc., and of " going up to " and " dwelling in " that house. When the correspondence or spiritual meaning of *house* is understood, such passages are seen to have something more than a local or Jewish significance. They are seen to be full of instruction for people of every age and nation ; for it is seen that at all times and in all places, even where there is no visible temple or place of external and formal worship, souls may be ever " going up to the mount of the Lord, to the house of the God of Jacob."

And Swedenborg further tells us that houses in heaven, like the best houses on earth, have many separate apartments,—inner-chambers and closets ; and these correspond to the more interior recesses of every soul, to the secret motives of every heart. They are the visible symbols of those interior states to which the devout believer retires when he wishes to be alone with God—to " commune with his own heart "—to examine himself in the light of divine truth. It is to such interior states—to these deeper recesses of the heart, that reference is had in the spiritual sense of the Lord's words, where He says, "When thou prayest, enter into thy closet ; " for there, in the secret closet of the soul, is the place for all genuine prayer and worship—for all real fellowship and vital union with Him who seeth in secret, and whose reward is sure.

And thus we find that, between Swedenborg's disclosures of the facts and phenomena of the spiritual world and his spiritual interpretations of the Scripture, there is no disagreement but perfect harmony. And this harmony is such as no human ingenuity could ever have invented; such, indeed, as clearly demonstrates the truth of both. If the law which determines the phenomenal world in the great Beyond, be the same as that according to which the Divine of the Lord forever descends to ultimates, according to which the inspired Word was composed, according to which creation is effected,— namely, the law of correspondence between the interior and exterior, or between cause and effect,—then we should expect to find in the teachings of the seer precisely the harmony to which we have referred, and which actually exists there.

Briefly to sum up what has been said :—

The heaven that Swedenborg tells us of is a thoroughly human heaven. And since it is human, there must be homes and consequently human habitations there. These, like everything else in the other world, are spiritual in their nature. This, too, is the testimony of both reason and Scripture. The houses in heaven are growths—creations—from within, and therefore in perfect correspondence with the states of their occupants. They are the normal outbirths of the loves which rule in the hearts of the angels—of loves which constitute their very being, and in whose exercise they live and find their supreme delight. Beautiful and magnificent are they, too, according to the breadth, exaltation, purity and intensity of their love; yet differing from each other as the angels themselves differ— thus enhancing the beauty and joy of heaven by their endless variety. And what is there in all this that is contrary to reason, to the teachings of Scripture, or to our highest conceptions of the wisdom and love and providence of God?

Then look at its practical tendency—its immediate and direct bearing upon the life and character of the believer. Is it not obviously good and wholesome? In the light of these disclosures we see that all the splendid habitations and magnificent palaces of heaven are but pictorial representations, under the great law of correspondence, of the ruling loves of the angels. They are the exact images of their dominant affections, reflecting with mathematical precision their inner life and character. It is each one's ruling love that fashions and adorns his house in the other world, the inner chambers and closets of which, with all their furniture, are but the correspondential images of his secret motives and hidden purposes. And he cannot possibly have or dwell in any other house than that which is in correspondence with his character.

So that, when our fleshly tabernacle is dissolved, if we would dwell in the beautiful mansions on high, we can hope to do so only by developing and carrying with us the angelic loves of which those mansions are the visible symbols. We must begin on earth to live the life of heaven; must imbibe here, and carry with us into the Hereafter, something of that heavenly spirit which creates for the angels their magnificent abodes; must begin here to find our life and delight in the performance of useful deeds from high and heavenly motives; must begin to make the Lord's unselfish love the sweet and familiar dwelling-place of our souls. For, according to the dispositions we indulge, the purposes we cherish, the plans of life we pursue, the motives we allow to govern us, we are actually building while here on earth our everlasting habitations;—building them beautiful and symmetrical like the palaces of heaven, if our ends of life be high and heavenly, but dark and dismal like the abodes of hell, if our ends be mean and selfish.

XX.

GARMENTS IN HEAVEN.

ANOTHER question which people are inclined to ask about heaven, is: Are the angels clad in garments? If so, are they all clothed alike? And if not alike, upon what does the diversity depend? What determines the character and quality of their garments? The following are Swedenborg's answers to these questions:

"Since angels are men, and live together in society like men on earth, therefore they have garments. . . . Their garments correspond to their intelligence. Therefore all in heaven appear clothed according to their intelligence; and because some excel others in intelligence, therefore they have more excellent garments. The most intelligent have garments that glitter as from flame, and some have garments that shine as from light. The less intelligent have bright and white garments without splendor; and the still less intelligent have garments of different colors.

"Since the garments of the angels correspond to their intelligence, therefore they correspond also to truth, for all intelligence is from divine truth. Therefore whether we say that angels are clothed according to intelligence or according to divine truth, it is the same thing. The garments of some glitter as from flame, and those of others shine as from light, because flame corresponds to good, and light to truth derived from good. The garments of some are bright and white without splendor, and those of others are of diverse colors, because the divine good and truth are less refulgent, and also variously received, with the less intelligent.

" That the garments of the angels do not merely appear as garments, but that they really are garments, is manifest from these considerations: that they not only see them, but also feel them; that they have many garments; that they take them off and put them on; that they lay aside those which are not in use, and when they come into use again they resume them. That they are clothed with a variety of garments I have witnessed a thousand times. I inquired whence they obtained them, and they told me from the Lord; that they received them as gifts, and that they are sometimes clothed without knowing how. They also said that their garments are changed according to the changes of their state; that in the first and second states they are bright and shining, and in the third and fourth states rather more dim; and that this also is from correspondence, because their changes of state are changes as to intelligence and wisdom.

"Since every one in the spiritual world is clothed according to his intelligence, thus according to the truths from which his intelligence is derived, therefore those in the hells, being without truths, appear only in torn, squalid and miserable garments, each one according to his insanity. Nor can they wear any others."—H. H. n. 177–'81.

21 *

Here, again, we are told that it is because angels are *men*, and live together in society like men on earth, that they are clad in garments—the same reason, observe, which was assigned for their dwelling in houses. The argument, brief as it is, when duly considered is seen to be one of immense force. It will bear expansion—requires it, indeed, that its full force may be seen and felt. In its expanded form it may be stated thus:

Man is endowed by his Creator with a certain constitution, physical and moral; and this constitution has its laws. His physical or material organization perishes, but the moral or spiritual, which is the *real*, never dies. And the laws of his immortal part remain forever the same. And belonging to this part of our nature, even when regenerate, are certain implanted instincts, wants and tendencies. And these must remain so long as man's spiritual constitution remains, or so long as he continues to be man. And while they remain, they impel him in certain directions, and necessitate a certain environment. For example, he is gifted with a social nature which impels him to seek the society of his fellows. And as this tendency belongs to our immortal part, it must exist in the Hereafter, and will therefore necessitate the existence of societies in the spiritual world.

Another of the laws or God-implanted tendencies of our moral nature, is that of spiritual affinity, which impels each one to seek the society of kindred spirits. This law or tendency can never cease until we cease to be human. Its active force in the Hereafter, therefore, necessitates the arrangement of angels and spirits into innumerable societies.

Another of the implanted instincts of our immortal nature, and which will therefore endure so long as the soul endures, is the love of home. And this love necessitates the existence of that visible symbol of home, the house, as the only means of fully satisfying this want of the soul. Hence, we are told, the angels have houses and live in them *because they are men*, with the wants, affections and tendencies of men, alive and active in them. And for the same reason, also, angels are clad in garments,—*because they are men.*

Remarks similar to those made respecting houses in heaven, are applicable also to the disclosure about garments there. For these have a moral or spiritual as surely as they have a physical use, even here on earth. They are required for the satisfaction of the soul, no less than for the protection and comfort of the body. Our spiritual nature demands them for the gratification of its God-given wants. And if it calls for them here, it will call for them in the world beyond. If garments on earth were worn merely for the body's comfort and safety, why are they not laid aside when the weather is such that the body does not need them ? True, this, or something approaching it, is done in some parts of our world. But what parts? Not where man's higher nature is most developed, and the angel-life in him is most conspicuous, but where this nature is most shriveled and debased—where the angel is most hidden beneath the bestial life, and man approaches nearest to the condition of the brutes.

As some evidence of the moral signification and use of dress among men, see how various are the garments of different people even in the same climate, country, city or village—various in color, form and material. This variety results from the variety of mental states— from a diversity of tastes which is its underlying and efficient cause; and it proves that garments are chosen to gratify an implanted want of the soul not less than an immanent need of the body.

The same truth is further evinced by the well-known fact that the soul of the same individual instinctively craves different garments when in different states. To-day you wear one that satisfies the demands of both body and soul. To-morrow some specially sad or joyous event occurs, and the soul requires a different garment —more sombre or more gay according to the nature of the event, and thus corresponding more truly with your mental state. Every one perceives how inappropriate a ball-room dress would be at a funeral,—*so* inappropriate, indeed, that our best feelings would be disturbed if not shocked by such unfitness. And why? Clearly because there are certain wants of the soul as well as of the body which garments are required to satisfy. And a brilliant dress on a solemn occasion fails to meet this requirement. Why do little children prefer garments of bright and gay colors? Not because these make their bodies more comfortable, but because they better correspond with, and satisfy the requirements of, their gay and glad-some spirits. For a similar reason old age usually prefers garments of grave and sombre colors; for such colors are in close correspondence with the sober thoughts of age, and therefore more satisfying to the soul's requirements.

Why is it, again, that children are so fond of new garments, and love to change their garments so often? While aged people are content to wear the same dress for years, and care little or nothing for change of style or color? The difference in their mental states furnishes the all-sufficient answer. The states of little children—their thoughts and feelings—change quickly and often; while those of the aged are comparatively fixed and stationary.

It is plain to be seen, therefore, that there is a meaning to garments as worn here on earth. They signify and reveal something of the wearer's mental state—which they could not do if they had not a spiritual as well as a natural use to subserve; if they did not meet a want of the soul as well as of the body. The universal human heart has ever had a perception of this truth; for in all ages men have recognized the propriety of different kinds of garments, corresponding to and indicative of different kinds and degrees of intelligence, and different stations and occupations in life. Thus the queen's or emperor's robe, the judge's gown, the bishop's surplice, the soldier's coat, the sailor's jacket, and the cobbler's apron, are each appropriate to the wearer's function. And if the positions and occupations of men in this world were always according to their intelligence and capabilities, then their garments, being according to each one's use or function, would correspond with and indicate the kind and degree of their natural intelligence, —as in the spiritual world each one's garments correspond with his spiritual intelligence.

To sum up the rational argument for the truth of Swedenborg's disclosure on this subject:

We have ample warrant for affirming that garments, even in this world, subserve a spiritual as well as a natural use; that they are required· not less to satisfy the wants and appetencies of the soul, than the immanent needs of the body. And as the soul is immortal, and retains all its wants and appetencies when released from the incumbrance of gross matter, it will desire garments in the spiritual world. And since all lawful desires (and the angels have no others) will be gratified in heaven, therefore its denizens must be clad in garments. And because of that great and universal law which determines the aspect of all outward things in the spiritual world, their garments must correspond to their states of intelligence, and change with the changes of their states —as Swedenborg has many times declared.

Let us now look at the Scripture testimony. The Bible makes frequent mention of angels, and always speaks of them as being clothed. Their garments, or the color and aspect of them, are often spoken of. Thus it is said of the angel that rolled the stone away from the door of the sepulchre, that "his countenance was like lightning, and his raiment white as snow." And when the weeping Mary looked into the sepulchre, the record says she saw "two angels in white, sitting, the one at the head and the other at the feet where the body of Jesus had lain." And Luke speaks of these two angels as "two men in shining garments." (xxiv. 4.) And in the Revelation the four and twenty elders are spoken of as "clothed in white raiment." They, also, that stood before the throne and the Lamb, were "clothed in white robes." And "white robes were given to every one of them" that were under the altar. Again it is said that the armies which the seer beheld "in heaven" following Him who was "called Faithful and True," and "on whose head were many crowns," were "clothed in fine linen clean and white." And of him "that overcometh" it is said, "the same shall be clothed in white raiment." (Chs. iii., vi., vii., xiii., xiv., xix.)

The testimony of the Bible, therefore, is ample and conclusive on this subject, and in complete accord with that of reason and the disclosures of the illumined Swede.

Then see how intimately these disclosures are connected with the deeper or heavenly meaning of the Scripture, and what light they throw upon many portions of it. For everything that appears in heaven, is in correspondence with something belonging to angelic minds, and is the visible image thereof. And garments, we are told, correspond to spiritual intelligence, and therefore represent the truths or thoughts that clothe the affections of the wearers.

"Both angels and spirits appear clothed in garments, and every one according to his truth. They who are in genuine divine truths appear clothed in white shining garments; and others in others. Some spirits do not know whence garments come to them, but they are put on while they are ignorant of it. And their garments vary according to the changes of their state as to truths. In a word, their intellectual is what is exhibited and represented by garments; for the intellectual of every one is formed by truths, and becomes of such a quality

as are truths from which it is formed. The intellectual
appertaining to the angels of heaven is in their internal,
hence they have white shining garments; the shining
is from the divine good, and the whiteness is from the
light of heaven, which is the divine truth. But the garments of those who are in things external without an
internal principle, are dirty and tattered, like those of
beggars in the streets and of robbers in forests."—A. C.
n. 10,536; also n. 5248.

From this we may readily understand the spiritual
signification of the garments of Jerusalem, and her
comely ornaments; and may see what is meant by the
"wedding garment," without which there can be no admission into the heavenly kingdom; and why we are
commanded to keep our garments clean, or to guard
against their defilement. Thus, in Isaiah we read:
"Put on thy beautiful garments, O Jerusalem" (lii. 1).
By Jerusalem is meant the Lord's church, viewed in-
dividually or collectively. And what are her garments but the truths of wisdom from the Word of God?
These are the appropriate clothing of whatever there is
of God's love in human hearts. They are, therefore,
the beautiful garments of Jerusalem. And when Jerusalem (the individual or collective church) is brought
into perfect marriage union with the Lord, and becomes
his own, this is the Divine testimony respecting her ornaments and apparel:

"I clothed thee also with broidered work and shod
thee with badger's skins; and I girded thee about with
fine linen, and covered thee with silk. I decked thee
also with ornaments, and put bracelets upon thine hands
and a chain on thy neck. And I put a jewel on thy

forehead, and ear-rings in thine ears, and a beautiful crown upon thine head. Thus wast thou decked with gold and silver; and thy raiment was of fine linen and silk and broidered work . . . And . . . thy beauty was perfect through my comeliness which I had put upon thee, saith the Lord God." (Ezek. xvi. 10–14.)

All moral or spiritual beauty is the Lord's own comeliness; for it is his own life in the soul of man. He stamps his comeliness on all who become spiritually conjoined to Him through obedience of life, and this it is that makes their souls beautiful. He clothes and adorns their minds with the precious and various truths of his wisdom. These are the beautiful garments and precious jewels wherewith He ever decks Jerusalem his Bride. And in the other world where all the inner qualities of the soul manifest themselves to the outward sense, those who have received the beautiful and precious life of the Lord, appear clad in garments of corresponding beauty.

And when the interiors of the soul are completely laid open—as is the case with all shortly after they enter the other world—or, what is the same, when the Lord comes in with his revealing light and life, it then becomes manifest whether that soul is and has been inwardly a worshiper of self and the world, or of the Lord in his Divine Humanity. If the former, he can have no permanent abode in the kingdom of light, but only in the " outer darkness," however fair and beautiful may have been his outward life and character; but if the latter, he is inwardly wedded to the Lord by love, and his thoughts thence proceeding are thoughts

22

of corresponding truth and loveliness. His mind is clothed with celestial intelligence; he has on "the wedding garment." And from this we may understand the meaning of the parable of the marriage of the king's son (Matt. xxii.), and why it is said that "when the king came in," and "saw there a man not having on a wedding garment," he gave commandment that he be taken away, and "cast into the outer darkness." All divine laws are self-executing. And the soul that has not become internally married to the Lord by a life of obedience to his precepts, is, by its own organic conditions, without the wedding garment, and therefore outside of the Kingdom—unclothed with celestial intelligence—in "the outer darkness."

And so we might extend our illustrations through many pages, showing again the intimate connection between Swedenborg's revealings of the spiritual sense of Scripture, and his disclosures concerning the spiritual world. And we find a similar agreement throughout his writings. Can a coincidence so striking and so often repeated, be the result of mere accident? If so, such a marvelous kind of accident never occurred before or since his time. And if it were an ingenious contrivance of the author, then he (the man of exceptional honesty, simplicity, and child-likeness of character) must be credited with such a degree of ingenuity and cunning as the world never before witnessed—yea, such as the human imagination was never capable of conceiving. Only things that are divinely true, parts of the grand and universal order of God, ever fit into each other in a manner so complete and perfect.

Then look at the practical considerations with which this disclosure, like all the others about heaven, is fraught. The garments of the angels, like their habitations and their whole environment, are indissolubly bound to themselves as effects to their producing cause. The quality and appearance of their dress are in perfect correspondence with their states of life, and change with those states. Their understandings are stored with the beautiful and precious truths of heavenly wisdom. These clothe and adorn their minds, and create for themselves, by the unerring law of correspondence, garments of corresponding worth and beauty visible to the outward eye.

And here, let it be borne in mind (for it is the *practical* lesson to be learned from this disclosure), we are daily weaving and working for ourselves the garments we shall wear in the great Hereafter. And we can wear no others than those we make, as it were, with our own fingers. If we are sedulously imbibing heavenly intelligence, seeking to have our minds clothed and adorned with the truths of wisdom from the Divine Word, as only those are who are careful to *live* or *do* the truths they learn, then we are weaving for our souls garments of heavenly texture and brilliancy. But if we are regardless of the Divine precepts, if we fail to clothe our minds with the truths of wisdom, as do those who neglect to apply these truths to life, then we shall have no garments, or none but filthy and ragged ones, in the Hereafter, to cover the shame of our nakedness. Therefore, saith the Lord: " Blessed is he that watcheth and keepeth his garments, lest he walk naked and they see his shame."

XXI.

CHILDREN IN HEAVEN.

IT is known that hundreds of thousands of little children are daily passing by death from the natural into the spiritual world. What becomes of all this infantile host? In what condition are they when their earthly bodies are laid aside? Are they infants and little children still? If so, who has charge of them? and what is done for them? and what their history and final destiny? Millions of bereaved parents are hourly asking these questions—mentally if not orally; and it would seem reasonable to expect that God, who has revealed Himself as an infinitely wise and loving Father, would some day give an explicit answer to such inquiries. He has done so through his own chosen and illumined servant. But before giving the answer, the reader should know what the generally accepted belief on this subject among Christians, was at the time Swedenborg lived and wrote; for this will show the dense spiritual darkness in which the Christian church had become immersed, and the imperative need there was of such a new revelation as he was divinely authorized and commissioned to make.

Many who have not made themselves familiar with the religious beliefs of a hundred years ago, will no doubt be surprised to learn that the cruel and worse than heathenish doctrine of *infant damnation*, was among the then generally accepted beliefs of all the churches in Christendom. The Roman Catholics believed and taught that all infants dying unbaptized, were doomed to eternal hell torments. And all the distinguished lights (?) and recognized authorities in the various Protestant churches —including Luther, Melancthon, Calvin and Beza, and many eminent professors of theology after them, the English and German churches, the Synod of Dort, and the famous Westminster Assembly of divines—believed that everlasting hell torments will be the portion of *some*, at least, who die in infancy and childhood.* This belief is seen to be one of the legitimate offspring of the doctrine of unconditional election and reprobation, which was generally accepted by all Protestant churches a hundred years ago.

It is needless to make any comments on this doctrine, or to attempt to prove its falsity. For in the light of to-day—the dawning light of the New Jerusalem which is being universally diffused—every one sees that it is not only false, but so monstrous and cruel that no intelligent and humane person thinks of accepting it. And although it may still linger in some of the creeds, or be fairly deducible from other articles there, the staunchest Calvinistic minister of to-day would hardly dare to proclaim such a doctrine before an intelligent congregation, or even hint his belief in it; or if he should, he might expect his people would very soon be on the lookout for another minister. How great, then, must have been the spiritual darkness of the church, when such a doctrine could have been generally accepted! And how

---

* See the many and high authorities on this subject quoted and referred to in Part I. of *Beauty for Ashes*, by the author.

great the need of a new and divinely-authorized revelation to disperse that darkness!

Turn, now, to Swedenborg's disclosure on this subject, and see how it squares with the teachings of enlightened reason and Holy Scripture. He says:

"Some believe that only the infants who are born within the church go to heaven, but not those born out of the church; and the reason they assign is, that infants within the church are baptized, and are thus initiated into the faith of the church. But they are not aware that no one receives heaven or faith by baptism, for baptism is only for a sign and memorial that man is to be regenerated. . . . Be it known, therefore, that every infant, wheresoever born—whether within the church or out of it, whether of pious or impious parents—when he dies, is received by the Lord, and is educated in heaven. He is there instructed according to divine order, and is imbued with affections of good, and by them with the knowledges of truth; and afterwards as he is perfected in intelligence and wisdom, he is introduced into heaven and becomes an angel."—H. H. n. 329.

We learn from this that *all* who die in infancy and childhood, go directly to heaven. They are not angels, however, immediately after their decease, for they lack the intelligence and wisdom necessary to constitute an angel. They have the same infantile mind which they had while yet in the flesh; for the death of the body works no change in the spiritual organism. So long, therefore, as they are without heavenly intelligence and wisdom, they are not angels, although in the society of angels.

"When infants die, they are still infants in the other

life. They have the same infantile mind, the same innocence in ignorance, and the same tenderness in all things. They are only in rudimental states introductory to the angelic—for infants are not angels. Every one after his decease, is in a similar state of life to that in which he was in the world; an infant in a state of infancy, a boy in a state of boyhood, a youth, a man, an old man, in the state of youth, of a man, and of an old man; but the state of every one is afterwards changed. The state of infants, however, excels that of all others in this respect, that they are in innocence, and evil from actual life has not yet taken root in them. And such is the nature of innocence, that all things of heaven may be implanted in it; for it is the receptacle of the truth of faith and of the good of love."—H. H. n. 330.

"As soon as infants are raised from the dead, which takes place immediately after their decease, they are taken into heaven, and committed to the care of angels of the female sex, who in the life of the body loved little children tenderly, and at the same time loved God. Because these angels when in the world loved all infants from a sort of maternal tenderness, they receive them as their own; and the little ones also, from an inclination implanted in them, love them as their own mothers. Each one has as many infants under her care, as she desires from a spiritual maternal affection."—Ibid. n. 332.

The condition, in the spiritual world, of those who die in infancy and childhood, is thus seen to be preferable to that of those who continue on earth. Their surroundings are more favorable to the growth of the heavenly graces. They are in better company. Their spiritual wants are more fully supplied; for those who have them in charge are wiser than the wisest mothers or nurses

on earth, and love them with a purer spiritual affection
—an affection that has supreme regard to their eternal
well-being.   Thus they are kept under the more immediate auspices of the Lord, and are freed from the manifold debasing influences that surround little children in
this lower sphere.   They inhale the healthful atmosphere
of heaven.   No blasting mildew—no foul breath from
hell falls upon them there.   They meet with no harsh
or unkind treatment.   So wisely are they led and governed, that their hereditary evils lie dormant—never become actual sins.   They witness in those around them
no exhibition of evil feelings, they hear no profane or
angry words, they look upon no wicked deeds.   Love
prompts and wisdom directs whatever is done to them
and for them.   Love breathes in every tone they hear;
love beams in every face they see ; love moulds the forms
and prompts the words and shapes the deeds of all around
them.   Even the gardens, trees and flowers, and all the
beautiful objects that greet their senses, are but the
visible and substantial forms of the angelic thoughts and
affections which are poured forth in a fresh and ever-
living stream into their open and receptive souls.

They are educated, too, in a far wiser manner than
children on earth.   They are instructed for the most
part by representatives which are surpassingly beautiful
and fraught with angelic wisdom.   Objects which delight
them exceedingly—all of which are correspondences re-
plete with instruction suited to their states—are presented
before them, and their signification fully explained ; and
thus their minds are gradually opened, and they are led
on by their angel teachers to the fulness of angelic wis-

dom, more rapidly and more pleasantly than children under even the very best instruction in this world. No compulsory processes are resorted to, but they are led by their affections; for the angels know how to insinuate heavenly intelligence into the minds of little children by means of objects which address and delight their senses. Describing the manner in which children are educated in heaven, Swedenborg says:

"Into their affections which all proceed from innocence, are insinuated such things as appear before their eyes, and are delightful. And as these are from a spiritual origin, the things of heaven flow into them at the same time; and thus their interiors are opened, and they become more perfect every day."

"Little children in heaven are instructed principally by representatives suited to their capacities, which, in beauty and fulness of wisdom derived from an interior ground, surpass all belief. Thus intelligence which derives its soul from good, is insinuated into them by degrees."—H. H. n. 337, '8.

And this, remember, was written more than twenty years before Froebel, the founder of the new method of educating little children known as the Kindergarten system, was born. Yet the latter system is a faithful imitation of the method pursued in heaven, as revealed through Swedenborg a hundred and thirty years ago.

But those who pass into the spiritual world during infancy or childhood, do not remain infants and children. They advance there as here to the full stature of manhood. They grow by the assimilation or accretion of the substances of the spiritual world, as children on earth grow by the assimilation of material substance. The body in each world is formed of substances homogeneous in their nature with its respective world. But they do not grow old there as here. They do not advance (in appearance) beyond the age of early manhood and womanhood, but retain forever the freshness and vigor of that early period. (See p. 227 for further remarks on this subject.)

But all children are born into this world with a certain hereditary evil taint. They inherit from foregone ancestry proclivities which, in their full development, incline them to all kinds of evil. This is what Swedenborg calls the natural or hereditary *proprium*, which he says is altogether infernal, and within or above which every regenerate soul receives from the Lord a new and heavenly proprium. This is what constitutes the new man—the new creature—the new birth from Above. And do not those who die in infancy, it may be asked, take with them this natural proprium? If so, what becomes of it? Does it never manifest itself in the world beyond? And if it does, how are their hereditary tendencies to evil to be overcome or got rid of?

It is true that children take with them into the other world all the evil proclivities with which they are born into this world. But their evils are never aroused or called into activity there, and are therefore never appropriated; that is, they never become *their own* by actual life. Their perverse tendencies gradually lose their strength by not being brought into exercise; for whatever is endowed with life, loses its vital force in the degree that exercise is denied it. This is a universal law. Every mental faculty and disposition as well as every bodily organ, acquires strength by habitual exercise, and loses it by long-continued rest. So with the hereditary evils of children in the other world; they remain quiescent, and never become actual sins by being ultimated. And the principal reason is, that they are so wisely governed that their evil proclivities are never aroused. The sphere of love and wisdom by which they are continually encompassed, exerts a restraining influence on their evil tendencies, while it quickens into life and action every innocent affection; and so their hereditary evils are kept in a quiescent state. But in order to convince them what they are by inheritance, and to induce in them a becoming humility, they are at times remitted into their natural proprium, and kept in it until they see and acknowledge their hereditary evil tendencies. Says Swedenborg:

"I have conversed with angels concerning infants, and inquired whether they are free from evils, because they have no actual evil, like adults. But I was told that they are equally in evil,—yea, that they, too, are nothing but evil; but that they, like all the angels, are withheld from evil and held in good by the Lord, yet in such a way that it appears to them as if they were in good of themselves. Lest, therefore, infants who have grown up in heaven should entertain a false opinion of themselves, and imagine that the good which they possess is from themselves and not from the Lord, they are sometimes let into the evils which they have received hereditarily, and are left in them until they know, acknowledge and believe that their good is all from the Lord."—H. H. n. 342.

All, we think, will admit the reasonableness of the great seer's disclosures on the whole subject under consideration. Some say they are too beautiful to be true. *Too beautiful to be true!* Is anything too beautiful or too good for the Lord to do? Is not He the very perfection of all beauty and all goodness? Did He not create man for heaven, and is it not his constant effort to bring all into the heavenly state? What is there, then, in the nature of the case, in the revealed character of God, in the laws of Divine Providence, or in the state of little children themselves, to prevent their lot in the other world from being precisely as Swedenborg has revealed it? Nay, is not the Lord's infinite mercy a sure pledge that such and so blessed will be their condition? And does not his Word give assurance of the same? What affecting tenderness and love for little children did the Saviour exhibit, when He called them to Him, put his hands upon them and blessed them! And how plainly did He declare their fitness for the realms above, when He said: "Suffer the little children to come unto me, and forbid them not, for of such is the kingdom of heaven" (Matt. xix. 14). Again, when He set a little child in the midst of the disciples, saying: "Verily I say unto you, except ye be converted and become as little children, ye shall not enter into the kingdom of heaven" (Ib. xviii. 3). And again when He said: "For I say unto you that their angels in the heavens do always behold the face of my Father which is in the heavens" (Ibid. v. 10).

It thus appears that Swedenborg's disclosures on this subject have the support of sacred Scripture as well as of sound and enlightened reason.

Then try them by that sure and infallible test which

infinite Wisdom has suggested—by their fruits. We know, or can readily infer, the inevitable effect of the Old doctrine on the minds of its believers. We know that it contains no solace for bereaved parents when death has snatched some little one from their embrace. It cannot suppress one sigh, nor mitigate one pang, nor minister one drop of comfort to their stricken hearts. Nay, the thought which it suggests of the bare *possibility* that their darling may be counted among the reprobates—forever doomed to the torments of the damned —is calculated to wring their souls with indescribable anguish. And what a reproach does the Old doctrine cast upon the character of the infinitely wise and loving Father! What a monster of injustice and cruelty does it make Him!

But the New doctrine as revealed through Swedenborg, while it accords with reason and Scripture and the unspeakable love and wisdom of God, is full of heavenly consolation for bereaved parents. It assures that weeping mother as she bends for the last time over the pulseless body of her darling child, that her precious one is still alive—brighter and happier, too, than ever before; that it has gone from the cold, dull earth to the warm, bright heavens; that it is already in the tender embrace of loving angels, and in due time will itself become an angel; that as soon as it left its earthly tenement and its eyes opened on the spiritual world, it beheld an angel mother smiling on it, and eager to fold it in her loving arms; that there this angel mother will love and tend it, and angel teachers instruct and guide it; that there it will play with other children who are

23

all learning to be good and wise; that there it will feel
no pain, and know no sorrow, and experience no want;
that there, enveloped in an atmosphere of sweetest love,
it will be forever shielded from all baleful influences,
and never know the polluting touch of sin; that everything which greets its senses there, will be full of instruction and delight; that its eye will behold none but
beautiful objects, and its ear listen only to love's sweet
notes.

And let that mother believe all this, as she surely
will if she studies the revealings which it has pleased
the Lord to make, and will she not derive support and
comfort from it?   Will she not find in it a balm for her
wounded spirit?   Will it not give her beauty for ashes,
the oil of joy for mourning, the garment of praise for
the spirit of heaviness?   Will she not dry her tears,
suppress her sighs, chide her murmurs, and with humble, cheerful trust look up, and say from the heart,
"The Lord gave, and the Lord hath taken away;
blessed be the name of the Lord."

Nor is the instruction which this new revelation imparts, less important than the comfort it affords.   Not
only does it enable us to give up our little ones with
more resigned and cheerful hearts at the call of the
Heavenly Father, but it presses upon us the importance
of governing and instructing them aright while they
remain with us.   It shows us that, if we would train
our children for heaven, we must endeavor to become
heavenly-minded ourselves.   We must have our affections so fixed on heavenly things, that the love of
heaven will shine out in our looks, tones, words and

actions; for then we shall be able to lead our children by their affections, as the angels do. We must endeavor to shield them against all corrupting influences, and to surround them by such a sweet and heavenly atmosphere as will strengthen all their good affections and stifle all the bad.

Such is the instruction which the new revelation on this subject suggests and emphasizes, by showing us in what way children are trained in heaven, and the happy results thereby attained. It shows us how the growth of their hereditary evils may be checked, and thus prevented from becoming actual sins. And how it enforces the duty of striving to make the home of our children a little heaven on earth! How it entreats us to suffer nothing "that defileth or worketh abomination or maketh a lie," ever to enter there! It tells us as in loud trumpet-tones, that all harsh and uncharitable judgments, all angry looks, resentful feelings and evil speaking, all impatience, discontent, discord and moroseness should be banished thence as soul-destroying fiends;—that the domestic altar should be shielded from every taint of sin as from a wasting pestilence,—swept clean of evil thoughts and words as of the seeds of death;—that it should be guarded and kept as the Holy of Holies where resteth the ark of God's covenant, where truth and purity and peace go hand in hand, and all are encircled with religion and love as with beautiful shining robes.

See how the Old and the New doctrine on this subject appear, when placed side by side! Look at them in the light of Scripture and reason and the revealed character of the Heavenly Father. Which has the stamp of truth most legibly imprinted on it? Which looks like the offspring of Divine Wisdom, and which like the work of men's hands? Do not the character and obvious tendency of the New revealings, clearly authenticate their heavenly origin?

XXII.

SEX AND MARRIAGE IN HEAVEN.

AMONG all of Swedenborg's voluminous works, there is not one which proves more conclusively his Divine illumination, than his treatise on Conjugial Love. Had any man written that book without having his mind opened to the light of heaven in an unusual degree, it would have been the miracle of miracles. In no other work ever published can there be found such exalted wisdom touching the character and relation of the sexes. In no other has the subject of marriage been discussed so profoundly, or its true nature and origin been unfolded so clearly, or so just and elevated views of it been presented—views calculated to produce such a deep conviction of the sacredness of this relation. We cannot conceive how a tolerably fair mind can read this work understandingly, without being made purer, wiser and better by it; nay, without being convinced that the truths here unfolded are such as no human mind could ever have reached by its own unaided efforts.

Hitherto the proper relation of the sexes has been but imperfectly understood; and even professing Christians have entertained extremely low, not to say false, ideas of the whole subject of marriage. They have generally looked upon it as a union of bodies rather than of souls; and regarded it, therefore, as a relation belonging exclusively to the natural world—rejecting, and sometimes scouting, the idea of anything like marriage in the great Hereafter. The moment a spiritual idea is admitted into the thought respecting marriage, and anything like a union of souls is conceded to be possible, that moment it is seen that the marriage relation must exist in the world beyond, or wherever souls exist.

On account of the low and merely natural view of marriage which has been generally held and taught, people have entered into this relation from low and earthly motives ; and innumerable evils have been the result. And before the evils resulting from a low and false view of marriage can be avoided, people must obtain a higher and truer view of it. The men and women of Christendom need to have their ideas on this subject elevated and spiritualized. They need to have the institution lifted up from the earth, to be shown the spiritual nature of the marriage relation, the spiritual uses it was meant to subserve, and the spiritual considerations from which it should be entered into, if they would realize the blessings it was meant to confer. There is no deeper need of Christendom to-day, however little it may generally be felt. And it was to satisfy this need, that the Lord has revealed through Swedenborg the heavenly doctrine concerning marriage, or the view which the angels take of this relation. And as the love from which marriages in heaven spring, is the foundation or

23 *

parent of all other heavenly loves, so the nearer marriages on earth approach in their nature to those in heaven, the more of heaven will there be in the hearts of men;—the more fully will the Lord's kingdom come and his will be done on earth as it is done in the heavens.

But are there really marriages in heaven? We will first hear Swedenborg's answer to this question, and then subject it to a careful examination in the light of reason and known facts; and finally, will explain the passage of Scripture which is commonly supposed to teach a different doctrine on the subject.

"Heaven is from the human race; therefore the angels of heaven are of both sexes. And because it was ordained from creation that the woman should be for the man and the man for the woman, and thus that each should be the other's, and because this love is innate in both, it follows that there are marriages in heaven as well as on earth. But marriages in heaven are very different from those on earth.

"Marriage in heaven is the uniting of two into one mind. The mind consists of two parts, one of which is called the understanding, the other the will. When these two parts act in unity, they are then called one mind. In heaven the husband acts that part which is called the understanding, and the wife that which is called the will. When this union which is of the interiors, descends into the inferiors which are of the body, it is perceived and felt as love. This love is conjugial love.

"Hence it is evident that conjugial love derives its origin from the union of two into one mind. This is called in heaven cohabitation; and it is said that they are not two but one. Therefore two married partners in heaven are not called two but one angel."—H. H. n. 366, '7.

The fundamental question to be first considered, is, whether the distinction of sex is preserved in the other world. Does a man remain a man and a woman remain a woman in the Hereafter? Or do they exchange genders, or all become of the neuter gender? The verdict of enlightened reason on this, as on other subjects, is clearly in agreement with Swedenborg's teaching. To suppose people to be of a different gender in the other world from what they were in this, were preposterous in the extreme. The preservation of one's sex is essential to the maintenance of his identity. If it were possible to change one's sex, the moment the change was effected he would cease to be the same person.

It is man's soul or spirit that is immortal. This, as we have repeatedly said, is the real man. And when the spirit leaves the body, it remains unchanged. It takes with it all its God-given instincts—all its innate affections, tendencies, wants and appetencies. The difference between man and woman in their physical structure, is apparent to all. The latter is usually smaller, weaker, of more delicate features, softer skin, and fairer complexion than the former. They differ, too, in their manners, gestures and tones of voice. Yet even as to their bodies it is plain they were made for each other,— that they belong together, and are parts of one and the same whole. So that, physically regarded, neither is complete without the other, because incapable of fulfilling all the ends of his earthly existence. The Creator's design is plainly written upon their physical organism, which is, that each is for the other—each but a part of a perfect whole.

But the body is only the manifested form of the soul or spirit within it. It therefore corresponds to the soul in every particular, being perfectly adapted to all its wants and capabilities. It thence follows that there must be a difference between the souls of the two sexes corresponding precisely to that between their bodies. For the logical inference from the great doctrine of correspondence is, that the masculine body must correspond to the masculine soul and the feminine body to the feminine soul.

And as a matter of fact, we find it is so. No truth is more obvious than this : that there exists an innate difference in the mental constitution of the sexes, just as wide and as strongly marked as that observable in their physical organism. Their souls differ precisely as do their bodies. For although we sometimes meet with manish women and womanish men, they are the exceptions and not the rule. We find them mentally no oftener than physically so. In general the feminine soul differs from the masculine, as woman's body differs from man's. But one is not *superior* to the other; only they are different. There would be as little propriety in speaking of the mental superiority of man to woman or of woman to man, as there would be in speaking of the physical superiority of the heart to the lungs or the lungs to the heart. The truth is they belong together, and are adapted to each other in their whole constitution, mental and physical. One is the complement of the other. When "they twain are one flesh," the man is complete—a whole man. Hence we read in Genesis that God created man in his own image; "male and female created He them, and blessed them, and called *their* name Adam," that is, *man*—for this is what Adam in the Hebrew means.   Accordingly Swedenborg says, that "in heaven two married partners are not called two but one angel."—H. H. n. 367.

Spiritually viewed, then, man and woman differ as do the will and understanding, or the heart and lungs, and are similarly adapted each to the other.   The masculine soul is preëminently intellectual, and the feminine preëminently emotional.   Or in other words, man is born into the affection of knowing, understanding and being wise; and woman into the love of man's wisdom, not in herself but in the man, and consequently into the love of conjoining herself with the intellect or wisdom of the man.   Accordingly Swedenborg says:

"The woman feels the delights of her love in the wisdom of the man, because this is its receptacle; and when love finds this receptacle corresponding to itself, it is in its enjoyments and delights."—C. L. n. 189.

And precisely this difference in their mental constitution, is indicated by the physical structure or form of man and woman respectively.   For the masculine form —being coarser, stronger, and more angular—is a form of the intellect; and the feminine form—being fairer, more delicate and beautiful—is a form of affection.   Not that man is wholly destitute of affection, and woman of intellect; but viewed in relation to each other, their minds are thus characterized—man being preëminently intellectual, and woman preëminently emotional or affectional.   Love is the native element of woman's soul, as truth is that of man's.   And so the sexes stand related like love and wisdom, will and understanding, or heart and lungs. And their mental difference is not the result of education or circumstances. It is inborn. It exists from their very creation. It belongs to their soul's constitution, and must therefore continue while the soul endures.

Now, the sexes being thus constituted, mutually desire conjunction with each other. The masculine soul instinctively yearns for union with some feminine soul, and the feminine for union with some masculine. And until this union is attained, each is conscious of an unsatisfied want; each has a sense of incompleteness—feels a lack of wholeness to his being. And the reason is, that the Creator has so constituted the human soul that no single one is complete or whole in itself, but only in union with another.

And because of this inborn constitution of the sexes, and because every soul takes with it into the other world all its innate characteristics, wants and appetencies, therefore man and woman must mutually desire to be joined in marriage in the great Hereafter, and marriages must exist in heaven. For the angels being of both sexes, and endowed with an ardent longing for union with each other, would be unhappy if such union were denied them. And as the conjunctive tendency was implanted in the sexes by God himself, it would be most unreasonable to suppose that its gratification would be denied in that highest state to which human beings are made capable of attaining — that is, in heaven.

Besides, the masculine and feminine soul being complements of each other, belong together from creation. Neither is complete by itself alone, but only in marriage union with its other half; just as neither lungs nor heart can perform its appropriate function except in organic union with the other. Marriages in heaven are, therefore, necessary to the completeness of the angels. No single angel would be a *whole* angel, without union with some other that is the complement of himself. And as everything in heaven is more perfect than on earth—the states of the angels, also, more innocent, pure and exalted than those of men—therefore we should expect the conjugial principle would exist there in greater strength and purity than on earth, and the marriage relation be found in its highest perfection. The heavenly life being the highest life, where but in heaven should we look for the best illustration of the truly conjugial affection and relation? Where else should we expect to find marriages so blissful or so perfect?

We have said that man and woman, like the lungs and heart, belong together as parts of one and the same whole. But as no two hearts and no two lungs are ever precisely alike, so no two hearts can ever be exactly suited to one and the same pair of lungs. It follows, therefore, that only one man and one woman can, from creation, be perfectly adapted to each other as parts of one and the same whole. Hence "the Lord provides that conjugial pairs shall be born." (C. L. 229.) Hence a true marriage—such a union of souls as exists in heaven—can take place only between two individuals who were created for each other.

That there are marriages in heaven may further appear, if we consider the highest use of marriage here
on earth. Its first use, like the first use of houses, garments and all material things, is natural and temporal.
But its principal and highest use is spiritual and eternal.
This is obvious from the fact, that the most unhappy
marriages are those where there is the least spiritual
affinity between the parties—the least approach to a
union of souls; and where the deepest want of the
spirit in this relation, therefore, is not met. Outward
circumstances may be of regal splendor; honor, wealth
and station may crown the wedded pair; but if there
be no internal and spiritual union, the bonds of external
marriage will be felt as a heavy burden grievous to be
borne—all the heavier and more grievous, perhaps, for
the splendor of the outward life. Neither of the parties
knowing aught of the sweet peace and comfort of love,
they will feel no support from, and no joy or delight in,
each other. On the contrary, they will both feel an unsatisfied want, a corroding canker, a gnawing worm, a
wasting consumption at the heart; and nothing but a
firm faith and well-grounded religious principle, will
prevent them from fretting life away in anxious longing
for a more congenial mate.

So deeply and so obviously is man's immortal part
involved in this sacred relation! So much does the soul
demand for itself in the marriage relation even on earth!
And so greatly does it suffer, too, when defrauded of its
just demands! And so egregiously do those parents
err, and such a fearful weight of responsibility do they
assume, who undertake to decide for their sons and

daughters what sort of conjugal alliances they shall form! And what a terrible mistake do the parties themselves commit, who, when about to enter into this relation, make mere external and worldly considerations rather than the deep and enduring wants of the soul, the basis of their choice!

Clearly, then, do marriages here on earth, be they fortunate or unfortunate, prove that the *soul* is deeply involved in this relation;—that it has a want herein which nothing else but union with some kindred soul can fully satisfy. And because it is a soul's want, it must endure so long as the soul endures; and in heaven, therefore, it cannot fail of its full gratification.

Observe, further, the spiritual uses of marriage on earth, in the connate character and obvious mental needs of the two sexes. Man is preëminently a form of the intellect, and in mind as well as body, is comparatively coarse, harsh, severe and angular. Alone, or disjoined from woman, he is like faith separate from charity, or truth apart from good, which Swedenborg says is represented in the spiritual world as something strong, powerful, hard and irresistible, at the sight of which good spirits are terrified. He, therefore, needs the softening, refining, mellowing influence of woman's gentler heart, precisely as truth or faith needs the softening and sweetening influence of charity. And woman being preëminently a form of affection, is comparatively weak, tender and delicate in mind as well as in body. Alone, or apart from man, she is like charity separate from faith, or like love without wisdom. She, therefore, needs the strengthening, supporting, guiding influence of man's

24

intellect. Man's intellect alone is cold—like the clear cold light of winter; it needs the warmth of woman's love to quicken in him the seeds of thought. And woman's heart alone is warm—like the warmth of a darkened chamber; it needs the light of man's intellect to enable it to impart health, strength and verdure.

And thus the soul of each is perfected by union with the other. Man's head is warmed by woman's heart—his harsh, stern features rounded and made beautiful by woman's love. And woman's heart is enlightened by man's head—her tender and delicate soul supported and made strong by the strength of man's intellect. Thus the two whom God has joined together—whose souls He has so constituted that they are " no more twain but one flesh "—are made all the more perfect, more human, more truly and completely *one*, by the union we call marriage. " Male and female created He them, and called *their* name Adam."

Now if—as the old theologies have taught—there are no marriages in heaven, either the angels must be less perfect than they would be with marriages, or the distinguishing mental characteristics of the sexes must be so entirely changed there, that each will be whole by himself alone, and will have no need of conjunction with the other.

And how clearly and impressively are the spiritual uses of marriage sometimes revealed here on earth!—A fond and devoted wife sees the partner of her bosom pursuing a downward and criminal course—plunging deeper and deeper into vice and infamy—gradually blinding his intellect, benumbing his moral sense, destroying his manhood. And see how that wife pursues her erring husband! How she clings to him as a part, and the stronger part, of herself! How she pleads with him on bended knees, with tearful eyes, in angel tones —only as love *can* plead! And how, also, she pleads with God and heaven in his behalf! How she waits and watches and prays—how she bears and suffers and forgives until seventy times seven, only as love *can* bear and suffer and forgive! And see, too, what triumphs she sometimes achieves!—the salvation of a wrecked and sinking soul!

Can this deep, mighty love which God has placed in woman's heart, which can work such miracles of healing here below, which has such power on earth to soften, subdue and bless, and which, from its very nature, so yearns for an intellect to cling to and guide it—*can* such love perish when the body dies? Will there be no sphere for its activity, no use and no reciprocation of it, in heaven? Then woman *as woman* cannot live in heaven. And if woman lives not there, what man having within him the soul of a man, would not say that heaven would be no heaven to him.

Again: the eternity of conjugial love, and the consequent existence of marriages in heaven, may be reasonably inferred from the fact that consorts who have lived together happily on earth, internally desire that this relation may be continued in the world beyond. And it is not the vicious and degraded in whom this desire is strongest. These know nothing of the pure delights of marriage; they have little or no respect for its sacred obligations here, and, of course, think and care but little about the relation hereafter. But they who have the intensest desire for the eternity of the conjugial tie, and the firmest belief that marriages do exist in heaven, are usually those whose state of life is nearest that of the angels—the wisest, purest, humblest, best—those who have experienced most of the exalted and spiritual delights of marriage here on earth. Yes: it is the most heavenly-minded consorts who most ardently long for the eternity of marriage, and who are least willing to admit that it exists not beyond the grave. It is painful to them to think of the utter cessation of the conjugal relation at death; for they feel that heaven without marriage would be no heaven to them.

"That they who are in love truly conjugial," says Swedenborg, "regard what is eternal, is because there is eternity in that love, and its eternity is from this: because that love with the wife and wisdom with the husband increases to eternity, and in the increasing or progression consorts enter more and more deeply into the blessedness of heaven, which their wisdom and the love of it at the same time store up in themselves. Wherefore if the idea of eternal should be rooted out, or from any accident escape from their minds, it would be as if they were cast down from heaven. What state consorts in heaven have, when the idea of eternal falls out of their minds, and the idea of temporary falls in in its place, came into open view with me from this experience: Once, from permission given, two consorts were with me from heaven; and at that time the idea of eternal concerning marriage was taken from them by a certain worthless spirit speaking cunningly; which being taken away, they began to wail, saying, that they could live no longer, and that they felt a wretchedness which they never felt before; which being perceived by their fellow-angels in heaven, the worthless spirit was removed and cast down; when this was done, the idea of eternal instantly returned to them, from which they were gladdened with gladness of heart, and most tenderly embraced each other."—C. L. n. 216.

Now, whose faith and perceptions on a subject of this nature are most trustworthy? Those of the vicious and profligate, or those of the pure and good? So surely upon it—so sure as there is a God who heareth and answereth prayer, the deep though unuttered prayer of his children on this subject—a prayer up-springing from a heart-felt want which his own boundless love has implanted—will not be all unheeded. And if their prayer is heard and heeded, there surely must be marriages in heaven.

Once more: Who are those that love the bonds of marriage most intensely? Who contemplate wedded life with the highest delight, and find in it the purest and most abundant joy? Not the carnal-minded and vicious, but the most spiritual and righteous—those whose walk with God is closest and humblest, and who discharge with the greatest fidelity all their daily duties. Consorts whose character is nearest like that of the angels—provided there be some internal fitness of each to each—experience a pure and heavenly delight in marriage which the vicious can never know. Therefore they love it best. And the farther they advance in the regenerate life, the more faithfully they do the Heavenly Father's will, the nearer they approach to that innocent, pure and loving state in which the angels are, the more closely do their hearts become wedded to each other,

24 *

and the higher and purer delight do they find in marriage. If this be so—and we know it is—the conclusion is irresistible that there must be marriages in heaven; and not only so, but that this relation must exist there in its greatest perfection, and the delights thence resulting be the sweetest and most abundant. And we should also infer that the farther the angels advance in the divine life, the more perfectly would the souls of consorts there be united, and the fuller and more perfect be their blessedness. Accordingly Swedenborg says :

" It was shown me what is the manner of the progress of the delights arising from conjugial love, this way toward heaven and that way toward hell. The progress of the delights toward heaven was into blessednesses and happinesses continually multiplying, till they became innumerable and ineffable ; and as the progression was more interior, it was into blessednesses and happinesses still more innumerable and ineffable, till it came even to the essential heavenly blessednesses and happinesses of the inmost heaven, or the heaven of innocence ; and this by a most perfectly free principle, for all freedom is of love, consequently the most perfect freedom is of conjugial love which is essentially celestial. Afterwards was shown the manner of the progress of the delights of conjugial love toward hell, in that they remove themselves by degrees from heaven, and this also from an apparently free principle, till at length there are scarce any remains of a human principle in them. The deadly and infernal principle in which they close cannot be described."—A. C. n. 2744.

In conclusion :—We have thus far examined Swedenborg's revelation on this subject, in the light of reason and known facts. Here, as on other subjects, he has spoken quite contrary to the current creed of Christendom, it is true; but it is equally true that he has spoken quite in accordance with the dictates of our highest reason and the teachings of a sound mental philosophy.

We see that marriages in heaven result necessarily from the nature, constitution and wants of the soul, and from the obvious fact that each one preserves his own identity in the Hereafter, and takes with him into the other world all that appertains to his immortal part—all his dominant thoughts, inclinations, dispositions and feelings. For marriage is a necessity of our human nature in its highest and most perfect state. It is one of the deepest wants both of man and woman—one that is woven, as it were, into the very fibres of our spiritual as well as natural being. Upon the whole constitution with which God has endowed human beings, He has written his great and beneficent design in this particular, as in characters of living light. And we may rest assured that He has nowhere written a word to the contrary; for He never contradicts Himself.

Thus do the great Swede's disclosures on this, as on all other subjects connected with the Hereafter, rest securely on the constitution of our whole nature, physical and spiritual, and are seen to be in perfect agreement with the wants, tendencies, capabilities, and everlasting laws of the human soul. Therefore they must needs agree with the teachings of God's Word; for this, too, is adapted to the wants of our spiritual nature, and contains in its bosom the laws of the human spirit. And because his pneumatology builds itself on such a firm foundation, therefore its truth is undeniable, and must endure so long as the human soul endures, and its laws and tendencies remain what they are.

But the Bible, says an objector, teaches that "in the resurrection they neither marry nor are given in marriage" (Matt. xxii. 30). How is this language to be understood, and how is its teaching to be reconciled with that of Swedenborg? Our next chapter will be devoted to the consideration of this question.

XXIII.

SEX AND MARRIAGE IN HEAVEN—SCRIPTURE TESTIMONY.

THAT there should be marriages in heaven, is something so reasonable in itself, and withal so desirable by those who have any true idea of the *spiritual* nature of true marriage, that Christians in general would readily believe it, did it not seem contrary to the explicit teachings of Scripture. Their highest reason favors the idea; the distinguishing characteristics of the masculine and feminine soul, seem to necessitate the relation in the Hereafter; and the deepest want of our nature and the best feelings of the regenerate heart, encourage the hope that it may be as the great seer has revealed. Yet they cannot accept Swedenborg's teaching on this subject, because of the Lord's words to the unbelieving Sadducees, quoted at the conclusion of the last chapter.

That pious minds should, in view of the Scripture re-

ferred to, feel some repugnance toward the new doc-
trinc—a repugnance all the stronger, too, in proportion
to their reverence for the Scripture—is not surprising.
And when opposition to any of the great Swede's revealings springs from such pious ground—from a belief
that they are contrary to the Word of the Lord—we
confess to a profound respect for it. We blame no one
for his opposition to the doctrines promulgated by Swedenborg, while he honestly believes that they contradict the Bible. We would not have a person accept a
word he teaches—nay, would counsel him *not* to accept
it—so long as it seems to him contrary to the teachings
of the Divine Word.

Yet we would urge all to remember this: that the
Lord reveals Himself in his Works as well as in his
Word; that both these Volumes are alike his, and
therefore alike sacred; and that his laws, from whichever of these sources ascertained, are equally divine,
and equally entitled to our reverence. We would beg
them further to bear in mind, that men are just as liable
to misunderstand and misinterpret one of these Volumes as the other. There is nothing to secure us absolutely against misunderstanding either; and the proofs
are abundant that both have often been misinterpreted.
Whenever these two Volumes, therefore, Nature and
Revelation, seem in conflict, we may be sure that the
conflict is only apparent, and arises from our misunderstanding one or the other; and it is the part of wisdom to endeavor to ascertain *which it is* that we have
misunderstood. As God's Word may help us to see
and understand Him in his works, so the revelation of

his will in his works may often aid us to a right understanding of his Word.   He is *our* Creator; and *some* of his purposes concerning us are written upon the human soul as legibly as they could be written in a book or on tables of stone, and as easy to be misunderstood. And among his purposes thus plainly written, is that in regard to the conjugial relation and its existence in the world beyond.   A marriage union of the sexes, not merely in this world but in heaven likewise, is legibly inscribed on the whole nature and constitution of man and woman, by God's own finger.

And now let us see if the passage in Matthew (xxii. 30) really teaches anything contrary to this—as many Christians think it does, and as at first sight, indeed, it appears to teach.

The question which the unbelieving Sadducees had put to our Lord on the occasion referred to, shows that they had no idea of marriage as an internal and spiritual relation—a soul union.   Their views of it were of the lowest kind.   They thought of it as a relation which might exist between one woman and any number of men; and *vice versa*.   The idea of an eternal adaptation of one man to one woman and only one, seems never to have entered their minds.   It was not, therefore, of real *marriage* that they were thinking when they put to our Lord the question: "Therefore in the resurrection whose wife shall she be of the seven?" for, as Swedenborg says, "there are *no marriages* elsewhere than in heaven; but beneath heaven [that is, among those in low or external states] there are only nuptial connections (*connubia*) which are tied and parted." (C. L. n. 192.)

Now it was simply of these *connubia* that the Sadducees were thinking, when they propounded to our Lord the question about the woman that had been married or *tied to* seven brethren. And the answer He gave them was the answer to the thought in their understanding; and it was the truth. It was as if He had said: "That of which you are thinking is *not* marriage, but only an external or nuptial connection. And as this is what *you think* is marriage, it is therefore what you inquire about. And in reply, I tell you there are no such marriages in the great Hereafter. Then and there, or in the resurrection, they neither marry nor are given in marriage, according to your idea of this relation; but are as the angels of God in heaven—constitutionally and organically adapted each to the other, as parts of one and the same whole."

The Lord's reply to the Sadducees, therefore, considered as an answer *to the thought* in their minds, was true even in its literal sense. But his words all have a meaning deeper than that of the letter. "The words that I speak unto you," He says, "are spirit and are life." (John vi. 63.)

A slight examination of the passage in Matthew, together with the context, will show us that reference is here had more especially to spiritual marriage, or the union of good and truth in human minds, and the consequent conjunction of such minds with the Lord. This is the spiritual or heavenly meaning of marriage, and the meaning which those attach to the term when it occurs in Scripture, who understand the Lord's words according to their spiritual sense. That such is the kind of marriage more particularly referred to in his reply to the Sadducees, is plain from the context. Before propounding their question they referred to what Moses taught respecting marriage with a deceased brother's wife—a plain matter of fact, so plain that it could not be misunderstood if its literal sense *alone* were the sense intended. Yet the first words in the Lord's reply, were: "Ye do err, *not knowing the Scriptures* nor the power of God." But they *did* know the Scriptures in their *literal sense*, and they understood the passage in Moses about marriage merely in that sense. But because the literal is not the true way of understanding the Scriptures, and because they knew nothing of the true spiritual signification of marriage, therefore the Lord says to them, "Ye do err, not knowing the Scriptures."

Besides, at the commencement of the chapter which records this conversation, the kingdom of heaven is compared to a marriage; and all who are invited to become subjects of this kingdom, are represented as *called to the marriage.* And in the Revelation we read: "Blessed are they that are called to the marriage supper of the Lamb." The Lord, too, is often called Husband and Bridegroom in the Word; and the church, composed of all who become spiritually conjoined to Him by a life of obedience to his commandments, is called his Wife and Bride. Thus in Isaiah: "Thy Maker is thy Husband; the Lord of hosts is his name." (liv. 5.) And in Matthew: "Can the children of the bridechamber mourn so long as the Bridegroom is with them?" And in the

Apocalypse the angel who talked with John, said: "Come hither, and I will show thee the Bride, the Lamb's Wife." (xxi. 9.) And in the next verse we are told who the Bride is—the Holy Jerusalem, the true church of the Lord. "And he carried me away in the spirit to a great and high mountain, and shewed me that great city, the Holy Jerusalem, descending out of heaven from God." And on another occasion the seer heard the voice of a great multitude in heaven, saying: "Let us rejoice and be glad, and give honor to Him; for the marriage of the Lamb is come, and his Bride hath made herself ready." (xix. 7.)

Do not such passages prove that marriage, when mentioned in Scripture, has a spiritual meaning? And that it signifies that conjunction of the Lord with his people, which is elsewhere spoken of as the reciprocal indwelling of the Lord in man and man in the Lord. And this takes place in proportion as we receive from Him love and wisdom, or in the degree that we learn truth, and, through religious obedience to its requirements, cleanse our hearts of all selfish and evil loves; for in that degree our interiors are opened, and we receive an influx of the Lord's life—we appropriate, as it were, the very Divine substance, the Lord's own flesh and blood. Hence He says: "He that eateth my flesh and drinketh my blood, dwelleth in me and I in him." The Lord's flesh is the good of his divine love, and his blood is the truth of his divine wisdom.

As man advances in the regenerate life, truths in his understanding become married to their corresponding goods in the will. And this union of truths with goods in the mind, is the spiritual or heavenly marriage; and in the degree that it takes place, the man is brought into a state of marriage union with his Maker. He is in the Lord, and the Lord is in him; and he delights to do the will of the Lord. In the degree, therefore, that this heavenly marriage takes place in any mind, the kingdom of heaven comes to that mind.

This union or marriage of good and truth in human minds, comes from the marriage of Divine Love and Divine Wisdom in the Lord; for these in Him are united like heat and light in the sun. And they proceed as one from Him, and are received by the angels as one. For the angels have no will contrary to the Lord's. They love to do what He loves to have them do. Thus they live in marriage union with Him, having in themselves—and this, from Him—the heavenly marriage of good and truth.

But the state of the unregenerate man is far otherwise. His will is opposed to the will of the Lord. Good and truth do not exist in marriage union in his mind. Evil instead of good loves are in his will, which are opposed to the truths in his understanding. He does not love to do what the truth teaches him he ought to do. And before he can come into the heavenly state, he must regard and shun as a sin against God the indulgence of every inclination which the truth condemns. Whenever we shun the indulgence of any evil as sin, that evil is gradually removed, and the opposite good affection takes its place. The truth in our understanding which revealed and condemned the evil, is thus married to its corresponding good in the will. And by a succession of such marriages the work of regeneration advances and the heavenly state is gradually perfected. But it is only the truths which we religiously obey while here on earth, that become married to goods in the will, and so remain with us permanently. Truths that are known and *not* obeyed, acquire no permanent abode in the soul. They may seem to be ours, but they are not until they become of the life—until they are brought down and obeyed, and thus become rooted, as it were, in the natural degree of the mind. We have no real interior affection for them, and when we come fully into the state of our interiors, as we shall in the other world, they will be taken from us, for we shall then deny and reject them. Accordingly it is written : " Whosoever hath not, from him shall be taken even that which he seemeth to have." (Luke viii. 18.) Truths that have been disregarded and disobeyed by us in the life on earth, cannot be married to their appropriate goods in the world beyond ; nor can the good and delightful things of heaven which are born of such marriage, be then and there given us. And this is the meaning of these words of the Lord, understood in their spiritual sense : " For in the resurrection they neither marry nor are given in marriage."

We thus see that this Scripture, rightly understood, is by no means opposed to the new doctrine concerning marriages in heaven. Even its literal sense, rightly interpreted, teaches nothing to the contrary. For there are no such nuptial connections in heaven as the Sadducees thought of as marriage, and about which, as the Lord perceived, they inquired of Him.

Then there are other passages of Scripture, which,

understood in their literal sense, clearly favor the doctrine taught by Swedenborg. As that, "a man shall leave his father and mother and cleave unto his wife; and they twain shall be one flesh." (Gen. ii. 24.) And these words of the Lord in answer to the Pharisees: "Have ye not read that He who made them at the beginning, made them male and female? And said, For this cause shall a man leave father and mother and shall cleave to his wife; and they twain shall be one flesh. Wherefore they are no more twain, but one flesh. What, therefore, God hath joined together, let not man put asunder." (Matt. xix. 5–7.)

We are here taught that man and woman were designed for each other from their very creation; that they are adapted, each to the other, and so joined together as parts of one and the same whole, by the Creator Himself. And it surely would not be said of beings created to live forever, that *God* had joined them together, if there were no joining of their immortal part —no mutual and organic adaptation of soul to soul. The beings that God joins together, must be organically fitted to each other as parts of one whole, and must therefore be joined for the full term of their existence. A man and a woman may be joined in an external union —a semblance of marriage—agreeable to human laws; and may separate in a few months for lack of mutual love, or of the proper organic adaptation of soul to soul. Can it be said of such that they were joined together by God? Every one can see that this would be charging the Creator with folly. Then extend the time, and suppose the parties joined in an external marriage for ten, twenty, or fifty years, and then to separate for lack of the proper constitutional adaptation of each to the other; could it with any greater propriety be said that they were joined by God? No: Man may join or *tie* together beings who are internally, constitutionally and mutually repugnant, and do not really belong together; just as they may join truth with evil, heaven with hell in their own minds. But all such alliances must, from their very nature, be sooner or later dissolved. But those whom God joins together, are and must be joined in the inmost ground of their being. And if created to live forever, they must (if joined by Him) be joined not for a day, but for the whole term of their existence; and *so* joined as, of twain, to make one flesh—one whole mind or person.

"Marriage in heaven," says Swedenborg, "is the conjoining of two into one mind. . . . Two married partners in heaven, therefore, are not called two but one angel."—H. H. n. 367.

"The most perfect and noble human form, is when two forms become one by marriage, thus when two fleshes become one flesh, according to creation. The mind of the man is then elevated into superior light, and the mind of the wife into superior heat; and then they germinate, blossom and fructify, as trees in the time of spring."—C. L. n. 201.

This, we see, is in perfect agreement with what we read in Genesis (v. 1, 2): "In the day that God created man, in the likeness of God created He him, male and female created He them, and blessed them and called their name Adam [or man]." It requires both the male

25 *

and female to make the âdâm—the man—that is the *whole* man. Therefore God called the name of the two conjoined—the male and female—*their* name, âdâm. And the Adam, including both sexes, is said to have been *in the likeness of God.* The reason is, that the female was created to be an image more especially of the Divine Love, and the male to be an image more especially of the Divine Wisdom. And as the union of Divine Love and Divine Wisdom is eternal, the conclusion is irresistible that the marriage of the male and female, whose union images that of these two principles in the Divine, must also be eternal.

We are further taught by the Lord, that "*for this cause,*" that is, because we were created male and female, " shall a man leave father and mother, and shall cleave to his wife;" which shows us that the conjugial relation is to endure when the parental, or the tie that binds parent to child, has ceased to exist. And endure how long? How long shall a man cleave unto his wife? Clearly so long as their distinctive natures remain what they are, and there exists such a mutual and organic adaptation of soul to soul, that they twain, by cleaving to each other, are no longer two but one.

The Bible, therefore, teaches that man and woman were created for union in heaven, as truly as it teaches that they were created for each other and belong together during their earthly sojourn. And if it teaches that marriage on earth was designed by Him who made us, it teaches with equal clearness that it was intended for man's highest or heavenly state, and that its duration will be coterminous with that of the soul itself.

XXIV.

CONJUGIAL LOVE—ITS NATURE.

BUT marriages in heaven, Swedenborg tells us, are quite different from marriages on earth. They are, like everything else there, more interior and perfect, and consequently more blissful. The love that binds in marriage union two parties in the realms above, is the true conjugial love. And this is not mere sexual love, which in itself is impure, and is felt by natural men and even by the lower animals. It is a pure spiritual affection. Souls in heaven are drawn together and held together by a love of what is really good and true—of what there is of the Lord *in* souls. A female angel looks and longs for wisdom in the male, for this is what delights her most. And in proportion as any male angel embodies the particular kind of wisdom with which she is most delighted, she loves him. And she loves him because of the Lord's wisdom which she perceives in him, and with which her soul yearns for conjunction. And the male angel looks and longs for love in the female, pure, innocent, tender, gentle, like the Lord's own love, for this is what delights him most. And he loves her in the degree that she embodies in herself the special kind of love that agrees with his special kind and degree of wisdom. And so it is the Lord's love which he perceives in her, and which is the life and soul of his wisdom, that is to him the peculiar attraction.

Thus consorts in heaven love only what there is of

the Lord in each other. And the more there is of the Lord in both—the more the man's understanding is enlightened by his wisdom and the more the woman's heart is warmed by his love, so much the more do they love and delight in each other, and the closer, therefore, is their union.

Moreover, conjugial love as it exists in heaven, is all from the Lord. It has its origin in the divine marriage of love and wisdom in Him; and thence it descends into angelic minds, and into minds of men who are nearest like the angels. This is clearly perceived by consorts in heaven; and they also perceive that the more faithfully they do the will of the Lord, the more are their minds opened to the reception of his love and wisdom, and the more do they experience of their heavenly delights in the love they feel for each other. And it is given them further to perceive that conjugial love corresponds to the marriage of the Lord with his church; for as husband and wife in heaven mutually love each other, so the Lord loves the church, his Bride, and forever wills that it should love and be conjoined with Himself, her Husband.

It thus appears, both from its origin and correspondence, how pure and holy conjugial love is, and what sanctity there is in marriage as it is viewed in heaven. The Lord himself being regarded as the source and centre and very essence of it, this love with the angels is not only free from terrestrial defilements, but is the fountain of all other angelic loves.

"If conjugial love," says Swedenborg, "be received from its author who is the Lord, sanctity from Him follows, which continually cleanses and purifies it. . . . Considered in its essence and from its derivation, it is holy and pure before every love with angels and men. . . It is the fundamental love of all the loves of heaven and the church, because its origin is from the marriage of good and truth ; and from this marriage proceed all the loves which make heaven and the church with man. Two consorts between whom or in whom this love exists, are an image and form of it; and all in heaven, where the faces are genuine types of the affections, are likenesses thereof. . . . Therefore if conjugial love be heavenly and spiritual, the loves proceeding from it are also heavenly and spiritual. This love, therefore, is as a parent, and all other loves are as the offspring. Hence from the marriages of the angels in heaven, are produced spiritual offspring which are of love and wisdom, or of good and truth."—C. L. n. 64, '5.

From this it may be seen that conjugial love is something quite different from the mere love of the sex. It is pure and heavenly in its nature, and can exist only with rational, regenerate, heavenly-minded persons. The love of the sex has supreme regard to self and self-gratification ; but conjugial love has supreme regard to the Lord and the things that are well-pleasing to Him. The love of the sex belongs to our carnal or animal nature ; conjugial love belongs to our spiritual and immortal part. The love of the sex is low—"of the earth, earthy"; conjugial love is from the Lord out of heaven, and is supreme above all other loves. The love of the sex exists with natural and even sensual men ; conjugial love, only with those who are, in some degree at least, spiritual and regenerate. Swedenborg says :

" The love of the sex is of the external or natural man,

and hence is common to every animal. Every man is born corporeal, and becomes more and more interiorly natural ; and as he loves intelligence he becomes rational, and afterwards if he loves wisdom he becomes spiritual. . . . If he stand still in the first threshold in the progression to wisdom, the form of his natural mind remains, and this receives the influx of the universal sphere (which is of the marriage of good and truth) no otherwise than do the inferior subjects of the animal kingdom—the beasts and birds—receive it; and as these are merely natural, man becomes like unto them [in the matter we are now speaking of], and so loves the sex in like manner as they do.

" But conjugial love is of the internal or spiritual man, because, as a man becomes more intelligent and wise, he becomes more internal or spiritual ; and in the same degree the form of his mind is more perfected, and this form receives conjugial love ; for it therein is sensible of a spiritual joy which is inwardly blessed, and from this a natural joy which derives soul, life and essence from that."—C. L. n. 94, 95.

But conjugial love may be said to be included in the love of the sex like a gem in its matrix. It is the spiritual internal whereof the love of the sex is the natural external. It is the love of the sex regenerated, spiritualized, cleansed of its defilements, lifted from earth to heaven. The love of the sex, like all other natural loves, is first in time—first in the order of development; but conjugial love, like all spiritual loves and the spiritual man himself, is first in end—first in the order of importance.

We thus see how the love between married pairs in heaven, called conjugial love, differs from the natural man's love of the sex—a love which often leads to unions here on earth which we *call* marriage, but which are as purely natural and external as is the love that leads to them.

In heaven there exists, we are told, the most delightful freedom—the freedom of perfect love. The love of rule, or of exercising dominion, one over the other, is wholly unknown among angelic consorts. Their souls are so perfectly united—every fibre of their hearts is so intertwined, each with the other's, that they have no separate and independent life ; nor do they desire to have any. Each lives in and for the other, and forever desires to live so. What one desires and wills, the other desires and wills also. One thinks no thought which the other does not think; one cherishes no purpose which the other does not cherish ; one feels no joy which the other does not feel; one breathes no prayer which the other does not breathe. Their everlasting bond of union is God's holy spirit of truth and love dwelling and operative in their hearts; and "where the spirit of the Lord is, there is liberty," for there is wisdom and there is love ; and " what is done from love truly conjugial, is done in freedom on both sides, for all freedom is of love, and each has freedom when one loves what the other thinks and wills " (A. C. 10,173). The least inclination to exercise dominion, or to force the will of the other, is foreign to the nature of conjugial love, and something which does not exist in heaven.

" The love of exercising dominion one over the other completely takes away conjugial love and its heavenly delight ; for conjugial love and its delight consist in this : that the will of one be that of the other, and this mutually and reciprocally. The love of dominion in marriage destroys this; for he who domineers wishes that his will should be in the other, and none of the other's reciprocally in himself. Hence there is nothing mutual, consequently no reciprocal communication of one's love and its delight with the other. Yet this communication and thence conjunction is the interior delight itself in marriage, which is called blessedness. The love of dominion completely extinguishes this blessedness, and with it all celestial and spiritual love. . . When one wills or loves what the other does, both enjoy freedom; for all freedom is the offspring of love. But when there is dominion, neither is free. One is a slave, and so is the other that exercises dominion, because he is led as a slave by the lust of domineering."—H. H. n. 380.

Marriage in the heavens being the conjunction of two minds into one, can exist only between one man and one woman. And so completely are their souls wedded, that their thoughts and affections never wander from each other. The husband never thinks of any female but his own wife with other feelings than those of charity and mutual love. If he should, that moment the blessedness of conjugial love would depart, and darkness would invade the souls of both. The wife would experience a dreadful sinking at the heart, as if the light of her life were about to be extinguished. And a similar result would follow, should the wife think fondly of any other man than her own husband.

"You two are one," said Swedenborg to a married couple in heaven. "And the man answered, We are one. Her life is in me, and mine in her. We are two bodies, but one soul. The union between us is like that between the two tents in the breast, called heart and lungs. She is my heart, and I am her lungs. But since by heart we here understand love, and by lungs wisdom, she is the love of my wisdom and I am the wisdom of her love. Therefore her love from without veils my wisdom, and my wisdom from within is interiorly in her love. Hence there is an appearance of the unity of our souls in our faces. I then asked, If such union exists, can you look at any other woman than your own? He replied, I can; but as my wife is united to my soul, we both look together. . . While I look at the wives of others, I look at them through my own wife whom alone I love."—C. L. n. 75.

" All of us here say that the husband is truth and his wife is good; and that good cannot love any truth but its own, neither can truth in return love any good but its own. If any other were loved, internal marriage which makes the church would perish, and there would be only external marriage to which idolatry and not the church corresponds. Therefore marriage with one wife we call sacredness; but should it have place with more than one among us, we should call it sacrilege."—Ibid. n. 76.

As the love of the sex which is external and natural, differs in its nature from conjugial love which is internal and spiritual, so also do their delights differ. The delights of the former are fleeting and transitory like all merely natural delights—becoming less and less delightful, too, the longer they are enjoyed; but those of the latter, like all pure and spiritual delights, are eternal and immortal — becoming more and more delightful the longer they are experienced. And since this love as it exists in heaven, is most innocent, pure and holy—the fountain-head, as it were, of all other angelic loves—so all heavenly satisfactions, joys and delights are gathered into this; for this love above all others opens the interior recesses of the soul, through which gush the streams of life pure from their eternal Fountain.

"As conjugial love," says Swedenborg, "is the fundamental love of all good loves, and as it is inscribed on the most minute particulars of man, it follows that its pleasures exceed those of all other loves, and also that it makes other loves pleasant according to its presence and its conjunction with them; for it expands the inmosts of the mind and at the same time of the body, as the delightful current of its fountain flows through and opens them. All pleasures from first to last are gathered into this love, because of the superior excellence of its use above all others, which is the propagation of the human race and thence of the angelic heaven; and because this use was the end of ends in creation, it follows that all the blessedness, happiness, gladness, gratifications and pleasures, which could possibly be conferred on man by the Lord the Creator, are gathered into this love."—C. L. n. 68.

"Conjugial love in its origin is from the marriage of good and truth, and this marriage is from the Lord. And because love is such that it wills to make another whom it loves from the heart, a partaker of, yea, to confer upon him, joys, and from thence itself to take its own; infinitely more, therefore, does the Divine Love which is in the Lord, will thus toward man whom He created a receptacle both of love and wisdom proceeding from Himself. And because He created him into the reception of these, the man into the reception of wisdom and the woman into the reception of the love of the wisdom of the man, therefore from inmosts He infused into men (*homines*) conjugial love, into which He might bring together all things blessed, satisfactory, agreeable and delicious, which proceed together with

life solely from his divine love through his divine wisdom, and flow in ; consequently into those who are in
love truly conjugial, because these alone are recipients.
Innocence, peace, tranquillity, inmost friendship, full
confidence and mutual desire, of mind and heart, of doing every good to the other, are named, inasmuch as
innocence and peace are of the soul, tranquillity is of
the mind, inmost friendship is of the bosom, full confidence is of the heart, and the mutual desire of mind and
heart of doing every good to the other, is of the body
from them."—C. L. n. 180.

The truth of all this must appear sufficiently obvious
to one who contemplates the effects of the love mutually felt by a young man and maiden in the warmth and
glow of its first summer; for in their innocent young
love there is something which allies it to the loves of
the angels. And when their love is reciprocated, what
a new world seems suddenly opened before them!
What fountains of new feeling are straightway un-
locked! What new and strange delights are kindled
in their bosoms! What floods of joy hitherto unknown, are opened! What exhilarating and fragrant
aroma diffuses itself through all the chambers of their
souls! And this new love which is felt as something
unspeakably delightful, at the same time quickens and
exalts all their other loves, and imparts to them a fresh
delight. They are more kind and tender and affectionate toward everybody. They clasp the whole human
family to their hearts. They feel a new and unwonted
affection for even the fields and flowers and the brute
creation, and seem to love things and persons that they
never loved before.

If such be the effects of youthful love here on earth in its first warmth and freshness, it is easy to believe that conjugial love in heaven, which is so much purer, deeper and stronger, is the parent and source of all other heavenly loves; and that into this love, as Swedenborg assures us, are gathered "all joys and all delights from first to last."

Then, to think of this love with angelic consorts as not only continuing forever, but growing stronger and purer and more delightful with every fresh accession of wisdom, and this through endless ages! And this, too, we can easily believe when we consider the origin and correspondence and spiritual nature of this love. And with equal readiness does the rational mind accept as true the following relation which Swedenborg says he received from a married couple who had been for ages in heaven, and from whom "there breathed forth a vernal warmth with a sweet-smelling odor as from the earliest flowers in gardens and fields."

"We have been consorts," said they, "now for ages, and continually in the flower of age in which you see us. Our first state was as the state of a virgin and young man when they unite themselves by marriage. And we then believed that that state was the very blessedness of our life. But we heard from others in our heaven, and afterwards we ourselves perceived, that that state was one of heat not tempered with light, and that it is successively tempered as the husband is perfected in wisdom and the wife loves that wisdom in the husband; and that this is done by means of uses, and according to those which each by mutual aid renders in society; also that delights succeed according to the degree of light and heat, or of wisdom and its love. . .

" These things being said, the man gave me his right hand, and conducted me to houses where were consorts in like flower of age with themselves. And he said that those wives, now seen as virgins, were in the world infirm old women, and the husbands now seen as youths, were there decrepid old men; and that they were all restored by the Lord to this blooming age, because they loved each other mutually, and from religion shunned adulteries as enormous sins. He further said that no one knows the blissful delights of conjugial love, but he who rejects the dreadful pleasures of adultery; and that no.one can reject these, but he who is wise from the Lord; and that no one is wise from the Lord, unless he *does uses from the love of use.*

" I also saw the utensils of their houses, all of which were in heavenly forms, and glittered with gold as it were flaming from the rubies set therein."—C. L. n. 137.

Such is a faint and imperfect outline of the new doctrine of marriage as it exists in heaven. Such the origin, correspondence, spiritual nature, ends and uses of love truly conjugial; and such its unutterable and everlasting delights. Can we conceive of anything in the nature of marriage more beautiful, more perfect, more desirable, or which carries more plainly on its face the very impress of heaven—the stamp of pure and eternal truth? It is such a view of the subject as satisfies the deepest want, the devoutest longing, and the highest reason of every regenerate soul; and we have seen how perfectly it agrees, too, with Holy Scripture.

And how do the views here presented exalt and dignify the institution cf marriage! What beauty and sanctity do they throw over it, and how do they lift it up from earth to heaven! Who is there, whose eye is

not dimmed by error or blinded by prejudice, that cannot
see in this heavenly doctrine something of the wisdom
and love and glory of the Lord? Who cannot here see
Him coming to the long beclouded minds of men on
this grand subject, with new and precious and convincing
truth—yea, "with power and great glory"?

XXV.

PRACTICAL CONSIDERATIONS.

WE have all along invited the reader's attention to
the practical bearing and value of Swedenborg's
disclosures concerning heaven. And we have done this
for two reasons: first, because no stronger evidence of
their truth can be offered than their obvious usefulness
when practically applied; and second, because upon no
single point, perhaps, is Swedenborg more generally
misunderstood than on this. The great *practical* value
of his teachings and revealings cannot be too strongly
emphasized. They all have relation to life, and come
close home to us as husbands, fathers, wives, mothers,
merchants, mechanics, members of society and citizens
of the state. All truth must have relation to life; for
what higher purpose can it have, or for what nobler end
could it be given, than to teach us how to live that we
may be most useful and most happy?

We have seen that the great Swede's disclosures concerning sex and marriage in heaven, rest upon a solid
foundation. Scripture and reason, the desires and hopes

of the best men and women everywhere, and the constitutional requirements of both sexes, unite in attestation of their truth. We have seen, too, what is the nature of marriage as it exists in heaven; also what true conjugial love is, whence it originates, who only can receive it and on what conditions, and what paradisiacal delights flow from its reception. From a union of souls in heaven, spiritual offspring (which are heavenly thoughts and affections ever fresh and new) are continually being born to the wedded pair; and these exalt and strengthen their love, as natural offspring do on earth—but in a far higher degree.

" The angels," says Swedenborg, " have conjugial love according to their wisdom, and the increments of that love and its delights according to the increments of wisdom. And the spiritual offspring that are born of their marriages, are such things as are of wisdom from the father and of love from the mother, which offspring they love from spiritual storge; which love adds itself to their conjugial love, and continually exalts it, and conjoins them."—C. L. n. 211.

We are taught to pray: " Thy will be done on earth as it is done in heaven." If marriages, then, really exist in heaven, their nature, when revealed, should teach us what marriages here on earth *ought* to be—yes, and what they *will* be when the Father's will shall be done here as it is done in heaven. What, then, is the practical lesson to be derived from Swedenborg's disclosures on this subject? What, in view of this new doctrine, will be the primary thought and chief aim of those contemplating marriage, or who have already entered upon it, if in their hearts they are really praying the prayer which the Lord taught his disciples?

Their first and controling thought will be of the Lord. As all true conjugial love is from Him, and He is the all-in-all of every true marriage, therefore their souls will first be lifted to Him in prayer. All who accept the heavenly doctrine on this subject, will see that there can be no real marriage except where there is a union of souls; and such, therefore, is the union they will desire and seek. They will see that their highest earthly bliss depends upon it. Any other union may, perchance, embitter their whole lives; or if not this, may deprive them of all the sweetness and delights of marriage. While there is, on the one hand, no heavier or more consuming grief than to be tied to an uncongenial and ill-adapted mate, there is, on the other, no purer earthly bliss than that experienced by consorts whose souls are wedded each to each. It is a bliss closely allied to that of heaven.

And not only are the happiness and spiritual growth of the parties themselves involved in this relation, but the character and happiness of their posterity, through successive generations. For children born of parents who are in love truly conjugial, inherit from them, to a degree above others, an inclination to the things of heavenly life—the truths of wisdom and the goods of love.

"Offspring," says Swedenborg, "born of two who are in love truly conjugial, draw from their parents the conjugial of good and truth;" that is, "they inherit, more than others, an aptness and facility for conjoining good to truth and truth to good, thus for becoming wise ; consequently also for imbibing the things of the church and heaven.

"I have heard from the angels that those who lived in the most ancient times, live at this day in heaven . . . in like manner as they had lived on earth, because love truly conjugial was with them ; and that their offspring inherited from them inclinations to the conjugial of good and truth, and that they were easily initiated into it more and more internally by the parents by education, and when they became of more mature judgment, were introduced into it as of themselves by the Lord."—C. L. 202, '4, '5.

We thus see what solemn and weighty considerations exist, to induce all who are contemplating marriage, to seek a truly conjugial union. And how can they expect to form such a relation, without looking devoutly for guidance to Him who is the light of all minds, and the source of all true marriages on earth as well as in heaven. There is no single act in life wherein the guidance of Divine wisdom is so much needed, as in that of marriage.

As soon, therefore, as a man begins to think seriously of entering into this sacred relation—involving, as it does, not only his own best welfare, but the character and well-being of his posterity—he should enter into his closet, the secret closet of his heart, and pray to the Father that seeth in secret, for the wisdom and guidance which he so much needs. And if he sincerely desires to be led of the Lord in a matter so momentous, and looks to Him with humble and supplicating heart, he cannot fail to be led in the right way.

" Every society of heaven," says Swedenborg, " consists of persons of similar character. They who are alike, are brought together not of themselves but of the Lord. In like manner conjugial partners whose minds are capable of being conjoined into one, are drawn together; and at first sight they deeply love each other, and see that they are conjugial partners, and enter into marriage. Hence all the marriages in heaven are of the Lord alone."—H. H. n. 383.

This is the case with those who have died in infancy or childhood, and been educated in heaven. They have never contracted any evil habits, and have learned and practiced the true worship. It is the indwelling of the Lord in their hearts which gives such perception. But it is otherwise on earth, mainly because children are not here nurtured, nor surrounded by such sweet religious atmospheres, as they are in heaven. They are not early taught to deny self, and to shun all known evils as sins. And sin always clouds the mind's clear vision. Forgetting or turning our backs on the Lord, as we do when we disobey his precepts, is what shuts out the light of heaven from the soul. And this light gone, we walk in darkness. And " he that walketh in darkness, knoweth not whither he goeth."

From the heavenly view of marriage that we have presented, it is further seen that, if one desires or hopes to form a true conjugial union, he must worship the Lord in his daily life; he must cultivate a reverence for the written Word, and shun as a sin all known evil. There can be no true worship without this; for it is not with words only that the Lord is truly worshiped. Words alone do not open the heart to the reception of the Divine life. It is works of filial obedience. It is devout and sincere reverence for the truth, and a resolute purpose to apply it to life. " He that *doeth truth*, cometh to the light."

Whoever, therefore, accepts the heavenly view of marriage as now revealed, will see the necessity of learning and doing the will of the Lord, if he expects to form a true conjugial union. He will see and feel the need of that wisdom which cometh from Above— the wisdom of a righteous and useful life. He will see that, without this wisdom he can never be really loved by a true woman; for a true woman can love only what there is of wisdom in a man. He will see the necessity, therefore, of becoming a form of heavenly wisdom before he can hope to be truly loved by a heavenly-minded woman. So soon as he begins to think of marrying, therefore, he will (if he accepts the heavenly doctrine on this subject) begin to think of learning wisdom from the Lord. He will begin, if he has not already, to regard and shun evils as sins against God. If he has any vicious habits—as of idleness, intemperance, licentiousness, profanity—he will straightway abandon them. If he has no useful occupation he will seek one. If he is false, dishonest, conceited, self-seeking, or worldly-minded, he will repent, humbly invoke the Divine aid, and earnestly set about the work of reformation. If he has scoffed at religion or trifled with holy Scripture, he will change his course and begin to cultivate a reverence for the Word and for all sacred things. For we are taught by this new revelation that the conjunction of a wife is with the rational, moral and spiritual wisdom of the husband.

"Of moral wisdom with the men are all the moral virtues which regard the life, and enter it, as are also the spiritual virtues which flow forth from love to God and from love towards the neighbor, and flow together into those loves. The virtues which pertain to the moral wisdom of men, are called temperance, sobriety, probity, benevolence, friendship, modesty, sincerity, obligingness, civility; also sedulity, industry, skilfulness, alacrity, munificence, liberality, generosity, activity, intrepidity, prudence; besides more. The spiritual virtues with the men are the love of religion, charity, truth, faith, conscience, innocence; besides more. The latter virtues and the former may in general be referred to love and zeal for religion, for the public good, for one's country, for his fellow-citizens, for his parents, for his consort and for his children. In all these, justice and judgment rule; justice is of moral wisdom, and judgment is of rational wisdom."—C. L. n. 164.

Such is the practical lesson which this new doctrine teaches every man so soon as he begins seriously to think of entering the marriage relation. And it teaches a similar lesson to every marriageable woman. By proclaiming a union of souls, and the spiritual uses of marriage as well as the spiritual nature of love truly conjugial, it teaches every woman who desires a true marriage, the necessity of elevating her thoughts and affections to things spiritual and divine, and of looking for some measure, at least, of heavenly wisdom in the man whom she is to call her husband. It teaches her that the supreme delights of marriage can never be known except to the spiritually minded and regenerate; and that if she loves a man who is destitute of heavenly wisdom, it is with a natural, selfish or worldly love which can endure only so long as the natural and worldly feelings are gratified. Wives in heaven, we are told, love only what is of wisdom in their husbands; and all true wisdom is from the Lord.

Every woman, therefore, who fully accepts this new and heavenly doctrine, will, before she gives her consent to marry, demand that her suitor shall give evidence not merely of some degree of worldly wisdom, but of that wisdom especially which cometh from Above; that he be a man of religious principle—a man whose ruling purpose it is to know and do the will of the Lord, who heeds the voice of duty sooner than the promptings of self-interest, and is ever ready to make personal sacrifice in defense of the right and the true. To such a man, a woman may safely give her hand and heart. But there is no security—almost no hope—for her future peace and welfare, if she consents to marry one who is devoid of religious principle. Nothing— no amount of worldly wealth, no rank, station, or connections however high and honorable, can compensate for the lack of this. And this every woman will plainly see, who understands and fully receives this heavenly doctrine of marriage.

Such is the practical lesson which this new doctrine teaches to young men and maidens—to all, indeed, who are contemplating wedded life.

And not less important is the instruction which the doctrine contains for those who have already entered the matrimonial state. It teaches both husbands and wives that they cannot know what true conjugial love is, nor have experience of its pure delights, save in the

27

degree that their souls become conjoined to the Lord by a life of use, and of religious obedience to the Divine precepts. The angels say that the marriage state becomes more blissful and perfect "as the husband is perfected in wisdom, and the wife loves that wisdom in the husband; and that this is done by means of uses, and according to the uses which each of them by mutual aid affords in society."—C. L. n. 137.

"No others come into conjugial love, or can be in it, but those who come to the Lord, and love the truths of the church and do its goods; because . . this love, considered as to its origin and correspondence, is heavenly, spiritual, holy, pure and clean above every love that is with the angels of heaven and the men of the church; and these its attributes cannot be given but to those who are conjoined to the Lord, and by Him consociated with the angels of heaven.

"That they come into this love, and can be in it, who love the truths of the church and do its goods, is because no others are accepted of the Lord; for these are in conjunction with them, and thence can be held in that love of Himself. . . . The truth of faith causes the Lord's presence, and the good of life according to truths of faith causes conjunction with Him, and thereby heaven and the church."—C. L. n. 70, '1, '2.

Thus the new doctrine teaches to married pairs the importance of beginning their wedded life with the Lord. It teaches the necessity of looking to Him and becoming internally conjoined to Him through a life of obedience to his precepts, before they can come into a state of genuine love towards, or of spiritual union with, each other. The reason is, that true conjugial love is from the Lord; and only those, therefore, can be in it and experience its delights, who are in Him and He in them. It is well known that husbands and wives feel the warmest love for each other when in the most faithful performance of all their duties; and it is the faithful discharge of our duties, which brings us into spiritual conjunction with the Lord. The voice of duty is the voice of God; and as often as we reverently heed that voice, we are clasped more closely in the Divine embrace. Apart from God and duty, there is not, and never can be, such a thing as true conjugial love on earth or in heaven.

It is evident enough, therefore, that this love is spiritual in its nature, and that only those come into it and experience its delights, who come to the Lord and learn and do the truths of his Word. And it is no less evident—from human experience as well as from the new revealings—that the more faithfully consorts perform all their duties, the more the husband increases in wisdom and the wife in the love of that wisdom, the more closely wedded will their souls become, and the more fully will they experience the delights of conjugial love. From which we may reasonably conclude that marriages must exist in heaven, and become ever more and more delightful as the souls of angelic consorts become more closely wedded to the Lord and to each other.— C. L. n. 216.

Such is the important practical lesson which the new doctrine concerning marriages in heaven inculcates. It teaches consorts on earth to begin their wedded life with the Lord. It reveals to them the necessity (if they would know the supreme delights of marriage), of living and acting continually from religious principle; the necessity of looking to the Lord and following after Him, of imbibing and cherishing a Christian spirit, and of performing all their duties with religious fidelity; in a word, of making the upbuilding of the kingdom of heaven in their hearts the ruling purpose of their lives. Having this for their grand and constant aim, they will indeed be helpmeets to each other in the highest and best sense; for they will be perpetually helping each other on their way to heaven. They will not strive to please by ministering to each other's natural proprium —pride, ambition, vanity, or love of self—for thus they would shut out from each other's hearts the Lord and heaven and all true love; but by kindness and gentleness, yet with perfect frankness one towards the other, by affectionate counsel, encouragement *and reproof*, by mutual aid in revealing and overcoming their evils, the soul of each will gradually become more closely conjoined to Him from whom all true love descends, and the golden chain that binds their hearts to each other, will grow continually brighter, stronger, and more golden.

Let married partners here on earth accept and adopt these heavenly views of marriage, let them be ever mindful of its spiritual design and uses, and never forget or turn away from Him who is the source of all love truly conjugial, and they will experience, in the internal wedding of their souls, a bliss which the world can neither give nor take away. And the pains, disappointments, bereavements, and manifold ills of life, instead of weakening their attachment, will serve to bind their hearts more closely together, and to augment instead of lessening the sweet comfort of love.

Why is it that the hearts of married partners often grow cold and colder towards each other as the years roll by? Why does married life with many, at first so sweet and joyous, after a while prove to be so dull, insipid, almost wearisome? The reason is obvious. They do not understand or do not accept the heavenly doctrine concerning marriage, nor do they know the heavenly nature of conjugial love. They have not entered into the relation from any exalted motive, or with any spiritual view of it, nor sought to fulfill its obligations from any religious principle. Having never looked to the one true Source for the joys they anticipated, having lost or strayed away from the path of duty, and excluded God and heaven and the things of religion from their affections and thoughts, no wonder their hearts have grown cold, and marriage worthless, and life itself wearisome. No wonder they have not found in this sacred relation the heaven they expected; for they looked in the wrong direction for it—to the things which are from beneath, and not to those which come from above. They expected a heaven where the Lord, religion and duty were unheeded or unknown; no wonder, therefore, that they were disappointed.

"Man was created," says Swedenborg, "that he might become more and more internal, and thus be introduced or elevated more and more nearly to the heavenly marriage of good and truth, and so into love truly conjugial, even so far as to perceive the state of its blessedness. The sole medium of such introduction or elevation, is religion.

27 *

" Hence it follows that where religion is not, conjugial love is not possible ; and where this is not, there is conjugial cold which is the privation of that love, consequently a privation of the state of the church, or of religion.

" The first of the internal causes of colds, is the rejection of religion by both parties. With those who throw back [or reject] . . the sacred things of the church, no good love is possible. If there is any apparent one from the body, still there is none in the spirit. With such persons goods locate themselves on the outside of evils, and cover them over as cloth shining with gold covers a rotten body. The evils which reside within and are covered over, are in general hatreds, and thence intestine combats against everything spiritual ; for all things of the church which they reject, are in themselves spiritual. And because love truly conjugial is the fundamental of all spiritual loves, it is manifest that there is intrinsic hatred of that."—C. L. n. 238, '39, '40.

It cannot be denied, therefore, that the legitimate tendency of this new doctrine of marriage, is most wholesome and benign. And this is the strongest possible evidence of its truth. Where in all the literature of Christendom can we find any teaching on the subject of marriage, so exalted and reasonable in itself, so refining and potent in its moral influence, so purifying and elevating in its practical tendency, as that contained in Swedenborg's treatise on Conjugial Love? Yet this is the book which, more than any other from the pen of the same illumined author, has been misrepresented, maligned, ridiculed, condemned and spit upon by the professed followers of Jesus Christ, and even by men claiming to be his ministers! Our sorrowful feeling for all such, finds its truest expression in those divine words, " Father, forgive them, for they know not what they do."

Let this new doctrine concerning marriage be generally accepted and made a *doctrine of life*, and what a change would shortly come over the face of human society! What different fathers and mothers should we have! What different sons and daughters! What a different atmosphere in all our homes! What a change would ere-long be wrought in the whole social, moral and religious aspect of Christendom! Married life would everywhere cease to be dull or insipid, and would be regarded as the very image of heaven on earth, as indeed it would be. And millions of hearts would feelingly and joyfully respond to the sentiment of the poet,

> " There 's a bliss beyond all that the minstrel has told,
>   When two that are linked in one heavenly tie,
> With heart never changing and brow never cold,
>   Love on through all ills, and love on till they die.
> One hour of a passion so sacred, is worth
>   Whole ages of heartless and wandering bliss;
> And, oh! if there be an Elysium on earth,
>   It is this—it is this! "

XXVI.

WORK IN HEAVEN.

WHENEVER a person contemplates a change of residence, one of the first questions he usually asks himself, is, How shall I employ myself in my new abode? And it is equally natural for those who are hoping some day to go to heaven, to ask, How shall we be occupied, or what shall we *do*, when we get there? Has Swedenborg answered this question? Yes—quite explicitly.

But first, let us see what Christians prior to his time thought about it. On this, as on most other questions touching the Hereafter, opinions were divided. Some believed they should sit upon thrones, and that their happiness would spring from the exercise of regal authority. Others, that they would feast with patriarchs and prophets on the daintiest viands, and that this would be unutterable bliss. Others, that they should dwell in a city with pearl gates and golden streets, be surrounded by more than princely magnificence, and that idly gazing on such outward splendor would make them supremely happy. Others, that there would be in heaven a complete release from all active employment, and that happiness would be found in utter idleness—its denizens forever quaffing delights without rendering the slightest service. Others, that heaven is a place abounding in spontaneous paradisiacal joys, where all things pleasant to the senses are daily born with endless variety, and where it is bliss to respire the fresh and ever-varying delights. Others (and some Christians of the present day may be included in this class) have supposed that acts of formal worship—oral prayer and songs of thanksgiving and praise—would be the chief employment of the heavenly inhabitants.

Such are the opinions which Christians have hitherto entertained. Does any one of them appear reasonable in the light of the present day? To conceive of human beings (for angels are all human) forever occupied in any of these supposed ways—what could be more absurd! Whichever supposition you choose, presents heaven to us as little else than a solemn farce. For all the above-mentioned ways of living, when regarded as regular *occupations*, fall far below the ordinary employments of people here on earth, in point of both dignity and importance.

Some may think this language too strong when applied to the last named occupation. But consider the subject for a moment. Is there no higher kind of worship than oral prayer and hymns of thanksgiving and praise? These, rightly regarded, are not *ends*, but simply *means* to an end. They are a means of opening the soul to a freer influx of the Lord's love and wisdom, and thus leading us to *act* in accordance with his will in the manifold relations of life. To regard them as anything more or other than helps to greater fidelity in the discharge of our ordinary duties, is to commit a serious mistake.

Suppose people on earth should devote themselves exclusively to praying and psalm-singing, making this their regular occupation: should we think they were thereby worshiping God in a manner most acceptable to Him? Would they thus be fulfilling the great end of their creation? Would the various wants and faculties of the soul find their full gratification in such exercises? Is this man's proper *employment?* So far from it, the individual who should make it the regular business of his life, would justly be regarded as insane.

Besides, what *use* would be subserved by it, if engaged in as a regular occupation? Would the growth of charity or the welfare and happiness of society be thereby promoted? And whatever does not tend to this end, cannot be really useful. God does not desire our prayers or praises on his own account. He desires them solely for our good. He knows them to be a means of opening our souls to the influx of his love and wisdom, and of helping us to obey more implicitly the precepts which require us to love and do good to our neighbor.

And does any one believe that a person's own happiness or growth in the heavenly graces, would be promoted by making oral prayer and psalm-singing the business of his life? Let the best man living devote himself steadily and exclusively to this for a single week, and the languor, listlessness and mental torpor thereby induced before the close of this brief period, would seem to him anything but heavenly delight. They would convince him that he was doing violence to his better nature—sinning against the laws of his spiritual being.

Acts of formal worship may be (we are told, are) occasionally engaged in by the angels; and these exercises are, in heaven as on earth, a means of spiritual improvement. But they cannot be the regular employment there, unless man's spiritual constitution is totally changed in the other world—a presumption not warranted by reason or Scripture. For man has many faculties and wants besides those which find their gratification in acts of formal worship. Each of these faculties has a definite mode of action, seeks its gratification in its own way. And they are wants and faculties of the soul, and must therefore exist so long as the soul exists. And if these faculties do not find their chief gratification in prayer and sacred song here, neither will they there. If this would not be useful as an *occupation* on earth, what reason is there for believing it would be in heaven? If it would not promote men's happiness here, why should it be the chief source of happiness there? And if those who should make it their sole occupation on earth would be regarded as insane, what, then (if it be the chief employment of the angels), would heaven be but a vast assemblage of lunatics?

Similar remarks will apply with even more force to the other ideas which Christians have entertained about life in heaven. In the light of to-day, they are all seen to be most unreasonable and absurd. Not one of them will stand the test of a rational examination. Sitting upon thrones, feasting daintily with the patriarchs, walking idly in golden streets, dwelling luxuriously in palaces of regal splendor—none of these things can confer real happiness, because none of them can adequately supply the soul's varied wants. And if it is desirable to have correct views on the subject, it is to the same extent desirable that some further revelation respecting it be vouchsafed.

Turn now to the disclosures made through Swedenborg; and see if they are as unreasonable as the beliefs which have hitherto prevailed. He tells us first, that there are innumerable occupations in heaven, every one there having some useful work to do, for which he is constitutionally fitted, and which he takes delight in* doing. No one can be happy or *be in* heaven without being actively employed. But work there is never fatiguing, as it often is on earth. It is the free, spontaneous and healthy exercise of the faculties;—is all joyous and delightful like the dearly-loved plays of children.

"There are," says Swedenborg, "so many offices and administrations in heaven, and so many employments also, that it is impossible to enumerate them on account of their great number. Those in the world are comparatively few. All, how many soever there be, are in the delight of their occupation, and labor from the love of use, and no one from the love of self or gain. Nor is any one influenced by the love of gain for the sake of maintenance, because all the necessaries of life are given them gratis,— their habitations, garments and food. From these considerations it is evident that they who have loved themselves and the world more than use, have no lot in heaven. For every one's own love or affection remains with him after his life in the world, nor is it extirpated to eternity."—H. H. n. 393.

And we are further told that every one's happiness in heaven, is in proportion to the importance of the use he performs there, and to the affection and earnestness with which he devotes himself to it.

"Every one in heaven is remunerated according to the excellence of his use, and at the same time according to his affection of use. No one that is idle is there tolerated, no slothful vagabond, no indolent boaster of the studies and labors of others; but every one must be active, skilful, attentive and diligent in his own office and business, and must place honor and reward not in the first but in the second or third place. According to these circumstances there is an influx among them of necessaries, of the useful things of life, and of the delightful things of life. . . The necessaries of life, which are given gratis by the Lord and which exist in a moment, are food, clothing and habitation, which altogether correspond to the use in which the angel is; the useful things are those which are subservient to these three things, and are a delectation to him, besides various things for the table, for garments, and in the house, beautiful according to the use, and shining according to its affections; the delightful things are those which are enjoyed with the conjugial partner, with friends, with companions, with all by whom he is loved, and whom he himself loves. From every affection of use proceeds that love which is mutual and reciprocal."—A. E, Vol. vi., p. 353.

But the Bible, we are told, speaks of the righteous after death as "*resting* from their labor." How is this language to be understood, and how is its teaching to be reconciled with that of the passage just quoted? We will let Swedenborg himself answer this question, or rather one of the wise ones he encountered in the other world. On a certain occasion three new comers from our earth, who had imbibed many erroneous ideas about heaven, and among others, that all active occupation would there cease, were led about by a wise elder, and shown various things which astonished them. At length "they were led in the city [called Athenæum] to the rulers, administrators, and their subordinate officers, and by the latter to the wonderful specimens of workmanship which are made in a spiritual manner by the artificers." And the narrative proceeds:

"After these were seen, the elder man again spoke with them concerning the eternal rest from labors, into which the blessed and happy come after death, and said: Eternal rest is not idleness, since from idleness is languor, torpor, stupor, and deep sleep of the mind, and thence of the whole body; and these are death and not life, and still less eternal life in which the angels of heaven are. Wherefore eternal rest is a rest which dispels these, and causes man to live; and this is nothing else but such as elevates the mind. It is therefore some study and work by which the mind is excited, vivified and delighted; and this is done according to the use from which, in which, and to which it operates. Hence it is that the entire heaven is regarded by the Lord as containing uses; and every angel is an angel according to use. The pleasure of use carries him on, as a favorable stream does a ship, and causes him to be in eternal peace and in the rest of peace. Thus is understood eternal rest from labors."—C. L. n. 207.

And many Christians of our day, especially such as are gifted with much spiritual insight, have come to the same conclusion without the help of Swedenborg,—so completely do his disclosures about life in heaven accord with the dictates of reason and common sense. How entirely in agreement with the above extract, is the following, for example, by the author of that remarkable discourse, "Religion in common Life," which has been so widely circulated:

"The true 'Rest' of the soul is that, *not of Inactivity, but of Congenial Exertion.* Labor is rest to the active and energetic spirit. To not a few minds, congenial activity, eager, absorbing, all but incessant, is the element in which they find repose. And the ardent and enthusiastic soul, conscious of power, and delighting in work that calls it forth, will sometimes seem to enjoy perfect serenity only in the whirl of occupation, as the bird on the wing, in the flow of joyous strength, while it cleaves the air at fullest speed, yet seems as if at rest, poised on its outspread pinions.

"For it is to be remembered that the toil that is unfelt is no toil; and the exercise of the mind's faculties on congenial objects, is not only unaccompanied by any irksome sense of toil, but is attended, and probably, were it not for the necessity of using gross material organs, would ever continue to be attended, with positive delight. Fatigue, waste, exhaustion, belong only to matter and material organization. The mind itself does not waste or grow weary, and but for the weight of the weapons wherewith it works, it might think, and imagine, and love on forever. Even with all its present drawbacks, a spirit of great power and energy, so far from resting, frets and feels ill at ease in inactivity. To it inaction is unrest and torture—no work so hard as doing nothing. Only in the putting forth of its energies, in the evolution of its inward power, in the devotion of thought and feeling to congenial pursuits, does it find itself tranquil, unburdened, at rest."—*Caird's Sermons*, pp. 251, '2.

Swedenborg further tells us that the diligent application of the mind to some useful employment from a principle of neighborly love, is an essential condition of happiness in the realms above; and that no one can have experience of the joys of heaven without such application, since the interiors cannot otherwise be opened to the Divine life, the influx of which is the cause of all true joy. He relates the following as instruction given by the angels themselves to certain novitiates who had recently entered the spiritual world:

"The delight of use arising from love through wisdom, is the life and soul of all heavenly joys. In the heavens there are most joyful consociations, which exhilarate the minds of the angels, fill their bosoms with pleasure, and recreate their bodies; but not until they have performed uses in their functions and employments. From these uses is the soul or life of all their joys and delights. And if this soul or life be taken away, accessory joys gradually become no joys, exciting first of all indifference, then disgust, and lastly sorrow and anxiety." —C. L. n. 5.

"There is a certain latent vein in the affection of the will of every angel, which draws his mind to the doing of something; and by this the mind is tranquillized and made satisfied with itself. This tranquillity and satisfaction form a state of mind capable of receiving the love of uses from the Lord; from the reception of this love is heavenly happiness which is the life of the joys mentioned above. Heavenly food in its essence is nothing else but love, wisdom and use together; that is, use, by wisdom, from love. Wherefore food for the body is given to every one in heaven according to the use which he performs; magnificent to those who are in eminent uses; moderate, but of exquisite relish, to those who are in uses of a middle degree; and ordinary to such as are in ordinary uses; but none to the indolent."—Ibid. n. 6.

"Learn what is meant by kings and princes, and reigning with Christ; that it is to know and do uses; for the kingdom of Christ, which is heaven, is a kingdom of uses. For the Lord loves all, and thence wills good to all. But good is use; and because the Lord does good or uses mediately by the angels, and in the world by men, so to them who faithfully do uses He gives the love of use and its reward which is internal blessedness, and this is eternal happiness. There are in the heavens as in the earth, supereminent dominions and the richest treasures; for there are governments and forms of government, and thus there are greater and less powers and dignities. For those of the highest rank, are palaces and courts which exceed in magnificence and splendor those of emperors and kings on earth, and honor and glory flow around them from the number of their attendants, ministers and guards, and from their magnificent vestures. But they who have the highest rank are selected from those whose hearts are in the public welfare, and who are only as to the senses of. the body in the fullness of magnificence for the sake of obedience. And because it is for the public welfare that every one should be of some use in society as in a common body, and because all use is from the Lord, and is done through angels. and through men as if by them, it is plain that this is to reign with the Lord."—C. L. n. 7.

"There are three things which flow as one from the Lord into our minds; these are love, wisdom and use. But love .and wisdom do not exist unless ideally, when only in the affections and thoughts of the mind; but they exist really in use, because they are simultaneously in act and bodily work; and where they exist really, there they also subsist. And because love and wisdom exist and subsist in use, it is use which affects us; and use is faithfully, sincerely and diligently to perform the works of one's office. The love of use, and therefrom a fixed attention to use, hold the mind together, so that it may not flow forth and dissipate itself, and wander about, and drink in all the lusts which flow-in from the body and the world through the senses, with their allurements, by which the truths of religion and morality with all their goods, are scattered to the winds. But a studious fixing of the mind upon use, holds and binds them together in use, and disposes the mind into a form receptive of wisdom from those truths; and then it exterminates the sports and mockeries of falsities and vanities."—Ibid. n. 16.

"The wise ones said: Man when first created was imbued with wisdom and its love, not for the sake of himself, but for the sake of its communication with others from himself.   Hence it is inscribed on the wisdom of the wise, that no one is wise or lives for himself alone, but for others at the same time.   Thence is society, which otherwise could not be.   To live for others is to perform uses.   Uses are the bonds of society, which are just as many as there are good uses, and the number of uses is infinite. . . Moreover, every love has its own pleasure, for by this love lives ; and the pleasure of the love of uses is heavenly pleasure, which enters succeeding pleasures in order, and according to the order of succession exalts them and makes them eternal.

"After this they enumerated the heavenly delights proceeding from the love of use, and said that they are myriads of myriads, and that they who are in heaven enter into them.   And with further discourses of wisdom on the love of uses, they passed the day with them until evening."—C. L. n. 18.

And the same thing in substance is often repeated in his writings.   In the light of these disclosures heaven is seen to be a state of intense activity.   Every angel has some useful occupation which he loves, and in the earnest pursuit of which he finds intense delight.   Without it, he could not really know what heaven is.   Its essential constituents, we are told, are love and wisdom ; but these are only ideal entities—mere abstractions— until determined toward and embodied in works.   They have no real existence but in *use*.   The angels say :

" Love and wisdom without use, are only ideas of abstract thought, which, after some stay in the mind, pass on as winds ; but these two are united in use, and there become a unit which is called a real thing.   Love cannot be easy unless it is doing, for it is the veriest active principle of life ; neither can wisdom exist and subsist except it be doing from love and with it; and doing is use. Therefore use is to do good from love by means of wisdom. Use is good itself."—C. L. n. 183.

Uses, therefore, or love and wisdom ultimated and fixed in deeds, are the essential things in God's kingdom. The angelic heaven is a kingdom of uses, and every angel is a form of some particular use. Use, moreover, is the containant of all true heavenly life, and every angel is happy according to the nature of his use, and to the affection and earnestness with which he devotes himself to it.

Such is Swedenborg's uniform teaching on this subject. Is it true? is the next and vital question to be considered.

It is generally conceded that God is the one infinite Source of life. He alone is Life Itself. And life is forever active. Life and inaction are incompatible ideas. The two cannot coexist. One forbids or dissipates the other, as surely as light disperses the darkness. God is Life, and Life is inseparable from action. Therefore He never has ceased and never can cease to work. He not only *did* create, but is forever *creating*. He not only *did* make, but is now and forever *making* men in his own image and likeness; yes, and making worlds, and fitting them for the abode and sustenance of human beings. He is everywhere and always working—always creating and preserving; for it is not in the nature of Life to cease from action. This is a central truth. As saith the incarnate Word: "My Father worketh hitherto, and I work."

Now, as He from whom creation sprang is forever

present in his own works, filling, sustaining and directing, therefore something of his own activity is stamped on all things which have been touched by his living breath, from the great orb that warms and enlightens us, down to the smallest atom that quivers in his beams. All things have an appointed use, a specific end and a determinate mode of action, because something of the Divine Love and Wisdom is in them all as their guiding and controling power. This is true of the sun's light and heat, of the air we breathe and the earth we tread, as well as of everything that lives and grows upon it. The smallest grain of dust is the containant of something of God's wisdom which directs it to its appointed goal, and of something of his love which impels it to the performance of its allotted work. And ascending to the realm of organic matter, the activity of life becomes more apparent. There is life of a low order in plants and trees; and it is ever at work there—ever busy at its appointed use. When its vital forces are so obstructed that their activity ceases in a blade of grass or the limb of a tree, straightway that blade or limb withers and dies.

Then look at animal life, especially as manifested in the higher orders. It not only courses in one continuous current through their veins and arteries, imparting health and activity to each separate organ, but it sets the whole animal in motion. Each creature has its sphere of use, and its determinate mode of action; and both its action and its use are according to the nature of its life. It must *act* as its life impels it, else it cannot enjoy its full share of happiness, health or content.

We know, too, that a certain amount of bodily exercise is indispensable to bodily health. Weakness and infirmity are the sure consequences of inaction, while exercise promotes health and vigor. And this is true alike of the whole body and each of its component parts. If any part is exercised more than the rest (provided the exercise is not carried to excess), that part is sure to outstrip the others in strength and vigor. Look at the blacksmith's brawny arm, and contrast it with that of one who has left that limb unexercised!

What, then, is the conclusion to which we are forced by the analogies of nature? Clearly this: That life in heaven must be one of intense. activity. The denizens of the celestial realms must be actively and usefully employed. Nature (and this is but the lowest plane of the Divine activity) in all her kingdoms is a vast theatre of action, and of action tending always to some useful end. Nothing is idle here; nothing stands still; nothing is inactive. Earth, sun and stars are always in motion. The air and the ocean pulsate continually. They have their tides, their eddies, and their currents, and through ceaseless activity are preserved in a salubrious condition. And the multitudinous forms of animal life all have a determinate mode of action corresponding to the nature and use of each. And not only is activity needed to the health and comfort of each, but indispensable to its complete development. And in the healthy condition of the human system, how active is every organ and every minutest part of it! Although their modes of action and the uses they severally perform are infinitely various, yet they are mutually adapted to each other, and work together in admirable harmony.

Life, then, under all its innumerable forms on earth, is forever active; and everywhere and always it has a definite mode of action corresponding to its nature or quality. Should we expect it would be less active in heaven than on earth?

But we have proof stronger than that from analogy, as well as more direct and positive. We know some of the laws that govern man's psychical nature, and some of the conditions indispensable to his happiness while in the flesh. And one is, the exercise of his mental as well as bodily powers, and their determination toward some definite object. *Activity* is inseparable from his mental constitution; and if his activity is not guided by the revealed laws of neighborly love, he will be active in doing Satan's work—active in seeking his own aggrandizement, and in cheating, robbing and spoiling others. And this misdirection of his powers brings sorrow and suffering both to himself and his neighbor.

Every one knows, too, that the idle man is never a happy man. The soul does not expand but collapses by idleness. It does not grow but withers under it. Man is not vivified but deadened by it. It is only by some kind of occupation requiring the exercise of our mental powers, that the mind is excited, vivified and delighted (C. L. 207). The most unhappy people in the world are those who have no regular occupation, and no clearly defined purpose in life.

But it is essential to our highest happiness here, not

only that we be busily but *usefully* occupied; and that
we work at our vocation from the love of serving or of
being useful. True human life everywhere has respect
to other beings outside of itself, and will ever seek to
ultimate itself in truly human acts. It is the love of
serving or doing good to others—at the same time acknowledging the Lord as the source of this love, and
of the disposition and power to do good. Because this
life is truly human, it must seek to ultimate itself in
deeds which tend to promote human welfare. If a man
really loves his neighbor, and knows how to serve and
bless him, he cannot leave the service unperformed; if
he should, his neighborly love would soon depart. True
love is ever active in doing for others. Soon as it ceases
to do—to bless—it ceases to be. The happiest people
in the world are those most actively engaged in some
useful occupation, and who work from the love of rendering themselves in the highest degree useful. These,
while on earth, enjoy a foretaste of heaven. They receive an influx of heavenly delights, just in the degree
that they use their gifts for the promotion of heavenly
ends. And on the other hand the goods and truths of
heaven with their delights, are lost or taken away if *not*
used for the benefit of the neighbor. The Lord plainly
teaches this in the parable of the talents. They who
used what was committed to them, gained thereby other
talents, and were pronounced " good and faithful servants " worthy of an entrance into the joy of their
Lord; while he who hid his talent, or neglected to use
it, lost through such neglect what was committed to
him, and was declared a wicked and slothful servant,
worthy only to be cast into " the outer darkness."

This, then, is an everlasting law—a law to which angels in heaven and men on earth are alike subject—that
the rich treasures of the heart are increased by being
used, and diminished if not used. Nothing is more certain than this. The more we exercise patience, the more
patient we become. The more we *do* justly, the more
are our hearts imbued with the love of justice. The
more scrupulously we obey the laws of the heavenly
life, the more delight do we find in obeying them, and
the more do we receive of the spirit of those laws. The
more faithfully and unselfishly we devote ourselves to
any worthy cause or useful calling—the more we give
of affection and thought and study and effort to the upbuilding of God's kingdom, the more is our affection for
the things of that kingdom strengthened, our capacity
for receiving them enlarged, and the freer and more
abundant is their influx. Agreeable to these words of
the Lord: " Give, and it shall be given unto you." Give
love and sympathy, and your love and sympathy will
increase. Give patience and kindness and tenderness and
generosity, and you will receive a larger measure of
these same graces. Exercise courage, and you will grow
more courageous. Do justly, and your sense of justice
will become keener and your love of justice stronger.
Practice the laws of the heavenly life, and fresh increments of that life and clearer views of its laws will flow
into your soul day by day. The more you do to enlighten and purify and bless others, the more of the light
and purity and unselfish devotion of heaven will be
poured into you from on high. As saith the incarnate
Word: " For unto every one that hath shall be given,

and he shall have abundance;" and "with what measure ye mete, it shall be measured to you again." There can be no reception of the heavenly life, without the giving, or the *effort* to give, of this same life,—that is, without the exercise of the heavenly graces; and the exercise of these involves the performance of heavenly uses.

Thus do reason, analogy, human experience and Sacred Scripture unite to prove that the denizens of heaven must be actively employed; and since they are all human, their employments must be human. They must be such employments as are suitable to human beings— such as proceed from and agree with true human love. But there is in heaven as on earth an endless diversity of character and state. Therefore we should expect an endless variety of occupations there as here. We should expect societies and individuals to have such occupations as correspond to their different states. Accordingly Swedenborg says:

"The employments of heaven are innumerable, and various according to the offices of the societies. Every society performs a peculiar office; for as the societies are distinct according to goods, so are they also according to uses, since goods with all in heaven are goods in act, which are uses. Every one there performs a use, for the kingdom of the Lord is a kingdom of uses.

"There are, in heaven as on earth, various administrations; for there are ecclesiastical affairs, civil affairs and domestic affairs.

"Ecclesiastical affairs in heaven are under the charge of those who, when in the world, loved the Word and earnestly sought for the truths which it contains, not for the sake of honor or gain but for the sake of the use of life, both their own and others. These are in illustration and in the light of wisdom in heaven according to their love and desire of use ; for they come into that light in heaven from the Word, which is not natural there as in the world, but spiritual. These perform the office of preachers.

" Civil affairs are administered by those who, while in the world, loved their country and its general good in preference to their own ; and did what is just and right from the love of justice and rectitude. Such men possess capacity for administering offices in heaven in proportion as their love of rectitude has prompted them to inquire into the laws of justice, and thence to become intelligent. The offices which they administer correspond exactly to the degree of their intelligence ; and their intelligence is then in like degree also with their love of use for the general good."—H. H. n. 387, '8, '93.

But employments in heaven are not the same as they are on earth. Here they are for the most part natural ; but in heaven they are altogether spiritual. And between natural and spiritual employments there is a correspondence like that between body and soul.

" The correspondence of natural with spiritual things, or of the world with heaven, is effected by uses, and uses conjoin them ; and the forms with which uses are clothed, are correspondences and mediums of conjunction in proportion as they are forms of use. . . The actions of man are uses in form, and are correspondences whereby he is conjoined to heaven, so far as he lives according to divine order.

" Every one in heaven is in his work according to correspondence ; and the correspondence is not with the work, but with the use of every work. He in heaven who is in an employment or work corresponding to his use, is in a state of life exactly like that in which he was in the world,—for what is spiritual and what is natural act as one by correspondence,—but with this difference: that he is in more interior delight, because in spiritual life which is interior life, and hence more receptive of heavenly blessedness."—H. H. n. 112, 394.

The employments of heaven exceed those of this world in number and variety as much as the denizens of heaven outnumber those of earth. The nature of some of them may be inferred from what is said of the various administrations there; and some are specifically mentioned.

"There are societies whose employments consist in taking care of infants; there are other societies whose employments are to instruct and educate them as they grow up; others who in like manner instruct and educate boys and girls who are of a good disposition from education in the world, and who thence come into heaven; others who teach the simple good from the Christian world, and lead them in the way to heaven; others who perform the same office for the various Gentile nations; others who defend novitiate spirits,—those who have recently come from the world,—from infestations by evil spirits; some who are attendant on those in the lower earth; some who are present with those in hell, and restrain them from tormenting each other beyond the prescribed limits; and some who attend upon those who are being raised from the dead.

"In general, angels of every society are sent to men, that they may guard them, and withdraw them from evil affections and consequent evil thoughts, and inspire them with good affections so far as they receive them freely. By means of these affections also they rule the deeds or works of men, removing from them evil intentions as far as possible. . . . But all these employments of the angels are functions performed by the Lord through them; for they perform them not from themselves, but from the Lord.

" These employments of the angels are their general employments. But to each one is assigned his particular use; for every general use is composed of innumerable others which are called mediate, ministering and subservient uses."—H. H. n. 391.

In heaven as on earth some employments are superior to others in point of dignity and importance; but no one there arrogates to himself the dignity, or thinks himself superior to others because of the superiority of his use. Personally the angels are all on a level; and they never think of the honor and dignity of any use as belonging to themselves, but to the Lord alone, from whom comes all their love of use, and their ability and skill in its performance.

" The wiser angels take charge of those things belonging to the general good or use; and the less wise, of such as relate to particular goods or uses; and so on. They are subordinated just as in divine order uses are subordinated. Hence also dignity is attached to every employment according to the dignity of the use. No angel, however, arrogates the dignity to himself, but ascribes it all to the use. And because use is the good which he performs, and all good is from the Lord, therefore he ascribes it all to the Lord. Wherefore he who thinks of honor for himself and thence for use, and not for use and thence for himself, cannot perform any office in heaven; for he looks backward from the Lord, regarding himself in the first place and use in the second. When use is spoken of, the Lord also is meant; because use is good, and good is from the Lord.

" From these considerations it may be inferred what

subordinations in the heavens are ; namely, that as every one loves, esteems and honors use, so also he loves, esteems and honors the person to whom that use is adjoined ; and also that the person is loved, esteemed and honored in the degree that he does not ascribe the use to himself, but to the Lord ; for in that degree he is wise, and the uses which he performs are performed from a principle of good.

"Spiritual love, esteem and honor are nothing else than the love, esteem and honor of use in the person who performs it ; and the honor of the person is from the use, and not that of the use from the person. He also who regards men from spiritual truth, regards them in no other way ; for he sees that one man is like another, whether he be in great dignity or in little ; that they differ only in wisdom, and that wisdom consists in loving use, and thus in loving the good of a fellow-citizen, of society, of the country and of the church. In this also consists love to the Lord, because all good which is the good of use, is from the Lord ; and love toward the neighbor also, because the neighbor is the good which is to be loved in a fellow-citizen, society, the country and the church, and which is to be done to them."—H. H. n. 389, '90.

Look, now, at the practical bearing of this teaching. What kind of influence is it calculated to exert on the lives of those who accept it? The teaching briefly summarized, is: That the kingdom of heaven is a kingdom of uses, and every dweller therein is a form of use ; that no one can experience the delights of heaven, until there is developed in him a genuine love of use ; that the heavenly inhabitants are all actively employed, each in that particular use which he loves and is constitutionally fitted to perform best ; that their innumerable

29 *

employments are all human—all answering the demands of true human love, and tending to the advancement of human happiness; that every angel does his appointed work, not from any selfish end, but from the exquisite delight he finds in rendering useful service; and that the higher the use, and the purer the love that one carries into its performance, and the more earnestly he devotes himself to it, the more exalted and abundant is his happiness.

Now, take this doctrine along with that other, that each one carries his own life with him into the other world, and what is the conclusion?　Why, that every person who would enter heaven, must first become a form of use in the kingdom of God; for such are all the angels. He must diligently cultivate, and to some extent acquire while here on earth, the love of use.　Every believer will, therefore, seek to know what his peculiar powers of body and mind qualify him to do best; and that he will do, thinking less of personal reward than of the use, and trying to work from a love of this latter.　Thus will he consecrate to USE—or, what is equivalent, to the service of God—all his powers of body and mind.　He will study to learn the highest use of them all, and will regard himself merely as a steward bound to use his Master's goods in a manner most agreeable to his Master's will.　He will not be idle, but an earnest worker.　He will not ask, What shall *I* gain by doing this or that? but Will it be *useful?*—will it benefit the church, the community, the country, or mankind?　He will not inquire, What occupation will bring me most of honor or emolument, but what one do my gifts of body and mind qualify me to perform best? For he will see that every occupation which is useful, is honorable and praiseworthy in the sight of God, so it be honorably performed.

And since God intended that all men should be brethren, therefore there is a mutual dependence and a bond of brotherhood among the innumerable occupations of men, from that of the monarch on his throne or the president in his chair of state, down to the humble scavenger and sable chimney-sweep. They are all fraternally allied—bound together like the innumerable parts of the human body. Therefore every one who labors faithfully in his calling, should be respected in his use and according to his use.

The belief has been entertained even by professed Christians, that labor is a curse inflicted on mankind as a penalty for the transgression of the first human pair; and the *literal* sense of the Bible favors this idea. Hence the conclusion, that in heaven there can be nothing in the nature of work, since the curse must there be removed. Hence also the idea, hitherto prevalent even in Christian lands, that there is something degrading and servile in work; and that they are the special favorites of heaven, whose circumstances relieve them from the necessity of doing any kind of work,—as if idleness were bliss.

With all such fantasies the doctrine revealed through Swedenborg is seen to be directly at war. Its obvious tendency is to exalt and dignify all useful labor; to make industry everywhere honorable, idleness everywhere contemptible. It shows us that persons who neither have nor desire any useful work, are living a life far removed from that of heaven ; and unless they change their course, and try to be of some use in the world, they will never reach the abodes of the blessed. And on the other hand it shows us that all who devote themselves to some useful occupation, and endeavor to discharge its duties with religious fidelity, are laying up for themselves treasures in heaven. They are offering to God the most acceptable worship; for how can we more truly glorify our Father in the heavens, than by diligently occupying ourselves about our Father's business?—employing the powers bestowed by Him, in serving and blessing our fellow men?—*working* under the promptings of his unselfish love, and the guiding light of his revealed wisdom? "*Herein* is my Father glorified, that ye bear much fruit." This—the faithful performance of uses from the love of use—is regarded in heaven as the truest worship.

"The real worship of the Lord," says Swedenborg, "consists in performing uses; and uses consist, during a man's life in the world, in every one discharging aright his function in his respective station; thus in serving his country, society, and his neighbor, from the heart, and in acting with sincerity in all his associations, and in performing duties prudently according to the quality of each. These uses are principally the exercises of charity, and those whereby the Lord is principally worshiped. Frequenting the temple, hearing sermons, and saying prayers are also necessary things; but without the above uses they avail nothing, for they are not of the life, but teach what the quality of the life should be. The angels in heaven have all happiness from uses and according to uses, insomuch that uses are to them heaven."—A. C. n. 7038.

Can we conceive of any doctrine more wholesome in its tendency, or more eminently practical, than this? It points us to a life of active, faithful, self-forgetting service, as the sure pathway to the realms of bliss; and tells us that all who hope to enter there, must begin on earth to tread this pathway,—begin here to become forms of use in the kingdom of God, as all the angels are. It adds new meaning and emphasis to the words of one of our poets:

> " *Work*—and thou shalt bless the day
>   Ere the toil be done;—
> They that work not cannot play,
>   Cannot feel the sun.
> God is living, working still;
>   All things work and move;
> Work, wouldst thou their beauty feel,
>   And thy Maker's love."

And affirms, as an absolute certainty, the reasonable conclusion of another, who sings so sweetly the truth which every gifted child of song cannot fail to see—

> " Surely there must be work to do in heaven,
>   Since work is the best thing on earth we know;
> Life were but tasteless bread, without this leaven—
>   A draught from some dead river's overflow.
>   .   .   .   .
> " Work is the holiest thing in earth or heaven:
>   To lift from souls the sorrow and the curse—
> This dear employment must to us be given
>   While there is want in God's great universe.
>
> " There must be work for us to do in heaven,
>   Else that were a less blessed place than this:
> The worthiest impulse to our earth-life given,
>   Must still be felt amid celestial bliss." *

---

* Lucy Larcom in the *Christian Union* for Oct. 9, 1884.

Let this New doctrine concerning life in heaven be generally accepted, and become thoroughly imbedded in the popular mind and heart, and what a stupendous change in human society would speedily be wrought! Heaven brought down to earth! The Father's will done here below, as it is done in the realms above! What activity, contentment, abundance, harmony, peace and joy would be here! Millions of human beings all praising God by the diligent and loving performance of uses, in the blessings of which all alike are sharers!

Look at the doctrine in a practical point of view, and see if it be not worthy the high origin claimed for it. Consider what must be its legitimate fruits, and judge it by this divine standard; "for every tree is known by its own fruit." Surely a doctrine, the obvious tendency of which is so good and wholesome, cannot be false, nor can it have emanated from the darkness of the abyss. For it bears upon its front the very signet of God, the impress of his unfathomable love.

XXVII.

THE THREE HEAVENS, AND HOW RELATED.

THE great merit of Swedenborg's pneumatology, and that which entitles it to the serious consideration of all thoughtful people, is, that it is based on the essential nature of the human soul. It is a legitimate outgrowth, as we have shown in the previous chapters, from the known laws of our mental and moral constitution. And since these laws are all God's own, and as eternal and unchangeable as Himself, therefore any system of pneumatology founded upon them, is founded upon the Rock of Ages, and will endure forever. On the other hand, any system which is not so based, or is not the normal outgrowth from our human nature, however beautiful it may be as a fancy sketch, rests on a sandy foundation, and sooner or later is sure to be rejected.

We have seen all along how intimately the whole economy of the spiritual world as revealed through Swedenborg, links itself with all that is known of man's spiritual and immortal part. We have seen that his disclosures concerning the essential nature of heaven, its form or order, its social arrangements, its employments, the personal appearance of its denizens, etc., are in strict accord both with the revealed laws of the heavenly life and the implanted instincts and potencies of our human nature. We have seen that, through the operation of the heavenly life within, the reported order, beauty and perfection of the heaven without, unfold themselves as naturally and necessarily as the plant unfolds itself from the seed or the flower from the bud under the influence of a vernal sun. And this becomes more apparent and striking the farther we push our inquiries into the abodes of the blessed as unveiled by the Swedish sage.

We come now to consider that trinal distinction of the angelic heavens of which Swedenborg so often speaks, to inquire into the grounds and origin of that distinction, and endeavor to ascertain if it has any solid or scientific basis; in other words, to inquire whether his alleged disclosure on this point is true.

Since the Lord alone is Life, and the only source of life to angels and men, therefore He is the all-in-all of heaven. But in Him there exists a trinal distinction— a trinity of divine *essentials*. These are, Divine Love, Divine Wisdom, and Divine Operation; called by Swedenborg the Essential Divine, the Divine Human, and the Divine Proceeding; and referred to in the New Testament by the terms Father, Son, and Holy Spirit. We have a good illustration of this Divine Trinity in the natural sun, the three essentials of which are heat, light, and their proceeding operation. These three are united in the sun, and are its *essentials;* for neither of them can exist apart from the other two. This illustration is perfect; for the sun's heat corresponds to the Divine Love, its light to the Divine Wisdom, and their joint operation to the sphere of the Divine Activity, or the proceeding influence of the Lord's love and wisdom.

And as man was created in the Divine image and likeness, therefore there must be in him a trinal distinction imaging, in some degree at least, the trinity in God. There being a manifest trine of *essentials* in the Divine Being from whom is all our life, there must of necessity be three discrete degrees of life in the soul which is the real man. And as the kingdom of heaven is within, it follows that there must be in general three heavens separated by discrete degrees. These are, we are told— and this is precisely as it should be—related like end, cause, and effect, or like Love, Wisdom, and Operation (or Use) in the Lord. And every man after death enters that particular heaven which has been previously opened and formed in him; for every one then comes into the state of his interiors, or into the enjoyment of just that kind of life which agrees with the kind of truth he had received and religiously obeyed. If only the lowest form of truth has been received, and the lowest degree of his mind opened, he enters the first or lowest heaven. If the second degree of his mind has been opened, he enters the middle or second heaven. And if the third degree has been opened, he enters the third or highest heaven.

Thus the heaven which each one will enter after death, will depend upon the kind or degree of life to which he has attained, or upon the heaven which has been opened and formed within him during his sojourn on earth. He cannot then receive and appropriate a higher degree of life, and therefore cannot enter any higher heaven. And in any lower heaven his measure or degree of life would not be full.

We thus see that the existence of three angelic heavens in general (there are innumerable societies in each of these heavens), follows as a logical conclusion from the existence of three degrees of life in man. And these degrees exist from the trinity in God, in whose image and likeness, the Scripture tells us, man was originally created. Many passages might be cited from Swedenborg in confirmation of what we have here said; but the following are sufficient:

"There are three heavens quite distinct from each other; the inmost or third, the middle or second, and the ultimate or first. They follow in order and are mutually related like the highest part of man, which is called the head; his middle, which is the body; and the lowest, which is the feet. . . The Divine which proceeds and descends from the Lord is also in similar order. Therefore, from the necessity of order, heaven is three-fold.

"The interiors of man are also in similar order. He has an inmost, a middle and an ultimate. For when man was created all things of divine order were collated into him, so that he was made divine order in form, and thence a heaven in miniature. For this reason also he communicates with the heavens as to his interiors, and comes among the angels after death; among those of the inmost, middle or lowest heaven, according to his reception of divine good and truth from the Lord during his life in the world.

"It is to be carefully noted that the interiors of the angels are what determine their situation in one or the other of these heavens; for the more their interiors are open to the Lord, the more interior is the heaven in which they dwell. There are three degrees of the interiors with every one, whether angel, spirit or man. They with whom the third degree is open, are in the inmost heaven; they with whom the second degree is open, are in the middle heaven; and they with whom only the first degree is open, are in the lowest heaven.

"The interiors are opened by the reception of divine good and divine truth. They who are affected with divine truths, and admit them immediately into the life, that is, into the will and thence into act, are in the inmost or third heaven, and are situated in that heaven according to their reception of good from the affection of truth. But they who do not admit them immediately into the will, but into the memory and thence into the understanding, and from that will and do them, are in the middle or second heaven. While they who live a moral life, and believe in a Divine Being, and care but little about being instructed, are in the lowest or first heaven.

" Hence it may be manifest that the states of the interiors make heaven, and that heaven is within every one and not without him; as the Lord also teaches (Luke xvii. 20, 21).

" All perfection also increases toward the interiors and decreases toward the exteriors; because interior things are nearer the Divine, and in themselves purer; but exterior things are more remote from the Divine, and in themselves grosser. . . Since the interiors of the angels of the inmost heaven are open to the third degree, therefore their perfection immensely surpasses that of the angels of the middle heaven, whose interiors are open to the second degree. In like manner the perfection of the angels of the middle heaven surpasses that of the angels of the ultimate heaven."—H. H. n. 29–34.

" It is known that there are three heavens, the inmost, the middle and the ultimate, or the third, the second and the first: all those heavens were represented by the tabernacle. . . The reason why there are three heavens is, that there are three degrees of life in man (for man who becomes an angel after death, constitutes heaven, nor have the angels or the heavens any other origin); the inmost degree of his life is for the inmost heaven; the middle degree of life for the middle heaven; and the ultimate for the ultimate heaven. And since man is such, or so formed, and heaven is from the human race, therefore there are three heavens. Those degrees of life in man are opened successively; the first degree by a life according to what is equitable and just; the second degree by a life according to the truths of faith from the Word, and according to the goods of charity toward the neighbor thence; and the third degree according to the good of mutual love, and the good of love to the Lord: these are the means whereby are successively opened those three degrees of life in man, thus the three heavens in him.

"But it is to be known that so far as man recedes from good of life, and accedes to evil of life, so far these degrees are closed, that is, so far the heavens in him are closed; for as the good of life opens them, so evil of life closes them: hence it is, that all who are in evil are out of heaven, that is, in hell. And since the heavens in man are successively opened according to the good of his life, as was said above, it is to be known that, on this account, in some the first heaven is opened and not the second, and in some the second heaven is opened and not the third; and that the third heaven is opened in those only, who are in good of life from love to the Lord."—A. C. n. 9594. See also A. C. n. 1642, '7, 3691, 5145, 9825, 10,130. D. L. W. n. 202, 236–9. Influx n. 16.

We have said that the three angelic heavens are related to each other like the head, trunk and extremities of the human body. The same is said in one of the above extracts; and in D. L. W. n. 202, that "the thoughts of the angels of the highest or third heaven are thoughts of ends, and the thoughts of those of the middle or second heaven are thoughts of causes, and the thoughts of those of the lowest or first heaven are thoughts of effects;" thus showing the three heavens to be related like end, cause and effect.

Now if the doctrine concerning the human form of heaven as developed in a previous chapter, be true, it follows as a logical sequence that there must be in general three heavens related like head, trunk and extremities. Otherwise the whole heaven would not be in the human form, that is, not in true human order. The head is not only the highest part of the body, but is in every respect superior to the other parts. It is the part in which are located the organs of sense, whereby the bodily movements are determined and the physical life preserved. Thus, in relation to the other parts of the body, the head is the supreme, guiding and directing organ. Hence in every larger or collective man, it is usual to hear the supreme and directing power called the head. A military general is called the head of the army because he plans and directs its movements. So a king or president, with his constitutional advisers, is called the head of the government; and his cabinet officers are called the heads of the several departments of the government. The principal teacher in a school is the head of the school; the best scholar in a class is the head of his class; the chief owner and director of a factory or mercantile firm, is the head of the establishment.

Thus, in every association or corporate body the member which is invested with, or acknowledged as having, the right to direct, is called the head. And the fact of his being a governing or directing member, implies that he is *in ends*, or in the thought of ends. And Swedenborg tells us that the angels of the highest or third heaven, who constitute the head of the Grand Man, are in the thought of ends.

But what can the head of an individual do without the body and extremities? The body serves as the means, and the extremities are the servants or operatives. Thus the head, through the intermediate agency of the trunk, sets the extremities in motion, and thereby accomplishes the ends at which it aims. The body or trunk, therefore, viewed in relation to the head, is seen to be a means or secondary cause ; and the act of the extremities, through this means, under the direction of the head, is the effect. Accordingly Swedenborg says that the angels of the second heaven, who form as it were the trunk of the Grand Man, are *in causes*, or in the thought of causes ; and that the first or lowest heaven, who constitute the extremities of the Grand Man, are *in effects*, or in the thought of effects.

We thus see that the three heavens, connected like the head, trunk and extremities of the human body, and really constituting these parts of the Grand Man respectively, are also related like end, cause and effect, —the angels of the highest heaven being more especially in ends, those of the middle heaven in causes, and those of the lowest in effects. And every individual viewed spiritually, is a miniature of the Grand Man, and therefore embodies in himself the same trine of end, cause and effect. He *aims* to do something—the *end*. He thinks of *how* he shall do it—the *cause*. And the act when *done*, is the *effect*.

But let us pursue our inquiry a step further, and notice the beautiful and striking correspondence between these three parts of the body and the three angelic heavens.

Looking at the parts more interiorly, we find that the principal contents of the head are the brain, which is the most refined, delicate and sensitive of all the bodily tissues. It is the seat of sensation, motion and life. It is the great centre of the nervous system, under whose vital influence or direction as it were, digestion, nutrition, circulation, and all the functions of the animal economy are carried on. Next in rank and office are the viscera of the thorax and abdomen, embracing the whole respiratory, circulatory, digestive and nutritive apparatus. These are less delicate in their structure than the brain, and endowed, so to speak, with a lower degree of life. They include, however, all the *means* whereby, under the direction of the brain and nervous system, the various tissues are supplied with their appropriate nourishment and sustained in healthy action. But the extremities are still lower in rank, farther removed from the centre of life, less refined and less delicate in their structure. They consist for the most part of coarser and harder materials, such as bones, muscles and cartilages—yet all admirably adapted to the uses they were intended to perform.

Now, corresponding precisely to these relative degrees of vitality, refinement, delicacy of structure, etc., in the principal constituents of these three parts of the body, are the relative degrees of life enjoyed by the angels of the three heavens, according to Swedenborg's disclosures. For he says that the angels of the third or highest heaven, who are also the most interior, are the most innocent and perfect, and in the highest degree of life, because spiritually nearest the Lord, the Fountain of life—that is, most like Him; that the angels of the middle heaven who are less interior, are in a lower degree of good and truth, less perfect, and farther removed from the Lord; and that those of the lowest heaven who are in the most external state, are still more remote from the Lord, thus in a lower degree of good and truth, and less perfect. All of which agrees with the universal law announced in these words, and often repeated by Swedenborg:

"All perfection increases toward the interiors, because interior beings are nearer the Divine and in themselves purer; but exterior things are more remote from the Divine, and in themselves grosser."—H. H. 34. See also A. C. 1799, 3405, 5146, '7.

It will be noticed, too, that Swedenborg's disclosures on this subject are in perfect agreement with the apostle Paul's testimony. For in one of his letters to the Corinthian church he says: "I will come to visions and revelations of the Lord. I knew a man in Christ about fourteen years ago (whether in the body I cannot tell, or whether out of the body I cannot tell: God knoweth): such an one caught up to the *third heaven.* And I knew such a man . . how that he was caught up into paradise, and heard unspeakable words which it is not *possible* (οὐx ἐξόν—see Schleusner's Greek and Latin Lexicon) for a man to utter" (2 Cor. xii. 1–4).

All Christians, therefore, who regard the testimony of the great apostle as credible, must believe that there are at least *three* heavens. And we may remark in passing, that Swedenborg's pneumatology shows us *how* Paul was caught up to the third heaven. It was not by any elevation through natural space, for heaven is not to be approached in that way; but by the opening of the third or highest degree of his mind, together with the spiritual senses belonging to that degree. In this way he had a vision of things in the inmost or third heaven, not knowing whether he was in the body or out of it. And his testimony in regard to the unspeakable words he heard, "which it is not possible for a man to utter," is in perfect agreement with Swedenborg's revealings. Concerning the speech of spirits and angels, he says:

"The speech of angelic spirits is incomprehensible. . . But the speech of angels is ineffable, far above that of spirits because above that of angelic spirits, and not at all intelligible to man so long as he lives in the body.

"The speech of the celestial angels [those of the third heaven] is distinct from that of the spiritual angels, and is still more ineffable and inexpressible. . . It is much more full and abundant, for they are in the very fountains and origins of the life of thought and speech."— A. C. n. 143, '5, '7.

But every angelic society, we are told, when viewed collectively, appears in the human form, which is the form of the whole heaven; "because, in the most perfect form which is the form of heaven, the parts bear a likeness to the whole, and the least reflects the greatest." Consistently with this, therefore, there should be a trine in each of the angelic heavens, and in each angelic society, simulating the three-fold division of the whole heaven. Accordingly Swedenborg says:

"That there are three heavens, is a known thing; consequently three degrees of goods and truths there. Every heaven also is distinguished into three degrees, for its inmost must communicate immediately with what is superior, its external with what is inferior; and the middle thus, by means of the inmost and the external, with both; hence is its perfection. The case is similar with the interiors of man, which in general are distinguished into three degrees, viz., celestial, spiritual and natural ; in like manner each of these into its three degrees ; for the man who is in the good of faith and love to the Lord, is a heaven in the least form corresponding to the greatest ; so in all things of nature. . . Hence it is that *three* in the Word signifies what is complete from beginning to end."—A. C. n. 9825. Also A. R. 876.

" All in heaven are collected into societies, and the societies exist in vast numbers, and each society in its own place forms three heavens."—L. J. n. 27.

And this, again, may be seen beautifully illustrated in the human body, the visible image of the order of heaven. For every muscle in the body is a bundle of fibres, and each of these fibres is a collection of smaller threads or fibrillæ. Every nerve is a collection of filaments, each of which is a collection of still smaller fibres. Every gland is a congregation of smaller glands, and each of these a conglobation of others still more minute. And the same three-foldness exists throughout all the kingdoms of nature. First, we have matter existing under three distinct forms, viz., solids, liquids, and gases— earth, water, and air—separated from each other by a discrete degree. Then there are the three natural kingdoms, mineral, vegetable, and animal. And each of these, again, is tri-partite. The animal kingdom is distinguished into beasts, birds, and fishes, corresponding to the three forms under which matter is known to exist, and respectively inhabiting the three elements, earth, air, and water. And in the vegetable kingdom we have grasses, shrubs, and trees, separated also by discrete degrees. And if we descend from generals to particulars, we shall everywhere find the same three-fold order ; for

the order as well as the things of heaven, are distinctly
imaged in things of earth.

"Everything in the world," says Swedenborg, "possessing the three dimensions, or called composite, is
constituted of discrete degrees." And "although the
progress of end, cause, and effect, is by discrete degrees,
yet of these degrees little or nothing is known in the
world."—D. L. W. n. 189, '90.

But if the three angelic heavens exist in accordance
with the eternal laws of divine order, having their foundation, as we have said, in the constitution of the human
soul, why, it will be asked, do we not see some illustration of this doctrine in the social or collective as well
as in the individual man here on earth? There can be
no law of human nature so deeply implanted as to determine the angelic heavens into one or another form,
which does not manifest itself with greater or less distinctness in this natural sphere. The veil of flesh which
is here thrown over the spirit, is not sufficient to hide
any of its deep-seated laws or fixed determinations.
The same law which draws angels of like character into
the same heavenly society, determines people everywhere
on earth to seek the companionship of those most like
themselves. And so with all biological laws. They
exist and are alike operative in both worlds, the natural
and the spiritual. Not more certainly does the form of
the eagle while yet unfledged and in its shell, point to
the future destiny of the bird and the element in which
it is to move, than do the laws and tendencies of our
human nature as manifested in the flesh, point to the
general order and arrangement of that world which is to
be our final home.

What is there, then, in the larger or collective man, in the arrangements of human society here on earth, that foreshadows the trinal order of the angelic heavens? If we look at bodies of people, such as kingdoms, states, towns, or smaller companies organized for the performance of some special use, what do we see?   In the most advanced civilization (for it is here that we are to look for the fullest development and best illustration of biological laws) we see in all these organized bodies, three distinct classes operating in as many distinct spheres, and requiring, for the due performance of their respective duties, different kinds of knowledge, or different orders of natural truth, yet all working together simultaneously, the will and wisdom of each uniting with that of the others in the final result.   These three classes are the principals, the agents, and the operatives.   The principals are in the thought of *ends*.   They have the direction, decide what shall be done, and set the others to doing it.   Thus they represent the head, and afford an illustration of the third or highest heaven whose denizens are in ends, or in the thought of ends.   The agents are in the thought of means or causes.   They know how the intention of the principals is to be executed.   They know what to do, and how to do it, in order that the end aimed at may be accomplished.   Thus they represent the trunk, and afford an illustration of the middle heaven whose denizens are said to be in causes, or the thought of causes.   And the operatives are in the thought of effects.   Their knowledge is more limited than that of the others—limited to doing, or knowing *how* to do, what their superiors direct.   They are mere obediences

—instruments in the hands of others. Thus they represent the extremities, the hands and feet, which are moved by the body under the direction of the head; and they are as necessary to the completeness of this larger or collective man, as the hands and feet are to the completeness of the individual. We have in this class, therefore, an illustration of the first or lowest heaven, whose denizens are described by Swedenborg as mere " obediences," and are said to be in the thought of effects.

To see how naturally and necessarily people arrange themselves into this triple order in an advanced state of society, we will take a case by way of illustration. Let us look at a country as a single individual in larger form. A government is therein instituted for a definite purpose. And when duly organized and its machinery is in successful operation, what do we find? One class of men whose special function it is to conceive, plan and direct in the affairs of state, and who therefore constitute its head. And in well-organized governments this head must consist of a deliberative and an executive department—a law-making and a law-executing power —functions corresponding perfectly to those of the cerebrum and cerebellum in the head of every individual. This head of the government or state, too, is in the thought of ends. It conceives, plans, points out, directs. It decides what the country will do; when it will go to war and when make peace; when and where it will purchase or sell territory; what foreign nations it will hold intercourse with, and what it will not; when and where it will erect fortifications, improve harbors, construct lighthouses, negotiate treaties, make internal improvements, etc., etc. It is this organized head, therefore, which sets the country in motion, and decides what it shall do. Thus it is manifestly in *ends*.

Next to the head or supreme class in this organized body, the state, we have another class who act as agents. They do not consider the wisdom or expediency of what the head decides to do. This is no part of their business. Therefore they have no need of the knowledge requisite for settling such questions. But they know how to execute the intentions of those above them— how to accomplish the objects at which the head aims. They consist of all those officials who are appointed as agents in executing the designs of government, such as postmasters, collectors of customs, civil engineers, army and navy officers, superintendents of national works, etc. This class are obviously in the thought of causes or means, having the knowledge of *how* to accomplish the ends which their superiors (the head) conceive and desire.

But this class of officials do not perform the manual labor that is necessary before the intentions of the head are ultimated. They do not sort, stamp and distribute the letters; they do not weigh, gauge and measure the imports; they do not carry the chain, arrows, compass, or theodolite; they do not shoulder the musket nor wheel the artillery; they do not handle the brick or trowel. But another class come in here, whose knowledge is more limited than that of either of the other two, and who are, therefore, lower in the scale of natural intelligence. They have not that reach of mental vision which belongs to the first or highest class, nor that su-

perintending and commanding talent, or that engineering
knowledge and skill which belong to the second class.
They do not know why a country needs a fortress here
or there, nor have they the knowledge or skill in military fortifications, which would qualify them to superin-
tend its construction. They are mere artisans, with less
of mental (but possibly more of physical) ability than
either of the other classes. Though unable to plan or
engineer a fortification, they understand masonry and
can lay brick and stone better than either of the classes
above them.

And so with all the operatives who perform the work
assigned them by the agents of government in each of
its several departments. They are verily the *hands* of
this organic body, which, set at work and directed by
the intermediate class or *trunk*, execute the plans which
the *head* conceives and desires to have executed. And
the work when completed is the product of the joint
labor of these three classes who sustain to each other
the relation of principals, agents, and operatives—highest, middle, and lowest—head, trunk, and extremities—
end, cause, and effect. And as the end flows through
the cause into the effect (which is the everlasting law of
influx), or as the head, by means of the body, puts the
extremities in motion, so this first class, by means of the
second, set the third or operatives at work; and the
combined knowledge and labors of the three are exhibited in the final result, which is the ultimate.

And wherever, in an advanced stage of society, a
work of any magnitude is to be done—as the construction of a railroad, the building of a ship, the erection

of a temple or factory—the whole body of men engaged
in it, will always be found distributed into three classes
holding to each other the relation of end, cause, and
effect. Which shows that the trinal distinction of the
angelic heavens as disclosed by Swedenborg, is no fanciful or arbitrary division, but one founded on the very
constitution of the human soul, and growing legitimately
out of it. As there is a trinal distinction in the Divine
Being, and three degrees of life in every soul, related
like end, cause, and effect, so we find in every larger or
collective man on earth, three corresponding degrees
similarly related. The conclusion, therefore, seems easy
and natural—yea, irresistible—that there must be three
discrete degrees of life in heaven, consequently three
heavens; and three discrete degrees of good and truth
in the Sacred Scripture, suited to the wants or states of
these three heavens respectively. So solid and secure
is the foundation on which this doctrine of the three
angelic heavens rests.

XXVIII.

ETERNAL PROGRESS IN HEAVEN.

THAT change of mind and heart whereby a man is
delivered from the bondage of selfish and worldly
loves, and brought under the dominion of love to the
Lord and the neighbor, is called regeneration. It is
the soul's birth into a higher life, even the heavenly.
It is not, however, a sudden but a gradual and progres-

sive change, like all truly divine operations. It goes on during the whole period of man's pilgrimage on earth. "There is," says Swedenborg, "no determinate period of a man's regeneration, in which he may say, 'now I am perfect;' for there are innumerable states of evil and falsity with every man . . . all of which must be so entirely shaken off as to no longer appear." (A. C. n. 894.) And it is clear that these states cannot be all changed in a moment. Selfishness cannot be eradicated or thoroughly subdued, and disinterested love implanted in the heart, in an hour. Character is neither formed nor changed suddenly. It is a thing of slow and gradual growth, like the progress from infancy to manhood. The kingdom of heaven cannot be instantly established and built up in any soul. It is always exceeding small at first—like a grain of mustard seed; but it *grows* until it becomes a tree, so that the birds may build their nests in the branches thereof. It is subject to the same divine law that governs all living things—the law of development, growth, progress.

And here the question naturally arises, Does this law of progress exist in heaven as well as on earth? Is there with the angels anything in the nature of spiritual improvement or growth?—Anything like a progressive advancement toward higher and more perfect states of life? The following is Swedenborg's answer to this question:

"Regeneration, or the implantation of heavenly life in man, commences from his infancy and continues even to the close of life in this world, and after death it goes on perfecting forever; and what is a secret, man's

31 *

regeneration in the world is only a plane for the perfecting of his life to eternity."—A. C. n. 9334.

"The arcana of regeneration are innumerable and scarcely at all known to man; for the man who is principled in good, is reborn every moment from his earliest infancy to the last period of his life in the world, and afterwards to eternity."—Ibid. 5202.

"The angels are being continually perfected by the Lord; yet they can never be perfected to such a degree that their wisdom and intelligence can be compared with the divine wisdom and intelligence of the Lord."—Ibid. 4295.

"While the church is being established in man, he is in truths, and by means of them good grows; but when established, he is then in good, and from good in truths which in this case grow continually. The growth is, indeed, small during his life in the world, because obstructed by cares for food and raiment and other things; but in the other life it is immense, and this perpetually to eternity; for the wisdom which is from the Divine has no end. Thus the angels and all who become angels when they come into the other life, are perfecting continually; for everything of wisdom is of infinite extension, and the things of wisdom are infinite in number; hence it may be clearly seen that wisdom is capable of growth to eternity."—Ibid. 6648. See also A. C. n. 894, 1941, 1610, 5122, 7541, 8325, 8426, 4803, 10,048.

Extracts similar to the foregoing might be greatly multiplied. What is here quoted is Swedenborg's uniform teaching on this subject; nowhere in his writings do we meet with anything contrary to this.

Now, it must be conceded that there is something in the doctrine here enunciated, which produces an agreeable impression upon the mind on its first announcement. It is a doctrine which we cannot help wishing, at least, might be true. It chimes in with every one's fondest hopes and noblest aspirations. Our highest conception of heaven demands for its full realization, that it should be a state of never-ending progress in knowl-edge, wisdom and love. And as soon as we begin to look at the subject from a rational point of view, the reasons multiply for believing that what is here announced, and is in such complete accord with the highest hopes of all enlightened minds, must indeed be true.

For, what reasonable objection can be urged against the doctrine? What is to hinder eternal progress in the realms above? There surely is ample room for it. There is only One Infinite and absolutely perfect Being. Compared with Him, what are the highest angels in respect to love and wisdom? Less than the fire-fly's tiny spark compared with the sun's majestic blaze. The angels themselves perceive and acknowledge that all the love and wisdom they possess is momentarily received from the Lord ; and without such perception and acknowledgment, they would not be in heaven — would not be angels.

There is, then, spiritually speaking, an infinite distance between the Lord and the angels. And the latter may, therefore, go on advancing forever *toward* the Divine perfections, yet never reach them—never become absolutely perfect. And as every increase in love and wisdom is accompanied by a corresponding increase of happiness, therefore the happiness of the denizens of heaven (assuming that the doctrine here announced is true), will continue to increase throughout the endless ages.

Eternal progress, then, is clearly among the *possibilities* of the angelic state; and this may be taken as presumptive evidence, at least, that the doctrine is true. For the Lord's essential nature is such that He must forever desire to draw all—angels as well as men—to Himself. His will toward all his children must be, that they continually " go on unto perfection,"—continually approximate the Divine likeness. And if such be his will, such is virtually his command to the angels; and such a command implies the capability of endless progress.

Furthermore, progress is everywhere an indispensable condition of the highest happiness. We must not forget that angels are human beings. They are all in the human form, and were once inhabitants of the natural world. They are all, therefore, gifted with human faculties which are subject to fixed laws. Now it is well known that progress is an essential condition of the highest happiness on earth. However learned, wise and good a person may be, the consciousness of having attained the utmost limit of human perfection, and of inability to receive any increase of knowledge, wisdom or love, while knowing that there exist degrees of excellence infinitely beyond his present attainments,—this would be a serious draw-back to his happiness. A person of very moderate attainments, if conscious of a steady increase in wisdom, and of possessing the capacity for unlimited progress, would be much happier than he who had attained a far higher spiritual eminence, but knew that all further progress was denied him. If heaven were an unprogressive state, therefore, it would be wanting in one of the conditions which we know to be essential to people's highest happiness on earth. Indeed we can hardly conceive of the angels as being *very* happy, if the capacity for still higher human excellence were denied them. Certainly the angelic state would be less happy *without* than *with* the condition of eternal progress.

The truth of this doctrine may be further argued from the intense activity which exists in heaven. Wherever there is life, there is activity; and the higher the life, the more intense the activity. And it is an eternal law that all our human powers—our intellectual and moral faculties not less than our bodily organs—are expanded and strengthened by exercise. The man who daily exercises his powers of memory, reasoning, calculation or analysis for a considerable length of time, finds that he thereby comes to remember, reason, calculate or analyze with ever-increasing facility. These faculties are improved by exercise. So with the moral feelings. A person who exercises himself habitually in deeds of kindness, grows more and more kind. The more one practises the laws of charity, the more he comes to love these laws, and the more charitable he grows. The more we sympathize with the unfortunate and sorrowing, the more tender and sympathetic we become. And on the other hand, by the unrestrained indulgence of our lower propensities—our pride, avarice, conceit and love of self—the more proud, avaricious, conceited and selfish we become through such indulgence.

Nothing, indeed, is more certain than that all the powers of the intellect and all the dispositions of the heart are strengthened by exercise. And the more they are exercised (provided there be no excess), the more does their strength increase. There is no exception to this law. And since it is a law of mind, it must exist wherever finite minds exist,—for bodily death works no change in the laws of our mental constitution. The mind is the man—the real person in human form. This is immortal, and its laws are unalterable. Whatever laws, therefore, are known to govern the mind or spirit when clothed with flesh, will surely govern it in the great Hereafter.

Now, the angels being all images and likenesses of the Lord, must reflect in some measure the light of his wisdom and the warmth of his love. They love others better than themselves; therefore it is their delight to communicate of their love and wisdom to others. Such being their character, their highest and noblest faculties are being brought into constant exercise. Their love of wisdom impels them to the fullest exertion of their intellectual faculties, and their love of each other finds its appropriate exercise in continued deeds of kindness and of use. And if the powers of the intellect and the dispositions of the heart are strengthened and improved by exercise, what then should result from the constant exercise of these powers and dispositions in heaven? What, but continual growth, expansion, improvement? —continual increase of heavenly riches?—continual progress toward perfection?

And this doctrine has also the support of holy Scripture. Thus in the parable of the talents, it is said that those servants who *used* (traded with) their talents, did thereby *increase* them—gained besides them two and five talents more; while he that received but one talent, instead of using, buried it in the earth, did thereby lose all that was given him. By which we are plainly taught, that the spiritual gifts bestowed by our Divine Master, are increased by being properly used; while, if we neglect to use them—neglect the healthful exercise of our God-given powers—fail to practise the revealed laws of heavenly charity, we lose at length, through such neglect and failure, the inclination and power to use them. We show ourselves unprofitable servants, unworthy the powers or gifts bestowed. Hence that Divine decree: "Take therefore the talent from him and give it unto him who hath ten talents. For unto every one that hath shall be given, and he shall have abundance; but from him that hath not, shall be taken away even that which he hath."—Matt. xxv. 28, '9.

Yes: The sure and everlasting law is, that heavenly treasures increase with the using. Heavenly dispositions and feelings are strengthened by exercise. Heavenly wisdom increases in proportion as the laws of the heavenly life are religiously obeyed. In respect to spiritual things, therefore, it is given to every one according as he gives; in other words, according as he *uses* the gifts that God has bestowed on him; agreeable to the Lord's own words: "Give, and it shall be given unto you; good measure, pressed down, shaken together and running over, shall they give into your bosom." When we exercise the graces of heaven, we impart unto others of our spiritual gifts; and by the very act of imparting, our souls are opened to a fuller reception of the same gifts and graces. This is one of the laws of our spiritual life. It must, therefore, be a law of life with the angels, who are simply human beings in a more advanced stage. And since they never desire any good merely for themselves, but are ever willing and anxious to communicate their delights to others, therefore they must be continually receiving fresh increments of love and wisdom from the Lord, and their progress must be unending.

Besides, there is a two-fold progress—progress through growth or the maturing of graces already acquired, and progress from the increase or multiplication of goods and truths. Every spiritual truth dropped into an honest heart, is as a seed sown in good ground. It springs up, and, if properly cared for, grows to maturity, and in due time brings forth fruit—the golden fruit of charity. And this fruit contains the seeds of new truths, which, falling into the same good ground, spring up and bear fruit, "some thirty, some sixty, and some a hundred-fold." And so, through the multiplication of truths and the fructification of goods, the mind of a regenerate man (and the same is true of an angel) becomes like a beautiful garden adorned with all manner of trees, flowers and fruits, ever increasing in fertility and beauty, and in the number, variety and richness of its products. *This* is the true paradise of God. This is the real meaning of that garden which it is said the Lord God planted eastward in Eden, and wherein He "caused to grow every tree that is pleasant to the sight and good for food; the Tree of Life also in the midst of the garden." And now, as in the most ancient times, He places in this garden every Adam whom He recreates in his own image and likeness, when He breathes into him the breath of true spiritual life, and makes him a *living soul.*

The Lord himself teaches in the parable of the sower, that *seed* has a spiritual signification. "The seed," He says, "is the Word;" and the Word is divine truth. And when the truth falls into humble and honest minds, and is received, understood and obeyed, the seed is said to fall upon good ground. "He that received seed into the good ground, is he that heareth the Word, and understandeth it; which also beareth fruit, and bringeth forth, some an hundred-fold, some sixty, some thirty."

"With a man who is principled in love and charity," says Swedenborg, "seed from the Lord is so fructified and multiplied that it cannot be numbered,—not so much during his life in the body, but incredibly in the other life. For while man lives in the body, the seed is in corporeal ground and among underbrush and thickets which are scientifics and gross pleasures, also cares and anxieties. But when these things are cast off, as is the case when he enters the other life, the seed is freed from them and shoots forth, as the seed of a tree when it springs out of the ground, shoots forth into a shrub and then into a large tree, and is afterwards multiplied into a garden of trees. For all knowledge, intelligence and wisdom, with their delights and felicities, are thus fructified and multiplied, and in this manner grow to eternity."—A. C. n. 1941.

If in heaven, therefore, there exist the precious seeds of truth, and the still more precious fruits of charity, there must be a perpetual multiplication of truths and fructification of goods in the minds and hearts of the angels; and this implies eternal progress.

Analogy also lends additional support to the truth of

32

this doctrine. All organic forms on earth enjoy but a transitory life. They are born, they grow to maturity, they die. But until they arrive at maturity, their state is one of constant progress. They are continually advancing with greater or less rapidity, continually increasing in strength, continually unfolding new beauties and capabilities. This goes on until the period of full maturity is reached. Then decay—and decay is but another term for death—commences. This is the case with every plant, tree, animal, and even with man considered in respect to his material organism. Death is not sudden but gradual when it takes place in an orderly way. It is the conclusion of a process, the whole of which from beginning to end is a dying process. Man is not dying for only a few minutes or hours, but usually for many years. He begins to die shortly after he has attained to the fulness of bodily strength and stature, and when the freshness and bloom of early manhood have begun to depart. But up to this time there is physical growth, progress, a continual unfolding of bodily powers.

Now, there is no death in heaven; consequently no decay. All is life there. And since in all living things on earth there is constant progress up to the time when death commences, therefore (reasoning analogically) we must conclude that progress in heaven is unending. Analogy justifies the inference, that, so long as there is orderly life without decay in any created subject, so long must there continue to be a progressive improvement in the recipient forms, and a constant increase in the fulness and perfection of that life.

Moreover, the angelic heavens are continually increasing in numbers. Every society there grows by the constant addition of new members; and every additional member being a new form of good and truth, adds something to the perfection of the society, just as every new instrument added to a band of music, exalts and improves the general harmony. In this way also every society, and consequently the whole heaven of angels, must be ever advancing toward a more and more perfect state— ever increasing in variety, wisdom, and consequent happiness.

Can there be any doubt, then, about the truth of Swedenborg's disclosure on this subject? Nothing less than everlasting progress would suit the nature or satisfy the wants of the human soul. Reason, analogy and holy Scripture alike bear testimony to its truth. No one in heaven remains stationary, or quite satisfied with his present attainments,—an inspiring and ennobling thought! There all are forever receiving fresh increments of wisdom and love, forever advancing toward the Divine likeness, forever drawing nearer to the eternal Fountain of all light, life, peace and joy. No one there ever thinks that he has attained to the *ne plus ultra* of knowledge, or that the intensity and purity of his love can never be increased. On the contrary they all perceive and acknowledge that what they know is as nothing in comparison with the fathomless abyss of knowledge in the Divine mind; and that their love, in its strength and sweetness, bears no comparison to the Lord's infinite love. While they are in this state of perception and humble acknowledgment, they are in a progressive, because in an open and receptive state.

Their joys, too, are forever multiplying, for these increase with the increments of wisdom and of love.

What, now, is the practical bearing of this doctrine? What is its obvious and legitimate tendency? Clearly this: to make those who cordially accept it, humble and earnest seekers after heavenly goods and truths; never satisfied with present attainments; unwilling to think themselves already wise or good enough, but always reaching after a wisdom more exalted; always *going on unto* perfection, yet never imagining that they have attained to it. It naturally suggests such reflections or inquiries as these: Should a person be content with that particular phase of religious truth which was adapted to the world centuries ago? Should we refuse to believe in, or neglect to seek after, higher aspects of truth than such as were suited to their eyes? We, who know so very little comparatively—should *we* cease to be receivers or learners, when the angels are inquiring and learning forever? Should mortals imagine that they have fathomed all the arcana of the Divine Word and the human soul—that they have reached the end of God's last chapter on things divine and spiritual —and fancy themselves so wise that they can afford to sneer at further alleged disclosures, when those shining ones in the courts above so humbly confess that all they know is as nothing in comparison with what they do not know? Should men on earth indulge the conceit of having already attained perfection, or be satisfied with any standard already reached, when the angels of the highest heaven are forever advancing in wisdom and in all angelic graces?

Oh, what a rebuke does this heavenly doctrine of progress, administer to that contracted, conceited and unprogressive spirit so often exhibited even among professing Christians!—that spirit which turns proudly and sometimes scornfully away from all new disclosures on the sublimest themes; and which—asking for no more and no higher truth—plumes itself on present attainments, as if the farthest boundaries of spiritual knowledge and heavenly wisdom had been already compassed!

O, God of boundless truth and love, be pleased to look with pitying eye on the foolish pride and self-conceit of the multitudes who treat with scorn and derision thy sublime revealings, and shed down on all thy children here below more of that humble, truth-seeking, wisdom-loving, progressive spirit of thy children in the realms above!

XXIX.

CONSOCIATION OF ANGELS WITH MEN.

WE have shown in previous chapters that heaven consists of innumerable societies of wise and happy beings, all of whom were once dwellers in the natural world; and spirits of a very different character, also of human origin, constituting a realm quite the opposite to that of heaven, have often been referred to. Thus we have, in these two realms, the clearly announced Bible doctrine of a heaven of angels and a hell of devils. These in the aggregate constitute the spiritual world—a world not remote from the natural, but inti-

32 *

mately present and associated with it as the soul is with the body. While clothed with material flesh, we are dwellers at one and the same time in both worlds; consciously and sensibly in the natural world, unconsciously, because of the closed condition of our spiritual senses, in the spiritual world. And every individual is internally and spiritually associated with one or another class of spirits, by whom he is daily and hourly influenced almost as the body is actuated by the soul. We do not see the spirits that are near and operating upon us, because our spiritual eyes are closed; but we may know their general character by attentively considering the nature of our predominant thoughts and affections,— the ends at which we aim, the prompting and governing motives of our lives. All these flow into our minds and hearts through the medium of spirits in close fellowship with us; and they take their character, therefore, from the character of the spirits. If our ruling purpose is supremely selfish—one that shuts out from the heart all reverent regard for the Word of the Lord and the good of the neighbor, we may know that infernal spirits are our invisible companions—that our souls are in fellowship with devils, inhaling from hour to hour the pestilential atmosphere of hell. But if our aims are good and heavenly, if we regard our neighbor's welfare as our own, and desire above all else to know and do the will of the Lord, then angels are our associates, our spirits receive influx from them, we walk and work in their company, and breathe the balmy air of heaven. This accords with the dictates of enlightened reason, and is precisely what the great law of spiritual affinity would lead us to expect. Accordingly Swedenborg says:

"All spirits are distinguished in the other life by this: they who desire evil against others, are infernal or diabolical; but they who desire good to others, are good and angelic spirits. Man may know which he is among, whether the infernal spirits or the angelic. If he intends evil to his neighbor, thinking nothing but evil concerning him, and actually doing evil when in his power, and finding delight in it, he is among the infernals, and becomes himself also an infernal in the other life: but if he intends good to his neighbor, and thinks nothing but good concerning him, and actually does good when in his power, he is among the angelic, and becomes himself also an angel in the other life. This is the criterion: let every one examine himself by it. It matters not that a person does not do evil when he either cannot or dare not, nor that he does good from some selfish regard: such abstinence from the one and performance of the other, have only their origin in the man's externals, which are removed in the other life where he is such as his thoughts and intentions make him."—A. C. n. 1680.

"There are innumerable societies in the other life, which are disposed and arranged by the Lord according to all the genera of good and truth, also those of an opposite character. . . . Every man is associated with these as to his interiors, that is, as to his thoughts and affections, although he is ignorant of it. Hence comes all which a man thinks and wills. . . . Such as is the good in a man, such is the society of angels with which he is associated, and such as is the evil in him, such is the society of evil spirits with which he is associated. Man invites to himself such societies, or places himself in their midst, since like associates with like. For example: he who is covetous, invites to himself the societies of such as are in a similar lust. He who loves himself in preference to others, and despises others, invites to himself similar spirits. He who takes delight in revenge, invites such as are in a similar delight; and so in other cases. Such spirits communicate with hell, and man is in the midst of them, and is ruled altogether by them, so that he is no longer under his own power and guidance, but under theirs, although he supposes, from the delight and consequent liberty which he enjoys, that he rules himself.

" He, however, who is not covetous, or does not love himself in preference to others, and who does not take delight in revenge, is in the society of similar angels, and by them is led of the Lord, and indeed in freedom, to every good and truth to which he suffers himself to be led. And as he suffers himself to be led to an interior and more perfect good, so he is led to interior and more angelic societies. The changes of his state are nothing else but changes of societies."—A. C. n. 4067.

"The angels attendant on man have their abode solely in his ends of life. So far as he has respect to an end of the same kind as that which influences the Lord's kingdom—that is, to the good of the neighbor, the general good, the good of the church—so far the angels are delighted with him, and join themselves to him as a brother; but so far as he is influenced by selfish ends, the angels recede, and evil spirits from hell draw near; for in hell none but selfish ends have rule."—Ibid. n. 3796.

All this is quite consistent with the preceding disclosures, as well as with the conclusions of a sound mental philosophy and the rational intuitions of the wisest and best men. And we observe that the law governing the association of spirits with men, is the same biological law according to which spirits themselves are arranged into different societies—the law of spiritual affinity. And the Scripture, too, furnishes abundant confirmation of the truth of this disclosure.

It teaches that spirits in the flesh are operated upon by opposite forces; that both angels and devils are intimately present with men; the former to enlighten, strengthen, uplift and bless, sympathizing with and helping us in our conflicts with selfishness and sin, and rejoicing at the sincere repentance of every sinner (Luke xv. 7); the latter to tempt, delude, mislead and destroy —described in the aggregate as a single individual, "our adversary, the Devil, walking about as a roaring lion, seeking whom he may devour" (1 Pet. v. 8).

The evil spirits have access to us and seek to retain dominion over us by virtue of our natural proprium or hereditary selfishness. And the purpose of the Lord's advent in the flesh, was to resist and overcome this malign influence, and place Himself in such a relation to mankind, that all who humbly look to and follow after Him, may be delivered from their state of spiritual bondage. Hence the rejoicing in heaven over the Divine incarnation, and the song of the angelic host at the hour of our Savior's birth, "Glory to God in the highest, and on earth peace, good will toward men"!

And now the promise of his Second Coming is receiving its fulfillment—a coming of Himself and his angels into closer fellowship with all open and receptive souls —a coming with the loud-sounding trumpet of spiritual truth, to gather into the fold of the good Shepherd all who have ears to hear—"his elect from the four winds, from one end of the heavens even to the other."

And the great *practical* value of the teaching in the above extracts, is additional evidence of its truth. For every one who examines himself in the light of these disclosures, may know the character of his invisible associates with as much certainty as he knows by sight the members of his own family. If his ends are supremely selfish and worldly, he may know that he is internally associated with infernal spirits, and will, when he enters the other world, choose their society in preference to that of others. But if he is seeking to know and do the will of the Lord, acknowledging his evils and striving to overcome them, he may be sure that angels are his spiritual associates, working mightily in his behalf; and that in the Hereafter he will desire no other companionship than theirs. This thought is inspiring, and can hardly fail to impress every sincere believer, and incite him to daily watchfulness, prayer, self-denial and righteous endeavor.